Reflective Teaching in Further and Adult Education

Third Edition

Yvonne Hillier

continuum

Continuum International Publishing Group

The Tower Building	80 Maiden Lane
11 York Road	Suite 704
London SE1 7NX	New York NY 10038

www.continuumbooks.com

British Library Cataloguing-in-Publication Data
A catalogue record for this book is available from the British Library.

ISBN: 978-1-4411-7550-2 (paperback)

Library of Congress Cataloging-in-Publication Data
Hillier, Yvonne.
Reflective teaching in further and adult education / Yvonne Hillier. – 3rd ed.
    p. cm.
 Includes bibliographical references and index.
   ISBN 978-1-4411-7550-2
  1. Adult education–Planning. 2. Adult education teachers–Training of. 3. Effective teaching. 4. Adult learning. I. Title.
LC5219.H54 2011
374--dc22
                                                            2011012973

Typeset by Newgen Imaging Systems Pvt Ltd, Chennai, India
Printed and bound in India

For my son Tim

Contents

List of Figures, Tables and Checklists

Figures

Tables

Checklists

X List of Figures, Tables and Checklists

Acknowledgements

The first edition of this book arose from a chance encounter with Anthony Haynes at a conference I was involved in organizing at City University in January 2000. For his original help and encouragement, I thank him.

Throughout my career, I have learned from many colleagues and students. Although far too numerous to mention, I particularly wish to thank my fellow part-time tutors from adult basic education days. I would like to acknowledge how much I have learned from my colleagues at The City Lit, from whom much of my practice in training and development stems. I have received much help in identifying and finding reference material from Tamsin Heycock and John Blanchard particularly for the second edition of the book. Jas Kaur provided efficient and effective administrative support, as well as genuine interest and encouragement. Thanks to my colleagues at the Learning and Skills Research Network for their support and ideas which have helped me think constructively about the new developments in the sector. I would particularly like to acknowledge the work of Steve Besley from Edexcel who continues to generously disseminate his policy analysis through the regular *Policy Watch* series. His work has had a profound influence on many of my colleagues, I know, and his approach to dissemination has been used by other network groups to good effect.

A particular thank you to Jill Jameson, my erstwhile writing partner from other ventures who has been so engaged and interested in my work on this book.

I would like to thank a number of people who have contributed to this third edition. Thank you to the reviewers who have helpfully identified areas that I may wish to change. Thanks to Liz Briggs for her help with editing references. A thank you to my colleagues from the University of Brighton who are involved in teacher training in the Learning and Skills Sector, particularly Irena Andrews and Phil Lugton with whom I have enjoyed numerous discussions about the way in which our sector is responding to the frenetic pace of change. I have continued to watch and learn from students undergoing their PGCEs and DETLS programmes here at the University of Brighton. Their enthusiasm for learning and a commitment to the sector they wish to work in gives me faith that we can survive the oncoming cutbacks and continue to build a system of learning for adults and young people.

In the past couple of years, I undertook my own personal learning. I returned to ballet classes, tried to improve my French and began playing the piano again. I can't say that my ballet has improved but I did pass a piano exam this summer. My teacher, Linda Battacharya, inspired me and helped give me confidence, even though I was physically shaking when I sat down to play my pieces and scales during the exam. We have often chatted about teaching and I want to thank Linda for her inspiration (and funny stories!) that ensured I passed. Being a learner again, in all these activities, has reminded me how important it is to be thinking about our teaching from the perspective of *experiencing* it as a learner.

I have many friends who have wished me well during the writing of the three editions book, ready to hear about my progress and able to provide reassurance when I doubted that I should be the one to write such a book. To them all, a grateful thanks. I owe both thanks and an apology to Jill Ross, who has always done far more than provided coffee and chats on Sunday mornings. In my doctoral thesis, my thanks for the coffee suggested that her role was solely to provide sustenance. In fact, she has always engaged with my thinking and writing at many levels – as fellow practitioner, and as interested and critical friend. So thanks, fully, to Jill.

My heartful thanks to my husband, John Pratt, for his support and particularly for his diligence with the index. A huge thanks to my family for their ongoing support and love, particularly when I have been showing every indication that I am finally becoming like their grandma!

Finally I would also like to thank my son Tim Hillier who helped with updating websites. He knows how particularly brave and selfless he has been during the past year and how proud I am of all that he has achieved.

Yvonne Hillier
September 2010

Preface to the Third Edition

I recently was invited to Australia to work with a colleague, Jane Figgis, and to run a series of workshops for practitioners and their managers in vocational education and training (VET). I was delighted and very surprised to discover that a number of participants had read my book and realized that, even though much of the policy focus relates solely to England and the UK more widely, there is a large proportion of what I have written about that has relevance for folk abroad. I also discovered that if I changed the accent and the acronyms, most of their experiences in Australia were similar to those of practitioners in the Learning and Skills System. I realized that we are confronted with frenetic policy activity, urgent demands for upskilling, reskilling and enabling young people and adults to be able to function in society. I could see that we all face the same dilemmas of finding scarce resources to meet long-lasting needs in ways that are equitable and sustainable.

Anyone reading the earlier editions of my book will see that the current landscape has changed dramatically in England. I found it difficult to write and update sections of the book while our new government has been changing ministries, quangos, agencies as well as educational institutions and practices. Arguably, this is why a third edition is required. Yet there are some generic aspects of teaching and learning which can be drawn upon and developed into the increasingly networked and electronic society in which we live and work. There will inevitably be new practices which come into existence as knowledge is created, often with a rapid expanse in technological practices.

We now face urgent, global challenges, not least the need to find sustainable means of producing resources to keep us warm, fed and watered. We need to help people learn to live peacefully with each other and to understand and respect differences in their cultures. We need to help keep our world safe for future generations to enjoy.

The Learning and Skills System has much to offer in response to these challenges. It can only do so, though, through the people who teach and support learning. You, the reader, will be one of these thousands of folk who have a part to play. I hope that you enjoy reading this book and find it helpful. The ideas here have been gathered from my own experience but informed and influenced by my peers, friends and learners in the field and I continue to appreciate the generosity of all those with whom I have worked and observed in their professional practice. I continue to believe that together, we can make a difference. I hope that by seeking to reflect on *your* evolving practice and to experiment with ideas that you, too, will enjoy being a member of this rich and varied community of practice

Yvonne Hillier
September 2010

Introduction

It is Monday and a new course is starting. The room is bare, except for tables and chairs arranged in rows. The room is at the very end of the corridor, on the second floor. There are no signs to it. It is chilly and one window cannot close properly, causing a draught to whistle through.

There is an old overhead projector which has a smudge on the glass, and a screen which has to be tied down with string. The whiteboard has been cleaned but traces of writing still show. A sign on the wall gives instruction for using a data projector but there is only a string of unattached cables on the floor.

Now people begin to drift in. Some walk in purposely and take their seats. Others sidle in uncertainly, checking the room number, choosing to sit near the door or at the back. Some do not arrive before the session starts.

And you, the tutor, must take this situation and develop it to one where people learn and, hopefully, enjoy their learning.

Many courses have good facilities. There is a large number of learning institutions that provide pleasant rooms, good audiovisual facilities, easy physical access and clear signposting. Yet even with such advantages, fostering an environment where people achieve what they want to learn is a demanding and complex process.

This book is designed to help people who teach adults: tutors, trainers, volunteers, instructors, care assistants. It will encourage them to think reflectively about their practice. It offers insights into teaching which can lead to solutions for current challenges. It recognizes that practitioners have a wealth of experience which they draw upon, explicitly or tacitly, when teaching. Some of these experiences have been gained in the classroom, but many come from everyday lives, experiences of life changes, interactions with family, friends, colleagues and with total strangers.

There has been a shift in recent years to talk of learning rather than teaching. Yet those who facilitate the learning do something which *is* teaching in its broadest sense. This book concentrates on teaching, while constantly focusing on the importance of what the learner needs.

The approach taken is that any aspect of the interplay between teaching and learning can be examined through a critically reflective approach. This interplay presents challenges to be dealt with. Such challenges could be seen as problems to be solved, although not in a negative sense; rather as new situations which demand different strategies and responses.

The world of teaching adults is vast, complex and fast changing. This book cannot effectively capture all the changes in both concept and delivery of adult learning. What it offers is an approach to teaching that may enable practitioners to meet the constant challenges of their professional practice.

I remember my first experience of moving from being a part-time tutor in adult basic education to working as an organizer, on a temporary contract while my boss was on maternity leave. I remember being told that there was another volunteer training course about to start and all the notes were in a folder. Please would I take this on during the next four months? I remember the trepidation with which I met the group of volunteers for the first time. I knew about basic education teaching: I had been doing that for some years. I possessed an overwhelming sense that adult basic education was an important and worthwhile programme. I could have talked for hours about my students. Yet here I was, supposedly in charge of a group of people and about to help them come to understand about 'good practice'. What was it – and was I sure my version was the same as everyone else's?

Perhaps it was my doubting that led me to investigate this thoroughly later. Then, it meant that I had to think about what I and my colleagues did to ensure that volunteers would feel able and be able to work with our students. By running the volunteer programme, I discovered that everything I had taken for granted about basic education practice needed to be examined. I found myself likening basic education to one of those large, multifaceted mirror-balls that hung from ceilings on dance-floors in the 1960s, shedding rainbow light in different directions. Each facet alone could be inspected, but together they formed the wonderful effect. The process of reflecting on my teaching had begun.

I first discovered the literature on reflective practice and the underpinning philosophy of critical theory 15 years ago. Returning to this literature when preparing this book, I found how much I enjoyed reading what were now very familiar words and concepts. I was relieved that the initial joy of discovery had not diminished: if anything, I found myself affirming my original commitment to the ideas and concepts of critical reflective practice. Reflective practice means that you can never be sure that ideas have been fully explored and developed. It is relentless in its quest for making explicit the tacit thoughts and feelings about your practice. This book is all about reflective teaching. It takes a fundamental stance that without critical reflection teaching will remain at best uninformed and at worst ineffective, prejudiced and constricting. It also takes the view that professionals can and do learn constantly from their everyday practices, and the aim of the book is to enable you, the reader, to maximize what can be learned from experience, reflection and public knowledge.

This book, therefore, looks at the mirror-ball, examining it facet by facet. With each section, a cameo or case study offers to start the process of critically analysing taken-for-granted assumptions. It asks readers to think about their situation, to place themselves in that uncertain place where familiar ideas have been removed and replaced by doubt. It encourages readers to think of their experiences as learners as well as teachers.

There are three parts to this book. Part I explains what reflective practice is and describes the context of teaching, primarily drawn from England, but with reference to the rest of the

United Kingdom and developments in Europe. It considers how the focus has moved from adult education to lifelong learning.

Part II deals with the practicalities of teaching. Each chapter starts with a question about a particular issue. This is followed by discussion of the current theory and practice and the contexts in which teaching occurs, including traditional face-to-face, distance and web-based learning. The chapters particularly address underpinning approaches to inclusive learning and equal opportunities throughout, rather than as separate issues.

Part III discusses how we can evaluate our practice, from the perspective of meeting the requirements of a number of 'stakeholders' concerned with adults and their learning. The final chapter analyses how we can promote our own professional development, to enable us to meet the challenges of the changing context in which we work.

Each chapter covers part of the Lifelong Learning UK (LLUK) Standards for teaching and supporting learning in further education in England and Wales. In England, all staff who are new to teaching in the Learning and Skills Sector must gain qualifications which have been set against these standards. There are three stages to a full qualification: the Preparing to Teach in the Lifelong Learning Sector (PTLLS), the Certificate in Teaching in the Learning and Skills Sector (CETLS) and the Diploma in Teaching in the Learning and Skills Sector (DETLS). Readers from Scotland, Wales and Northern Ireland will find the LLUK standards helpful when reflecting on their practice. Readers from outside the UK will find the standards often a useful insight into how the further education sector is defining and promoting a high level of professionalism for all staff concerned with supporting learning. Most practitioners will recognize the content of the standards and be able to compare these with their own national policies and practice. For example, in Australia, the requirement for practitioners is to hold a Certificate at Level 4 in their qualification system, whereas in England, the full DETLS award is the equivalent of the second year of a full-time three-year bachelors degree or can be awarded at postgraduate level.

Many of you reading this book will be engaged in gaining a teaching qualification. One of the challenges for training people who work in the Learning and Skills Sector is that there are generic issues around teaching and learning, and subject-specific issues, which are difficult to cover in one programme. There are some programmes run by higher education institutions that are able to provide 'core plus option' content, so that a language teacher, for example, can take a module on the specific issues around teaching a foreign language, as well as the core modules on assessment. I feel there is a tension between ensuring that people can work in subject-specific areas, and relating these to the more generic issues of teaching and learning. There is an enormous sharing of information in most teacher training programmes that could not happen if people learned in their own subject areas exclusively. On the other hand, there are numerous occasions when people complain that the content is not relevant to them. A criticism by Ofsted (Office for Standards in Education) (2003) has been that the programmes do not 'stretch' people enough in the final year of study, and merely repeat what might have been covered in the first two stages of an earlier teacher training award. Research sponsored by the Learning and Skills Development Agency (LSDA) has shown that practitioners do value their training, particularly for the more practical aspects if covered early enough in their teaching careers, but throughout the programmes, it is the reflective aspect that they value (Clow and Harkin, 2003). This book addresses the generic issues of teaching and learning which I hope you will apply to your particular context. The first part, which addresses a critical reflective approach will help you begin to achieve this.

Throughout the book, you will find suggestions that you can adapt and apply to your own professional practice. The ideas in this book represent a professional lifetime of working with adults. I have gained many of these from my observations of colleagues and students which I have subsequently tried out myself and adapted accordingly. Some of these ideas you may be using already: others may seem alien or you may dismiss them as being inappropriate. I hope that you will create your own ways of facilitating the learning of adults which, with experience, turn into a repertoire of strategies and techniques upon which you can draw. I hope that you will experiment and look for opportunities to try out new ideas, and be ready to learn from the highs and lows of your professional practice.

When reading each chapter, take time to think about your own professional practice. Think of examples about which you can ask yourself such questions as 'What surprised me about this?', 'What perplexed me about that?', 'What happened when I did this?' By taking the familiar and challenging the reasons for acting in taken-for-granted ways, I hope that you will be able to become a reflective teacher facilitating the learning of adults.

Part 1
Reflective Practice and Policy in Adult Learning

Reflective Practice

Reflective practice in training and development: an example

Four professional trainers and teachers are meeting on a Tuesday night. Mary is a counsellor and trains people who wish to become counsellors. Justin works for a voluntary organization and provides training in finance and management. Hannah works in further education and teaches about the use of technology. Usha provides educational guidance to learners in higher education.

They sit in a circle. The greetings have taken place, they make themselves comfortable and three look expectantly to Hannah who is 'presenting'.

Hannah begins by reminding everyone that she has been working on a new project recently. She describes how it was created in response to a European-funded initiative, with very little time to plan it carefully. She explains that she identified what she felt was a problem that needed a resolution. The aim of the project did not seem to meet the actual needs of the client group – women who had limited computer literacy and who were working in an organization that was restructuring. These women would be vulnerable to unemployment within the next few months. They were taking a course which was not going to help them find work immediately. Instead, the course offered a qualification which provided access to higher education. How was Hannah going to plan a curriculum which would not only meet the objectives of the project but also enable the learners to have jobs?

At this point, Justin, Mary and Usha ask questions. These help clarify points that Hannah has made, often asking for jargon to be explained, or raising questions of fact: about the timing of the programme, the people involved in preparing the course, the people responsible for putting the programme proposal to the funders.

At this stage, the four begin to shift in their seats. The three members of the group who have been questioning move forward and show signs that they are becoming more careful with their questioning. They ask why Hannah is worried about the two apparently opposite aims – of the project and the learners. What is difficult for her to reconcile about these? Is she saying that the learners don't want to go into higher education and only want to work? Is she saying that there is no likelihood that they will be able to find work after they go into higher education? Is she saying that she thinks they may fail? Is she saying that the course is not going to help them succeed in higher education?

With each of these questions, Hannah hesitates before answering. She hasn't thought of her own perspective influencing so strongly her views of the project. She can state clearly her own ideas about education and what it is for. She does not like having to compromise when a project is set up with different objectives. Perhaps she thinks education is always about empowerment, but feels that the learners may be cheated in some way; she cannot honestly say that gaining entrance to higher education is a poor alternative. Who is she to say what people should and should not do?

An hour has passed and each member of the group is tiring. Have they uncovered some underlying assumptions that have directed Hannah's approach to her work? Can she reframe her perspective as a result of the discussion this evening?

Hannah decides that she will look again at the project's aims and discuss these with her line manager. She will contact the educational guidance co-ordinator and discuss the options for her learners. The group agree who will present next month. They stand up, stretch and agree where to go for something to eat. The reflective practice session has ended.

What was going on in that session? The same presentation could lead to completely different ideas if it was repeated, or if it had other members present. There is no view about what *should* be done about the project described, but it establishes that one's perspective on a professional matter can be 'unpacked'. The members had all been part of a Masters programme and studied reflective practice as a module on their course. They have read widely about the theory of critical reflection and about being a professional. They decided independently to set up their own reflective practice group after going through this process during the module. Why did they go about discussing an issue in this way? They were following a particular model known as the DATA process (Peters, 1994) which asks them to do the following:

- Describe the problem, task or incident which represents a critical aspect of practice which needs examination and possible change.
- Analyse the nature of what is described, including the assumptions which support any action taken to solve the problem, do the task or resolve the incident.
- Theorize about alternative ways to solve the problem, task or incident.
- Act on the basis of this theory.

This model provides an opportunity to step back from the urgency of dealing with the problem, task or incident. More importantly, by working with a group of colleagues or peers, it is possible to reframe the incident using a variety of perspectives which the individuals in that group offer. This is an important aspect of reflective practice. It is very difficult to reveal our own assumptions without the help of a 'critical friend'. This chapter will examine the philosophical and theoretical roots of reflective practice and discuss how reflective practice can be used in professional practice.

Why reflect critically on practice?

Why should we reflect critically on our daily practice? What can it achieve? There are two main reasons for doing this. The first is that we often have practices that are convenient in the short term but in the long term do not actually help people to learn effectively. For example, many learners ask for handouts when they attend a formal learning situation or for the PowerPoint presentation to be uploaded on an intranet. Handouts and downloaded files enable learners to catch up on any missed session and they enable the teacher to clarify what is to be covered in a session. Now, with the increasing use of information technology, there is almost a competition to see how beautiful and entertaining these handouts can be. Yet many learners take the handout and then ignore the content. How a handout is used is important for how well a person will learn. Simply having a set of handouts will not guarantee that, as if by osmosis, the content will transfer to someone's brain! So, if we think good teaching means having lots of smart-looking handouts for our learners because they think they have the content of the course, then in the long run, they will not learn so much and we may have to develop further teaching sessions to help them cover the material.

A second and more fundamental reason for thinking critically is that we do not teach in a vacuum. We are products of complex social and personal circumstances that affect anything we do. Some of the things that we think are a result of the influences of ideology, what Gramsci (1971) called hegemony. For example, in the Western world, there is a prevailing view that intelligence is important and that qualifications are vital for good jobs. The kind of education one has can often determine the kind of qualifications one gains and the type of work one does. As those in positions of power who make decisions about the education system in the UK, including those in government, the legal system and the professions, have been overwhelmingly beneficiaries of a system that values particular types of education and qualification, we continually reproduce what is desired for those who have been on the receiving end of it. This situation is hegemonic. We do not often question the underlying idea that education and qualifications are in themselves 'good things'. In other words, the state system provides the context in which some of our values are reinforced and others are neglected.

Now, some of our assumptions are a lot easier to question than others. If I say that I think meeting learners' needs is very important, most people reading this book would agree with this view. However, if I then say that I think meeting learners' needs means always doing what the learners want, people might start to challenge this. What if a learner has a very narrow definition of what is needed? What if I know that there is a whole range of alternatives that the learner simply has never heard of? It becomes easy to challenge me on this view. However, if I said that being learner-centred is a fundamental value in my teaching, it would be hard to challenge me, and I would certainly resist such challenges. Yet when we begin to look very carefully at that statement, we can begin to see that I have a lot of assumptions that may be quite false. Am I sure that the learners' needs are paramount? It may be that the learner does not *need* something but likes to have certain desires satisfied. For example, a learner may wish to have a set of notes for every session. This is not absolutely necessary, but it is something that she has come to expect. This is where a learner's needs are actually 'wants' that are misplaced. What if I think I am meeting learners' needs when really I am teaching in my preferred way and it does not take account of my learners' needs? The teaching/learning situation is one where the tutor wields power, not just in explicit ways like deciding if particular work meets assessment standards, but in less obvious ways, such as deciding what will be learned, and how.

I remember a colleague who had worked in what was then known as adult basic education for many years. She believed that learners should not have to work for qualifications in literacy and numeracy because it was more important to them to learn that they had dignity and that they should have confidence in themselves. She felt that having to undertake work that was assessed would only remind them of their previous failures. Yet when Wordpower and Numberpower (which are qualifications in basic skills) were first introduced, she found

that her learners developed a lot of confidence by achieving these, and it was through publicly recognized awards that they felt they could gain self-respect. Her previous assumptions
had been based on challenges to the establishment and the value of qualifications. She had
not thought of how the learners wanted to belong to that establishment. Now, we could go
further and question whether people should need qualifications to earn self-respect and we
would return to the current debates about lifelong learning and the need for a workforce
that is qualified.

So far, I have suggested that it is possible to challenge our taken-for-granted assumptions
about meeting learner needs because this may not be the most appropriate course of action
to take. Another result of trying to meet learners' needs is that it is almost impossible to
achieve this for everyone. It is important not to be too self-critical by the idea that we should
be meeting all our learners' needs. Brookfield (1998) reminds us that

> A critically reflective educator knows that while meeting everyone's needs sounds compassionate
> and learner-centred it is pedagogically unsound and psychologically demoralising. She knows that
> clinging to this assumption will only cause her to carry around a permanent burden of guilt at her
> inability to live up to this impossible task. (p. 133)

Critical reflection

So, when we reflect, we not only challenge our assumptions about why we do what we do, we
can also help ourselves identify where we feel lacking and why we may be setting ourselves
unnecessarily unachievable standards. How can we reflect on our approaches to our practice? What can we do? What can we uncover in the process?

Brookfield's critical lenses

There are many ways to help us think reflectively. The Peters (1994) model asks us to think
of a concrete example and then to step back and allow ourselves to test out our assumptions
about that situation. Brookfield (1995) suggests that we can look at a situation from our own
viewpoint, from our colleagues' viewpoint, from our learners' viewpoint and from theoretical literature. He calls these the four critical lenses. Brookfield identifies critical reflection
as a fundamental approach to teaching. He suggests that not only teachers but also learners
should develop an approach which demands the 'hunt for assumptions'. It is like detective
work, seeking out clues to our current behaviour.

Critical incident analysis

One way to begin this process is to start with a 'critical incident'. This idea was developed by
Flanagan (1954) and essentially asks us to think of an example which especially illustrates
a general point. So if we want to think about what it is like to be a learner, we can think of a
situation where we recently acquired a new skill. For example, I began learning British Sign

Language a few years ago while working at The City Lit, which has a Centre for Deaf People. I wanted to learn to communicate with my colleagues who were deaf, particularly as we had started working together on a course for sign language teachers, all of whom were deaf. I remember particularly the excitement of being able to communicate by showing expression on my face, and the immense difficulty in trying to read someone else's finger-spelling. I really enjoyed trying out the signs when we worked in pairs and small groups. I remember one evening feeling completely useless when it came to watching our tutor finger-spell and to take it in turns to say what he had just said. Critical incident analysis would ask the following: What were the characteristics of that situation which helped me to learn? What was difficult? Is there anything about these characteristics that we think we could attend to with our own learners? Doing this revealed for me that I enjoyed small-group work where I learned not only from putting into practice what we had covered as a whole group but also from the fun of making silly mistakes in a small group. I hated the sense that in the large group we were all so exposed; I cringed for people (including myself) who had temporarily forgotten the correct sign or finger-spellings.

So what can be learned from this particular example? If *we* remember feeling anxious about trying out our new skill in public, perhaps in front of our fellow-learners, then why do we ask our *learners* to do this? Can we justify putting them through such emotional terror? If we think it really is important for people to practise their new skill, is there a way we could enable them to do this without an 'audience'? These are the kinds of questions we can ask when we have a critical incident to analyse. In a way, we identify problems, based on our own experiences, for us to examine further.

Problem-solving

In fact, Burgess (2000, p. 54) makes the point that if we learn something, we usually start with problems; in particular 'those which arise when our knowledge bumps up against our ignorance'. He argues that we can effectively describe the logic of learning using the philosophy of Karl Popper. In this we start with a problem, and we try out a solution. We try to eliminate errors in the solution and refine it. This in turn leads to a new problem which we set about solving. This process can be shown as:

P1 – TS – EE – P2

where P1 is the first problem, TS is a trial solution, EE is error elimination and P2 is the second problem arising from the process.

Suppose you teach a practical subject like art, where the learners work throughout the session on their project. Some learners always seem impatient for advice and call across the room for help. You find it difficult to ask them to wait and so other learners do not have as much attention. This is your first problem. Perhaps you decide that you will introduce a system where, when the learners arrive, they write their name in sequence on a whiteboard in the classroom and then you systematically move around the room looking at people's work in the order in which they arrived. This helps solve the problem of some learners calling out, as they now understand there is a system, and everyone will be seen during the session. So you have begun to eliminate some of the problems in the previous situation. However, you now find that some learners do not really need your advice when it is their turn and others cannot get on because they are waiting until much later in the session for their turn. You have unintended consequences arising out of your first trial solution: so you now have errors in your first solution which you need to eliminate. You may decide that your solution should also include using coloured pens, so that people can write their names in blue to mean that they are happy to get on with their work, and red to mean that they need to speak to you quite soon. This new procedure may lead to a new problem, and so you have to devise further solutions.

Significant events

Another way to reflect critically has been offered by Willis (1999) when he suggests that we should look at the 'expressive knowledge' contained within our analysis of a significant event. He draws upon the reflective cycle of Smyth (1989) which uses 'episodes of practice' which are experienced by the practitioner. These episodes are similar to critical incidents. The reflective cycle begins by describing a significant event or practice. It then enters a phase of 'informing', that is, interpretative reflection, looking for significance or typicality of the event being reflected upon. The next part of the cycle involves 'confronting', where colleagues assist the practitioners to face up to their theories in practice and how these compare with their espoused theories. Finally, the cycle moves to reconstructing, which is the process through which practitioners devise new ways of proceeding, consequent upon their analysis and evidence of practice. This cycle helps to develop our awareness of what is in our 'lifeworld'.

Willis argues that this cycle produces expressive knowledge. This is generated by a person adopting a receptive listening stance, which allows an element of the world to present itself for contemplation. The individual can then attempt to construct a 'text' or story which accounts for that experience in its wholeness: 'The tool for this project is not the surgeon's analytical scalpel but the poetic pen or artist's brush' (Willis, 1999, p. 93).

Willis' approach starts with a phenomenon, which is something which appears to someone. It is about people holding their gaze on the phenomenon itself. Willis proposes that the phenomenon can be subject to three modes of reflection: contextual reflection, dispositional reflection and experiential reflection.

Contextual reflection

Here an episode of experience is reviewed in terms of the contextual forces, for example, time, place, race, class, policies, which have influenced and shaped it. In Hannah's example it would involve thinking about when the project was proposed, who was going to fund it, who was going to benefit from it. Contextual reflection 'sets the scene'.

Dispositional reflection

Here the predispositions of teachers and learners to the teaching/learning project are identified. It is a person's orientation which influences the action, for example, preferences, aspirations, feelings and personal reactions to purposive activity. With Hannah, her own views about widening participation but not setting people up to fail is an example of dispositional reflection. It is reflection on feelings and attitudes.

Experiential reflection

Here the lived experience of the learning episode is considered. The person reflecting on the purposive activity tries to think back to what the event was like as an experience. It focuses on the 'whatness' of the experience (Willis, 1999, p. 105). When Hannah undertakes her project, she will be able to reflect on the experience of running it – something which is concrete.

By undertaking this reflective cycle, Willis argues that it is possible to consider the difference between what we think we are doing and should be doing, particularly for a beginning practitioner who might not have been aware of the 'expectations they may have about a form of practice and the actual reality as it is experienced' (1999, p. 110).

If we look back at Hannah's example, her discomfort is the starting-point for reflection and critical scrutiny. She has been using theory while she has been working on the project, even though she might not have been aware of it. Reflection will help Hannah to look at theory now that she has stepped back from her everyday practice and she can begin to examine her newly articulated ideas. She can move from simply 'muddling along' and relying on a commonsense approach that is comfortable. Reflection will challenge her concepts, beliefs, assumptions and values (Carr and Kemmis, 1986).

Critical reflection: drawing upon informal theory of practice

We have seen an example of how a specific problem can be examined in terms of what assumptions are being brought to bear when the person identifies it as a problem. These assumptions, be they profound or workaday, constitute the theoretical basis of people's actions. There is no practice without theory, even if it is unstated. In this example, the theory includes ideas that adult education is for individual empowerment. We could compare this with governmental and European initiatives to widen participation in higher education. We can look at an individual lecturer's perceptions of the purposes of education and training. We could consider the motivation of both lecturer and learners. In short, we have in this example a microcosm of the situation of teaching adults, which can be analysed using existing theories from a number of disciplines including social science, philosophy, history and politics.

One of the enduring criticisms about the practice of teaching adults is that it is divorced from theory. Indeed, many readers may be thinking that this section is going to get too theoretical and that perhaps they can skim it, or put it away for another day! In my research with basic education practitioners (Hillier, 1994), many involved in the study mentioned that they did not read books but they did have their own ideas. Their daily practice was steeped in theory but they would not have been able to articulate it. Theory, on the other hand, could and did describe and explain much of their practice.

Sometimes we define one thing by what it is not, and often we say theory and practice are opposites. So practice deals with concrete, immediate realities and theory deals with general, abstract concepts. This is quite misleading. Carr (1986) argued that the assumptions that practice is non-theoretical and theory is non-practical underestimate the 'extent to which those who engage in educational practices have to reflect upon, and hence theorise about, what, in general, they are trying to do' (p. 162).

What, in fact, is happening is 'theory-guided practice' where what we do presupposes a conceptual framework, even if we are not terribly good at articulating it or even aware of it. However, we can, at times, decide to use theory to guide our practice. In fact, Griffin (1989) goes so far as to claim that our practice and our theory are interlinked:

> There is no adult education practice that does not express theory and no adult education theory that does not arise directly from adult education practice . . . the knowledge base would be the practice. (p. 136)

The link between theory and practice, therefore, means that theory is 'grounded' in practice and the latter is not some kind of 'thoughtless behaviour which exists separately from theory' (Carr and Kemmis, 1986, p. 113). When we teach, our practice is formed by our experience, by the way we make sense of what we do. If we try out a new way of teaching, the results of trying this new way help us decide whether or not to use it in the future. We develop knowledge which can be called practical knowledge, and this is concerned with 'appropriate action in the world' (Usher and Bryant, 1989).

By focusing on knowledge that is practically derived from solving problems, the gap between theory and practice is bridged. This knowledge is not the abstract, generalized kind but is 'situational' in that it is 'socially located, very often complex and problematic and consciously and intentionally carried out' (Usher and Bryant, 1989, p. 82). This can be called 'informal theory'. However, it is often taken for granted, it may be seen as simple common sense and is private and unique to the practitioner. So we need to try and make explicit the implicit nature of this theory, and once it has been made explicit we can critically examine it. Without critical analysis, informal theories held by practitioners and their practical knowledge arising from their experiences risk 'remaining at the level of anecdotal, idiosyncratic reminiscence' (Brookfield, 1993, p. 75).

Once again, the idea of tacit knowledge is apparent when we think of how much professionals know. Polanyi (1962) once said 'we know more than we can tell'. If you have observed an experienced colleague teach, that person will have an enormous amount of personal knowledge which is being operationalized. If you then ask your colleague to provide a running commentary on why she was behaving in the way she did, she would find it extremely difficult to do so. This is because she is using what Schön (1983) called 'knowledge in action', and needs to step out of that in order to talk about it.

Another example of public and private knowledge was demonstrated by Nonaka and Takeuchi (1995). They found that people joining a new organization are socialized into certain ways of doing things quite quickly. Some of these procedures are public knowledge; for example, in a further education college, filling in learning contracts must be done, and everyone who is involved in teaching a group of learners is told about it. However, there are implicit things that are not even discussed, often involving how people relate to each other, or what they wear. Yet newcomers work out for themselves, for example, what the dress code is. If asked, people may stop and think and then discuss 'this is how we do things around here' but this knowledge is often implicit and has been acquired without an induction programme to spell it out. An interesting activity for us is to try and think about what is publicly known by our colleagues about our workplace and what we seem to know without having talked about it.

When we think carefully about our teaching, we demonstrate our commitment to improving our professional practice. We want to find out about the consequences of our actions. Pollard (1997) calls this reflective teaching and argues that to do this effectively needs a range of qualities: open-mindedness, active concern with aims and consequences of teaching, ability to employ methods of enquiry, ability to employ self-reflection and also collaboration with peers, ability to engage in a dialogue with colleagues.

We need, therefore, a commitment to the systematic questioning of our teaching as a basis for development (Stenhouse, 1975). We should be concerned to question and test theory in practice in the use of these qualities.

Theory

So far, I have talked about theory in a particular way. In this book, you will read many references to theory. What does theory mean to you? Is it a set of formulae that you apply to a mathematical or scientific problem because there is a proof to be made? Is it a hunch that you have when you are trying to work out why someone or something behaves in a certain way? Is it what explains the way that machines work? People use the term 'theory' in a variety of ways. When we think of teaching, there is a complex set of circumstances in which we can use a variety of theories to describe, explain and predict behaviour. I find very appealing the idea that a theory helps us to describe a particular set of circumstances, explain these and then enables us to predict what is likely to happen in future situations. For example, why is it that some people lack so much confidence when they enrol on a learning programme? If we knew why, perhaps we would be able to plan our behaviour and approach to our teaching more effectively. If we could predict that y will happen if we do x, we will be more able to plan for successful learning. Throughout this book, I will be asking you to think of questions that say 'If only I knew how' or 'If only I knew why.'

So when we talk of theory, we can mean formal theories that stem from disciplines including history, psychology, sociology, philosophy and politics. It is no wonder that teachers and trainers decide that there is too much theory and not enough discussion on practice! However, when we begin to scrutinize our practice, we see that it is not divorced from these important theoretical considerations. If we want to understand why we are being asked to introduce a new form of accreditation into our programmes, then it helps to know about the recent political context. If there is a policy to encourage unemployed people to work, this may limit the opportunity for them to study and acquire new skills and knowledge. Those of you who were working in further and adult education in the 1990s will remember the changes in rules governing unemployment benefit, where people were only allowed 16 hours of study compared with a previous 21 hours. Changes to the delivery of many courses, particularly access courses to higher education, were a direct result of this government policy.

At a more local level, staff in educational institutions and in training organizations have conflicting ideas about how to recruit and teach their learners or trainees. If you are currently taking a course in how to teach, you will have noticed that you have many similarities with your colleagues' ideas, but also many differences. In many cases, we simply do not know what is the 'best way' to do something, or why certain situations occur. Now, we can have our 'hunches' and these are the basis of our informal theories. These informal theories contrast with the formal theories which are given status because they have been publicly examined and because we tend to think that theory, and in particular anything scientific, must be true. Brookfield, as ever, provides a timely reminder that if we think about what he calls 'universal theory', that is, formal public theory, it does not help us adapt to local conditions, in which, 'learners' actions contradict our beautifully reasoned analysis' (Brookfield, 1995, p. 209).

The tendency to believe that a particular theory is true directs our behaviour and attitudes, to the exclusion of other competing theories. The world is rife with differing views on how to deal with poverty, for example. One of the major influences on philosophy of science in the twentieth century was Karl Popper (1962, 1968). He argued that we cannot establish the truth of any given theory. However, we can learn a lot by finding that our theories do not work. For example, we may have a tried and tested way of introducing a new concept to our learners. We do not know why it works necessarily, but every time we use it, our learners learn. Now, this is as good a theory as we have for the time being; but if on one occasion we find that our learners do not learn, we sit up with a jolt. We then know that our theory is not foolproof in practice. We probably learn more from it not working than when it does. People often say they learn more from the mistakes they have made. If we apply this to our own practice, then instead of feeling miserable when we make mistakes, we can be far more positive and ask ourselves what we have learned. Our challenge is to tap our potential for learning from experience and to replace our blind spots with insights, something Pollard (1997) calls 'developing dreams and ideals into realities' (p. 69). How does this help us when we go about critically reflecting on our practice and when we begin to identify theories which describe this practice?

What do we mean when we say practice? In teaching, it is often referred to when we are training – we have teaching practice when we are newcomers to the study of education, we may be placed with experienced colleagues and given the opportunity to work with their learners or trainees over short intensive periods of time. We may be asked to undertake microtraining or microteaching practice during in-service training, particularly a feature of the LLUK validated teaching qualifications. We also talk about 'good practice', which can refer to a code of conduct, an underpinning approach or standards for which we must strive. The standards in England by LLUK, devised by one of the national training organizations are based on ideas of good practice and set out what practitioners can aim to achieve, starting with standards for new entrants to the profession through to those who have gained experience and teaching qualifications. In addition to the standards which define what people should do, there is a set of skills and attributes which relate to how people should behave, and qualities they should possess. This second set of skills and attributes may help define a set of values, and begin to define 'good practice' in our work.

If our practice incorporates theory, how do we know what is 'good'? We need to apply a critical approach to both our practice and the theory that informs it. One school of thought attempts to do this and applies an approach using critical theory.

Critical theory

Critical reflection is concerned with theory–practice connections. Critical reflection draws upon critical theory. Critical theory is a development based on the Frankfurt School which comprised a group of philosophers in the early part of the twentieth century who questioned the knowledge which is derived from the scientific or positivist paradigm.

The important point that critical theorists make is that we tend to believe that scientific knowledge is objective, that it is 'true' and that practical problems can simply be dealt with if we apply our scientific principles to finding the solution. In other words, the scientific way is seen to reign supreme. The solutions to our problems exist if only we investigate them enough. If you think about how the medical profession has, until recently, been perceived to be almost irrefutable, and how much people believed that their doctor would be able to make them better using scientific knowledge, or on a more everyday level, how washing powder is sold on the basis that it has been scientifically tested, then you can begin to see how much we take scientific theories as fact. The Frankfurt School seriously challenged the idea that scientific theory should be so powerful. The proponents of this School (including Adorno, Horkheimer and later Marcuse) stated that objective knowledge was simply unattainable. They argued that certain kinds of 'grand theory' directed our way of looking at the world so much that we could not see how influenced we were by these theories. We could not 'step out' of our viewpoint – we were 'blinkered' in our perspectives. Now, when we suggest that we should think critically, it means that we should try to find these taken-for-granted ideas.

For example, in the past, most women in the Western world believed that they should be the homemaker and that men should be the main financial provider. It was the natural order of things. With the onset of feminism (and this onset goes back much further than the 1960s), challenges to this view were made. If you now put this in the context of what one teaches, then some of the classes and curricula on offer in the past would not now be tenable. An interesting project is to look at old prospectuses of adult and further education institutions and to see how courses have changed and how they are advertised. In many cases, the curriculum designed for men and women reflected the dominant view of what men and women should study: car mechanics for men, cake decorating for women.

If the discussion on critical theory seems removed from our own teaching, let us return to our first example of critical reflection. When we think of Hannah, we have to ask ourselves whether there is an underlying viewpoint, an ideology which is operating and directing all of us to 'gaze' in a particular direction. If we look ahead, we do not see what is behind us. We need to direct our gaze to the areas out of our view.

What happens if we do reflectively criticize our taken-for-granted thoughts? What happens to the 'action' as a result? It requires reflection on our experiences so that 'formal study is informed by some appreciation of reality' (Brookfield, 1990, p. 50). Brookfield recommends that we can go beyond the 'nitty gritty' of our daily practice in the classroom or training room by 'questioning and then replacing or reframing an assumption which is accepted as representing dominant common sense by a majority' (1993, p. 66).

Thinking reflectively

To challenge our assumptions, we have to begin by thinking reflectively. What is reflection, exactly? One of the earliest exponents of thinking reflectively was John Dewey. His writing is accessible, thought-provoking and relevant, even though he was writing in the early part of last century. He identified five general features of reflective thinking:

1. Perplexity, confusion, doubt due to the fact one is implicated in an incomplete situation whose character is not fully determined. For example, if we had a group of learners who were thinking of dropping out from their studies, we may wonder how to tackle this. Instead of assuming that it is their problem, we may start to doubt the view (in any programme of learning, there will be drop-out), and be perplexed why that is.
2. Conjectural anticipation – a tentative interpretation of the elements. In our example, we may begin to wonder if our drop-out rate had anything to do with the clash between assessment deadlines

and busy times for families like holy festivals and holidays. We may wonder if our drop-out rate had something to do with difficulties in public transport, or difficulties with finance.

3. Careful survey (examination, inspection, exploration, analysis) of all attainable considerations which will define and clarify the problem at hand. In our example, we may want to research the learners' perspectives, how they see the situation, as well as obtaining facts about transport, childcare, ability to pay, and the timing of major festivals and holidays.

4. Consequent elaboration of the tentative hypothesis. Once we have our facts and figures and people's perceptions, we can begin to think of ways of dealing with our problem of drop-out. We may decide that we should alter the timing of the programme, or seek a college-wide solution to some of the transport difficulties and financial arrangements. We do not yet know if these ideas will work.

5. Taking one stand upon the projected hypothesis as a plan of action, doing something overtly to bring about the anticipated result and thereby testing the hypothesis. Now we have formulated our hypotheses, we can choose to take one in particular and see what happens when we introduce our new measure.

There are two points to note about Dewey's approach. The first is that the use of careful survey and elaboration makes this a reflective approach rather than a simple rushing into a trial and error approach to action. Second, Dewey suggested that hypotheses are formulated and then *tested* through taking action (just as Popper proposes when we attempt to test out our ideas and learn when they do not work). By doing this, we take an inquisitive approach to our actions in the world. As teachers, we can use this approach to take action based on our reflections. In other words, we can learn from our experiences, be proactive in trying out new ideas and solutions to existing problems, and be aware that any action we take leads to new challenges.

In our example at the beginning of this chapter, Hannah will learn from her experience, particularly if she is thinking reflectively. However, what can help her to learn beyond the survival stage, that Argyris and Schön (1974) call 'single-loop learning'? In other words, what can she do to avoid simply focusing on the context of her practice but rather to 'problematize' this practice? To progress, she needs to use 'double-loop learning' which involves systematic questioning of her understanding of the situation at hand. Argyris (1982) explains that double-loop learning occurs when 'the basic assumptions behind ideas or policies are confronted . . . hypotheses are publicly tested . . . processes are disconfirmable "not self-seeking"' (pp. 103–4).

The ethical dimension to reflective thinking

I want to sow some seeds of doubt at this point. It is all very well saying that we can think reflectively and try out solutions to problems we have identified, but how do we know we have identified the real problems? My definition of the problem arising from a given situation may not be the same as your view: who is 'right'? Furthermore, my identification of a problem and the solution may simply relate to what is called 'technical rationality' (Schön, 1983), in other words, I am finding a means to an end. I want my learners to learn, and I want an efficient way to do this. I may not be taking into account the notions of equity, or challenging what it is the learners should learn, and why. What about practising in ways that are 'morally good'? Here, we are moving away from the idea that we simply have to find efficient ways to go about the business of teaching and learning, to the idea that there are things that we *should* do; that is, there is a *normative* aspect to our theory and practice.

I want to introduce some terms which help us understand why theory and practice are often discussed as though they were completely different things. The Greeks did not have this problem. Aristotle, in particular, talked about two kinds of action: *poiesis* and *praxis*. The first means making action, doing something to bring about a particular artefact or product into existence. It is particularly linked with the idea of *techne*: that is, in order to make something, you need to know how to do it, and this form of knowledge is what we would recognize as technical 'know-how'. With teaching, we do not actually bring about the creation of goods or products. So for us the interesting term is *praxis*, which is concerned with bringing about something which is 'morally good'. We must be careful not to see *praxis* as a form of 'technically correct' behaviour: it is much deeper than that. It is concerned with ethical, social and political action. When we think of *praxis*, we, therefore, begin to think about how we are influenced by our culture, our upbringing, our socially situated selves. We act in this world in ways that are defined by our personalities, our religion or philosophy, and by our ideologies, much of which we are unaware. One of the major proponents of *praxis* was Paulo Freire (1971, 2002) who worked with peasants in Brazil, and helped them to see that their need to gain literacy was not simply so that they could read and write, but so that they could take action in the world to improve their situation. *Praxis* is, therefore, concerned with political action. It is something that Carr and Kemmis (1986) describe thus:

> Praxis has its roots in the commitment of the practitioner to wise and prudent action in a practical, concrete, historical situation. Praxis is always risky; it requires that the practitioner makes a wise and prudent practical judgement about how to act in this situation. (pp. 190–2)

So *poiesis* is non-reflective action which leads to the creation of something and *praxis* is a reflective form of action which is capable of transforming the theory that influences it. In *praxis* there is an emphasis on commitment to action. However, commitment to action is still not enough if we are searching for the wisest course of action. How do we know that our practice is prudent? For this, we need another approach where our action which has been informed by reflection which makes judgements about what is the 'best' way. This is the Greek term *phronesis*. I particularly like this term. It means practical knowledge that is defined as rightness of action. It aims to go beyond practice which is routine, habitual or unquestioned. It requires acting 'rightly and appropriately' (Doyal and Harris, 1986), and a 'prudent understanding of variable situations with a view to what is to be done' (McCarthy, 1984, p. 2). Of course, what is appropriate cannot be easily established and is open to challenge. Yet searching for ways to act rightly and appropriately is an important goal for us. It is a constant search and ensures that we do not become complacent. Carr, in articulating the importance of *phronesis* for Aristotle, described it as 'the most supreme intellectual virtue and an indispensable feature of practice' (1986, p. 171).

I am not suggesting that we can discover one 'right way' morally. We know that there are cultural differences in how we define what is morally 'right'. We can, however, be open to debate about the moral and ethical dimension of our work. It is only by acknowledging the difficulties we encounter in deciding how to act in this world rightly and appropriately that we can begin to work towards achieving this goal. So, our search for reflective teaching is based upon an ancient Greek concept of *phronesis*. Without it, the person 'who lacks *phronesis* may be technically accountable but never morally answerable' (Carr, 1986, p. 171). You will notice within the LLUK standards that there is a series of values listed. These help direct the way in which we undertake our professional practice and begin to help us identify and debate our code of practice as professionals who facilitate the learning of others. I do not think we should consider these values as given or unproblematic. I believe they should form the basis of a professional dialogue, continually reminding us that we are searching for practice which is never complacent.

Can reflection *change* practice?

It is one thing to think reflectively about our practice and use this in a wise way. Have we established that critical reflection can actually change practice? As one writer, Collins, reminds us:

> As adult educators operating within this overall text, we can spark debate and 'trip the light fantastic' with talk about critical thinking skills . . . without making any tangible difference to our own practice. (1991, p. 50)

Can we change practice and make it more effective, more underpinned by theories that are the best we have? Our informal theories have little likelihood of developing into 'good practice' if they are not critically examined and tested. Talking to colleagues about what we do 'unwraps the shroud of silence in which our practice is wrapped' (Brookfield, 1998, p. 136). If we reflect critically, we can begin to formulate propositions from our own personal, informal theories which then become public and testable. We can then begin to advance both our practical and theoretical knowledge, taking into account the important interplay between what is happening in practice and what sense is being made of our practice by others. Examining our practice is, as Popper noted, 'not the enemy of theoretical knowledge but the incentive to it' (1962, p. 222). Thus:

> Theories are not bodies of knowledge that can be generated out of a vacuum and teaching is not some kind of robot-like mechanical performance that is devoid of any theoretical reflection, both

are practical undertakings whose guiding theory consists of the reflective consciousness of their respective practitioners. (Carr and Kemmis, 1986, p. 113)

We have, therefore, ideas of theories in use and taken-for-granted ideas about what we do, ideas which can be seen as knowing how and knowing that, and occasionally ideas about knowing why (Ryle, 1949); Eraut (1994) succinctly sums up the difficulty in examining theory which gets used in practice as:

the failure to recognise how theory gets used in practice, that it rarely gets just taken off the shelf and applied without undergoing some transformation. The process of interpreting and personalizing theory and integrating it into conceptual frameworks that are themselves partly inconsistent and partly tacit is as yet only minimally understood. (p. 157)

Thinking reflectively seems to be quite a dangerous undertaking. We are actively challenging the comfortable, taken-for-granted parts of our professional selves. The words that Dewey, back in 1916 and 1933, uses to capture such demands are significant:

one can think reflectively only when one is willing to *endure* suspense and to *undergo* the *trouble* of searching. To many persons both *suspense of judgement* and *intellectual search* are *disagreeable*, they want to get them ended as soon as possible. They cultivate over-positive and dogmatic habit of mind, or feel perhaps that a condition of *doubt* will be regarded as evidence of *mental inferiority*. It is at the point where *examination* and *test* enter into investigation that the difference between reflective thought and bad thinking comes in . . . to be *genuinely thoughtful*, we must be willing to *sustain* and *protract* that state of doubt which is the *stimulus* to *thorough inquiry*. (1933, pp. 15–16; 1916, p. 176, my italics)

This approach relates to a concept of professional practice. John Elliot (1991) wrote that all worthwhile professional learning is experiential. We should look at real practical situations which are problematic, complex and open to a variety of interpretations from differing points of view. This provides opportunities to develop capacities that are fundamental to competent professional practice. Thus our acquisition of knowledge proceeds interactively with reflecting about practical situations.

The critical reflective practitioner

Donald Schön (1983, 1987) developed his ideas about the reflective practitioner in response to three criticisms of the prevailing positivist epistemology of practice. First, that in many professions there was a separation of means from ends; that is, the end point was more important than the process of getting there, a criticism particularly levelled at 'outcome-based' projects in education and training. The second criticism was that there is the separation of research from practice, with researchers not working with practitioners and practitioners not finding out about recent research. Third, and building upon the first two criticisms, Schön argued that there is a separation of knowing from doing. He subsequently developed his 'epistemology of practice' to argue the importance of *practical* knowledge. His ideas have been widely applied in professional practice, particularly in teacher education and the nursing profession.

His first notion is that our practical knowledge stems from our 'knowing-in-action'. This is where our action is dealing with everyday situations that are not unusual or problematic. It is the 'nitty gritty' of normal work. Sometimes, we are tempted to call this type of knowing 'instinct' or 'intuition'. So when we watch a skilled practitioner at work, very often that person would not be able to articulate what is known about that everyday activity, it is such a part of the 'unconscious competence'.

Schön built upon his work with Argyris on the idea of 'theory-in-use'. This is the 'body of informal beliefs relevant to deliberate human behaviour' (Argyris and Schön, 1974, p. 8; Bateson, 1958). Schön recognized the difficulty for many people that they are unable to describe their theories in use. Often, people have 'espoused theories' and find that they do not actually do what these theories suggest. For example, many of us will have experienced working in organizations which state that they are committed to a quality and diversity policy, but their practices, organizationally and individually, do not actually align with these principles. I have noticed that educational and training institutions are often the worst offenders at not enabling their own staff, particularly non-teaching staff, to engage in learning activities.

As we cannot state our theories in use and as a consequence cannot move our thinking from single-loop to double-loop learning, we, therefore, need to reflect on our action. While we are teaching, we may reflect on certain aspects: is the group engaged in the task at hand, do they look bored, should I move on to a new topic now? Schön calls this reflection-in-action. The most important aspect of reflection for Schön, however, is the reflection that goes on after the action has taken place: reflection-on-action. Here, he recommends that we think critically about what has taken place, and it is the combination of theories in use and reflection-in-action and reflection-on-action which leads us to knowing-in-practice.

Schön's work is immensely popular and has influenced a generation of teacher educators among many other professional disciplines. He is not without his critics. Newman (1999) has argued cogently that a better alternative to describe reflective practice is 'critical practice', where practitioners can adopt the 'different social contexts in which they find themselves' (p. 159). His argument is based particularly on criticisms of just how critically reflective Schön's case studies are. It is particularly relevant to the difficult notion of how to challenge what we have so badly articulated, that is, our tacit knowledge. Reflective practice has become a byword for a range of practices and meanings which do little to challenge our tacit assumptions and implicit, informal knowledge. For example, Brookfield (1998) reminds us that:

> Critical reflection on experience should move us beyond the dichotomous Animal Farm type slo-
> ganising of 'large lectures bad, small group discussion good' that bedevils much conversation on
> experiential learning. (p. 140)

Schön based his work on professional practice. He was concerned with the development of critically reflective practitioners, people who would be competent professionals, seeking to improve their practice. This raises the question of what is a competent professional? Michael Eraut (1994) has devoted much research and thought to this issue. Eraut talks about being professionally competent in a variety of ways. When we first train to be adult educators, we may have reached a minimum level of competence in order to work with our learners, trainees, clients. There are sets of standards in most professions that specify what a new-comer to the profession must be able to do. However, that level of competence is not enough for someone who has been practising for some time. Dreyfus and Dreyfus (1986) identify that one can progress from being a novice to a competent professional, and on to become an expert. Often, becoming competent requires a deal of conscious thought. If you have taken up a new hobby or sport, the first few months of learning what to do require immense concentration. Only when you have gained a level of skill can you undertake your activity without thinking about it so much: this is called 'unconscious competence'. It is like being able to ride a bicycle without having to remember how to keep your balance. In fact, if you do think about it, sometimes you wobble rather alarmingly! Yet, what is desirable is for our competent professionals to help us improve our own practice and become competent ourselves. So we need to have a way of thinking about all the things which have become 'unconscious' for the benefit of others.

What are the characteristics of competent professionals? Again, Eraut suggests that such people have learned not just about their discipline, but also about the people with whom they work, who to talk to about particular issues, who to ask for advice, who will know how to mend something. There was a television commercial a few years ago which was used by one of the motorists' organizations which showed someone being in trouble and needing help. Although a passer-by could not help, the memorable saying was 'I don't know but I know a man who does.' When we are faced with situations about which we are unsure, then knowing who to ask is a valuable part of our professional knowledge. If you are work-ing part-time for your institution, it is very easy to miss out on these valuable sources of knowledge. With the growth of technology and use of the internet, and through the use of social networks and Wikipedia, more people are able to tap into these sources of knowledge, which admittedly are not always well established or tested.

Where can you share your ideas with your colleagues and develop your knowledge about your professional practice? There are professional organizations which currently belong to the post-compulsory sector in education. The Learning and Skills Network (LSN) (formerly the Learning and Skills Development Agency (LSDA)) is very much involved with further education colleges in the design and delivery of development projects which investigate issues in teaching and learning. A network which shares the interest in undertaking research by further education practitioners is the Learning and Skills Research Network (LSRN) which encourages membership by individuals within both further education and higher education. Projects which can inform practice and help establish new methods and approaches are particularly considered at the annual LSRN conference. Other research networks which help to disseminate teaching and learning ideas include Research and Practice in Adult Literacy (RaPAL). There are interest groups which use mailbases which you can join where you can share and discuss your own interests and read about those of your colleagues. The Institute for Learning (IfL) is another important membership organization. See Chapter 10 for further ideas.

What happens when you critically reflect on your teaching?

There is a danger that we can become 'critically reflectively correct' people where we talk endlessly about *praxis*, *phronesis* and emancipatory practice. Our colleagues will yawn and ignore us! Yet what are the benefits of critical reflection? One of the great exponents of critical reflection is Jack Mezirow. His fundamental approach is based upon the idea that we should critically reflect on our assumptions (CRA) so that we have a principled approach to our thinking; in other words it is impartial, consistent and non-arbitrary. This is a tall order. If we do begin to adopt this approach, the results will be transformative. Mezirow called critical reflection of assumptions and self-reflection on assumptions the 'emancipatory dimensions of adult learning' (1998, p. 191).

By reflecting critically, instead of continuing with our feelings of self-doubt, that we are imposters in our classrooms, or that we are failing as teachers and racked with guilt, we can become positive in our search for new understandings of our practice and more ways to deal with the challenges that confront us continually. We take control over our professional practice, acknowledging that we cannot transform everything, but aware that we can identify the spheres in which we can. It is a truly emancipatory process.

Practitioners as learners

By now, many of you may be wondering what you can rely upon when thinking about the most appropriate course of action with your learners. I have suggested that you have underlying private theories about why things work and, therefore, how to teach, but these are not tested by others, if they are even articulated. I have then argued that this informal theory is subject to all sorts of 'deceptions', influences of culture and ideology which create assumptions which are not easily identified and, therefore, not easily challenged. As Crotty (1996, p. 280) noted 'When we attempt to describe what we have never had to describe before, language fails us.' So what is to be done?

Perhaps a starting-point is to think of professional practice as a journey. At the beginning, you have to be 'kitted up'; in other words you have to have the necessary equipment and knowledge about how to plan your journey and what to take with you. This is like initial professional education and training. However, once you start travelling, you will meet different situations and people, you will naturally grow older and will have found particular strategies and methods to help you on your way. This is experience which you gain and from which, if you reflect critically, you can learn. There is also a lot of information that you can obtain along the way, too. This is the formal knowledge that is public, a bit like tourist information, maps and timetables. You have to make use of them to plan your particular journey, and you will come to know some of this information very well. Yet your choice of mode of travel may not be the most effective. Sometimes you will not know this until you meet up with other fellow-travellers.

Developing professional practice

Intimately connected with reflective practice, then, is the way in which we act as professionals. One of the characteristics of professional behaviour is adhering to a set of values and views about how to practise. The Learning and Skills Sector can draw upon a number of professional practices, as it comprises such a vast array of specialist subjects. However, within the teaching and learning arena, the main source of an articulated code of practice is the set of LLUK standards. There are additional standards for school teachers created by the General Teaching Council (GTC). Both sets include statements that the professional practitioner engages in continuous professional development, with the aim of improving their skills and deepening their knowledge.

As the LLUK standards focus on the role of the professional, and you will find that you are required to keep a professional diary, or learning log, throughout your teacher training programmes. I am not going to prescribe how you should keep such a log, or even create exercises for you to undertake upon reading any chapter in this book. However, I do suggest that you write down thoughts as and when they occur to you, as you will be surprised at progress in your thinking as time goes by, and these 'scribbles' will provide you with an important source of information when you are asked to look back over your programme and identify how you have developed your thinking and understanding of this vast and complex area.

Conclusion

This chapter started with a practical situation. It then discussed what a reflective process was. This raised questions about thinking reflectively and how we, as practitioners, have many informal theories about our professional work. This led to thinking about theory and what it is and how it can help us. Critical theory was introduced as a way of challenging the supremacy of the scientific paradigm. Finally, the idea of professionalism and competence was discussed, showing that professionals continually seek more knowledge about how to improve their practice. In this way, we realize that not only do we teach but that we also constantly learn about our teaching. Throughout this book, you will be asked to think of yourself as a learner. What does it feel like? Can you remember when you struggled to learn something? Can you remember when you learned something easily? Can you use your experience when you work with your own learners? In other words, can you reflect on your experience and learn from it, transferring your knowledge about learning into knowledge about teaching. Can you teach reflectively?

We are accountable to many people when we teach: learners, colleagues, funding providers, members of communities, and we know that the demands of the various 'stakeholders' are often competing. Critical reflection does not claim to offer answers to these deeply serious problems. It is something that Maslow (1968) described as 'the crucial, unresolved, human questions'. As Eraut (1994) carefully points out, learning from experience is quite problematic. What, precisely, do we learn from experience? We may learn to repeat past mistakes, simply because we have not even thought that there could be alternative ways of doing things.

So, perhaps we can argue that it is not the fact that we can change the world through critical reflection, or indeed can guarantee that we will change our daily practice, but that we have a more developed view about what we do than before we began to think reflectively. Our position is now 'informed by other positions' (Warnke, 1987, p. 169). We can draw upon different forms of learning: learning from initial education and training, learning from books and formal, public knowledge, and learning from experience. Even though

> we can never know just how much we're cooking the data of our memories and experiences to produce images and renditions that confirm our own prejudices and instincts . . . the critical journey has to start somewhere and examining our autobiographies as adult learners is one obvious and fruitful (though usually neglected) point of departure. (Brookfield, 1998, p. 135)

We will have begun our journey of critical reflection. The first stage involves examining the policy context in which our practice operates. Then we can begin to reflect on the practical nature of our teaching, which will now be informed by the 'bigger picture' in which we work.

LLUK standards

This chapter will help you work towards all of the standards, but through a critical reflection of what they mean, how you use them and what impact they have on you and your learners. In particular, you will be able to work towards some of the personal skills and attributes and towards reflecting upon and evaluating one's own performance and planning future practice.

Further reading and information

Further reading

If you are interested in the philosophy of science, then the way in which scientific knowledge is constructed and challenged makes fascinating reading. I would recommend you begin with Chalmers' *What is This Thing Called Science?* (1982) and continue with *Empiricism, Explanation and Rationality* by Doyal and Harris (1986).

A helpful discussion on reflective practice can be found in the writings of Stephen Brookfield.

Brookfield, S. D. (1995) *Becoming a Critically Reflective Teacher.* San Francisco: Jossey-Bass.

Brookfield, S. D. (1998) 'Against naive Romanticism: from celebration to the critical analysis of experience', *Studies in Continuing Education*, 20, 2, pp. 127–42.

Carr, W. and Kemmis, S. (1986) *Becoming Critical.* Lewes: Falmer.

Dewey, J. (1916) *How We Think: A Restatement of the Relation of Reflective Teaching in the Educative Process.* Chicago: Henry Regnery.

Eraut, M. (1994) *Developing Professional Knowledge and Competence.* London: Falmer.

Freire, P. (2002) *Pedagogy of Hope: Reliving Pedagogy of the Oppressed.* London: Continuum.

Mezirow, J. (1998) 'On critical reflection', *Adult Education Quarterly*, 38, 3, pp. 185–98.

Pollard, A. (1997) *Reflective Teaching in the Primary School.* London: Cassell.

Schön, D. (1983) *The Reflective Practitioner.* San Francisco: Jossey-Bass.

Schön, D. (1987) *Educating the Reflective Practitioner: Towards a New Design for Teaching and Learning in the Professions.* San Francisco: Jossey-Bass.

Willis, P. (1999) 'Looking for what it's really like: phenomenology in reflective practice', *Studies in Continuing Education*, 21, 1, pp. 91–112.

Useful websites

Association of Teachers and Lecturers – New 2 Teaching (www.new2teaching.org.uk)

Institute for Learning (www.ifl.ac.uk)

Learning and Skills Improvement Service (LSIS) (www.lsis.org.uk)

Role of the further education teacher (https://nextstep.direct.gov.uk/planningyourcareer/jobprofiles)

Policy in Lifelong Learning

Chapter Outline

Most managers in the Learning and Skills System have an enormous pile of papers, many of which cite the latest announcements of new government initiatives, analyses of White Papers and helpful summaries of policy from among others the Learning and Skills Network (LSN), the Learning and Skills Improvement Service (LSIS), the National Institute for Adult and Continuing Education (NIACE) and EdExcel (an awarding body). By the time you read this chapter, many of the ideas and developments discussed below will have been superseded by newer initiatives, and changes in government. A lesson, then, from examining policy in lifelong learning, is that it is very fluid, fast changing and requires continual monitoring to ensure that we are able to critically engage with it. We are all asked to implement policy at national, regional and local level. If we have no idea where such policies come from, or why we are being asked to implement them, we cannot be effective, nor can we challenge them when we see that their aims are misleading or unhelpful. This chapter attempts to draw a map of the current policy context of lifelong learning, and sets out strategies for analysing policy. It addresses the following questions:

- What is policy?
- How is it made and what underlies it?
- How can policy be examined?
- What is lifelong learning?
- What is happening in lifelong learning policy?
- How does this affect practitioners and learners?

What is policy?

There are numerous definitions of policy, but most agree that it is difficult to define! One metaphor is that policy is an elephant, we can all recognize one but we find it hard to describe. This metaphor works well because it is usually difficult to change policy, in the same way that it is to move an elephant. Policy analysis is a huge area of study, and space does not permit a detailed examination of it. If you want to read further, Parsons (1995) provides a summary of definitions of policy analysis from the literature, including thinking about it as a way of dealing with 'the public and its problems' (Dewey, 1933). I find that the best way to think about policy is as an intention to undertake action to address a particular issue, or problem. Richard Hoppe (2010) discusses how policy-makers need to focus their energy on identifying a problem rather than simply finding solutions. Policies can be developed at global, international and national level, regional and local level, all the way through to an individual level, such as having a policy never to go overdrawn at the bank!

One way to look at policy and how it is developed is to think of a cycle (Figure 2.1), where a problem or issue is identified, the policy is devised as a way to tackle this issue, and then it is implemented. Monitoring the implementation of the policy is intended to ensure that it is effectively introduced and undertaken, and evaluation is intended to occur when the aims of the policy have been reached. Sceptics among you will instantly realize that policies do not often work through this cycle unhindered.

One of the major problems for policy implementation in the education sector is that a new policy is often introduced before an existing one has run its course. It may affect other parts of the education sector, which are themselves subject to policy implementation, or more usually these days policy 'overload'. Indeed, the permeability of public policies is a characteristic that has to be considered when creating and implementing them. For example, if we wanted to create a policy to address drop-out in colleges among young people, we might find that we need to consider a number of aspects of their lives, including how much part-time work they are undertaking, their family circumstances, the time it takes them to travel to college, the timetabling of their programmes, as well as the subjects they have

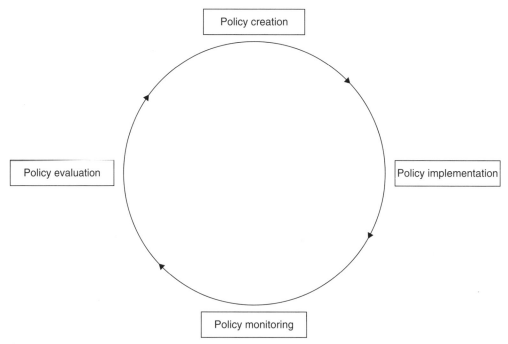

Figure 2.1 The policy cycle

chosen to study, and the college's own systems of pastoral and learning support. We would not be able to develop a policy to encompass all these factors as some are completely outside our control, for example, if people have family responsibilities, or a part-time job. Even if we decide to offer childcare vouchers, or suggest a limit to how many hours our learners should work part-time, we cannot guarantee that this will ensure that our young learners continue to come to college. So, when we talk about policy implementation, we need to remember that it is not a simple case of creating a 'good idea' to solve a problem, set this idea into train and assume that our solution will work. Policy-making and implementation is complex, dynamic and challenging.

How is policy made?

The idea of policy-*making* can be examined from the perspective of rational decision-making. Hogwood and Gunn (1984) provide a useful way to do this by examining how issues become noticed enough to reach a policy-making agenda. This phase is often known as agenda setting. How such issues are filtered so that only some reach the agenda is another aspect of policy-making and this process is known as issue filtration. Not all issues reach an agenda of policy-making. This entire process is not necessarily rational, particularly as people supporting an issue will have vested interests or strong beliefs and often, groups of people will disagree about what an issue is in the first place! Hoppe (2010) provides a number of examples from the UK and the Netherlands which show how an issue is through of differently and leads to very disparate policy solutions.

We can examine policy in a number of ways:

- as it reaches the agenda;
- as it becomes formulated and refined;
- as a statement of problem definition;
- as it is implemented;
- as it is changed;
- as it leads to new policy formation.

One of the ways in which policy reaches the agenda, is refined and implemented, is through negotiation with stakeholder groups. Government has attempted to negotiate formation of policy through consultations, which help to refine and reformulate a policy which has been developed by civil servants, for example. This provides opportunities to create ownership, and help ensure its success. It is important that you are aware of consultations that take place, so that you and your organization can respond and help influence the development of policies that will affect your professional lives.

How is policy examined?

Policy analysis aims to understand how problems and processes may be contextualized. Policy can be seen as a form of problem solving, and in a Popperian sense, we can test the effectiveness of policy in its ability to solve problems, but we must also take account of the unintended consequences of that policy.

Policy *analysis*, therefore, leads to policy *evaluation*. Again, we can make choices between a 'positivist' approach to evaluating the underpinning theory of our policy-making, where we choose between theories based on our tests against empirical evidence, or we can argue that all theories are social constructions, which takes a more relativist stance. Parsons (1995) advocates a far more pragmatic approach by considering policy analysis to be essentially a 'boot-strapping activity' (p. 73), where no one theory or model is adequate to explain the complexity of the policy activity of the modern state. On this view, analysis of public policy involves the 'appreciation of the network of ideas, concepts and words which form the world of explanation within which policy-making and analysis takes place' (Parsons, 1995, p. 73). With any policy examination, then, we need to decide what our viewpoint is, and then to seek out the effects of the policy according to the criteria which our viewpoint, or model, directs us to look for. With this in mind, we can now begin to examine the particular policies affecting our professional practice.

As most of you reading this book will be working in the Learning and Skills System, you will be particularly affected by policies which have been developed to address the major issue of enabling people who are no longer in the school system to gain knowledge and skills. This area is not only huge, but it also relates to many other aspects of public policy, for example, health, work and citizenship. It would be impossible to capture this vast arena of public policy-making in one chapter. I am going to concentrate on recent policy-making, in particular that involved with the concept of lifelong learning, and identify areas that are of fundamental importance to a practitioner. I will signal aspects of policy-making and implementation that you might also wish to pursue and give you advice on where to find out more. First, we must consider what we mean by the term lifelong learning, and then look at the policies that are currently in place.

What is lifelong learning?

Lifelong learning, as the name implies, is about learning that takes place throughout a person's life. It is meant to be continuous and, therefore, does not stop at the end of compulsory schooling. Lifelong learning is also called lifetime learning, continuing education, and within Europe terms like 'education permanente' attempt to capture the meaning of learning throughout life. For the purposes of this book, I want to concentrate on learning that takes place primarily in institutions set up to help young people and adults learn. However, as you will see below, the boundary between childhood, young adulthood and adulthood is becoming more blurred as far as the learning opportunities provided for them in institutions are concerned.

The second difficulty is defining what counts as learning. The OED defines learning as 'to get knowledge of (subject) or skill in (art etc.) by study, experience or being taught'. The definition of learning is very fluid and allows us to focus on what is being learned, by whom and how. What about people who go on holiday and take a trip to a local museum, escorted by their tour guide? They find out all sorts of things they did not know about before. They have learned a great deal. Does this count as learning? Is the tour guide therefore a teacher? If you ask your colleagues to name the ways in which adults can learn, you will probably find that you have a long and varied list. In most cases, the learners do not *have* to learn. They are no longer in a compulsory education sector. In fact, they are taking up learning opportunities that are on offer in the post-compulsory sector and in many cases they learn outside the formal education and training sectors. My definition of informal learning has a defining characteristic that it is always occurring. It may be unplanned, it may be a result of serendipity. It is *prevalent* but often unrecognized. People would not be able to use mobile phones, find their way in strange cities or use new foods without learning informally how to do so (Hillier, 2010).

Where do people learn? Structures and settings

Some of the learning that takes place does so in formal settings, like schools, colleges, universities, training organizations. In fact, this type of learning is defined as *formal learning*.

Other learning takes place entirely independently, through reading magazines, belonging to an interest group, watching television or surfing the internet. This type of learning is often called *non-formal* or *informal* learning. Many of the policies you will read about in the following pages are concerned with formal learning. Huge funds are available from the government to support formal learning by adults. Much of this is directed at younger adults, to encourage them to gain qualifications which will enable them to be economically active. A lot of this provision is found in further education colleges. You may think that all of further education is aimed at young people and helps them gain qualifications. In 2009, there were 909,700 young learners aged 19 and under and nearly 2 million adults – a total of 2.9 million learners, participating in the Learning and Skills System, excluding schools and higher education (Dataservice, 2010).

A much smaller proportion of funds is available for those who simply want to learn about a new hobby or interest. This form of learning is often known as *adult and community learning*, and much of this kind of provision takes place in local education authority institutions and school premises. Trying to map what opportunities are available, and where and how these are funded, is a difficult task. Not all learning is funded through the government's Department for Education (DfE) or the Department for Business, Innovation and Skills (BIS). People who work in the health sector, for example, may be funded through hospital trusts and health authorities. Trades' unions are now involved in funding learning, particularly through the Learning Fund. Unison, the union for local government workers, is heavily involved in providing 'opportunities for learning, through its work with shop stewards and in recent years with its Return to Learn campaign, in association with the Workers' Educational Association (WEA). Voluntary organizations are involved in the provision of learning opportunities. Housing associations enable those involved in tenants' associations to develop the skills of working in committees and urging action by local government. Prisoners can learn while serving their sentences. People in care can take part in learning programmes, as can people in community groups. In fact, people have opportunities to

Places where people can learn
  - Adult and Community Learning Institutions
  - Armed forces
  - Further Education Colleges
  - Distance and Open Learning, for example, learndirect, National Extension College (NEC)
  - The Open University
  - Libraries
  - Prisons
  - Public venues including pubs and drop-in centres in shopping centres
  - Specialist and Designated Colleges
  - Training Organizations
  - Voluntary Organizations
  - Web-based learning
  - Work-based Learning Programmes

Figure 2.2 Principal provision of learning in the Learning and Skills Sector

learn in an ever-increasing number of ways. The education programmes of television, radio and of course the opportunities from the internet bring learning opportunities into the home and workplace.

Figure 2.2 shows the current provision of education and training, demonstrating that provision of learning covers a range of different purposes.

Why do people learn?

When you first meet a group of learners, you may spend a little time asking them what they want to achieve from their learning programme. Even if you are running a one-day workshop, it is always helpful to find out something about your learners' motivations and aspirations.

Professionals have developed their own views about why adults learn. These views constitute models of adult learning. With liberal education it is assumed that people want to learn for learning's sake. In other words, they enjoy learning and they continually wish to do so (Brookfield, 1988; Jarvis, 1990; Schuller and Watson, 2009). They are not driven by some functional need like seeking a qualification in order to find work or advance their career. They simply enjoy finding out about things. This model of adult education is one which can be seen in many local authority (LA) forms of provision and in university extramural departments. It can also be seen in courses put on by art galleries, museums and a host of societies. It is, however, the area of lifelong learning which is most subject to cuts because it is seen as being less important than learning for employment. Tom Schuller and Jenny Williams (2010) argue strongly for a change in the way that lifelong learning is funded, precisely because a small rebalancing of funding away from younger learners will have a profound effect on provision for adults.

The radical model of adult education subscribes to the view that education has a transformative potential. Here, people learn in order to make changes to their social and political situation. Theories of radical education derive particularly from the work of Paulo Freire (1972) who worked with peasants in Brazil and enabled them to gain literacy skills through a process of 'conscientization', in other words becoming aware of their disadvantaged position. The radical model of adult education is particularly strong in community education, where workers facilitate the empowerment of local people to fight for improvements in their situation. The work of Tom Lovett in Northern Ireland and Liverpool is an example of this type of community education (Lovett, 1988; Westwood and Thomas, 1991; Mayo and Thompson, 1996, 2005).

There are *work-related* purposes for learning. Traditionally, further education has been the site of vocational learning, through full-time programmes for young people, day-release programmes for people in work, and evening courses for those who cannot have time off during the day to study. Increasingly, further education has expanded its provision to cover even younger people from 14–19 years, adults wanting evening classes similar to those in adult education institutes, and continuing professional development for a large number of professions. Generally, but not exclusively, further education has always offered accredited programmes. The more liberal adult education providers have also found ways to offer credit for their programmes, often with Open College Credits or through awarding bodies which are more prescriptive in what they accredit. Some courses disappear from the curriculum and others take their place. The rise and rise of technology courses, and the increasing demand for these, replaces other previously popular courses. You may wish to obtain a number of prospectuses from local colleges and providers to see if you can identify whether there is an explicit model of adult education reflected in the range of learning opportunities advertised.

What counts as learning and who provides the opportunities to do so keeps changing. Richard Edwards (1997) challenges the idea that people learn in neat categories of provision and that provision comes solely from formal educational institutions. Models of adult education draw upon the underlying cultural and ideological forces that direct and to some extent control our lives. Thus, the purposes of what we do as educators and the reasons why people wish to engage in learning must also be considered in light of the ideological context (see, for example, Collins, 1991).

The range of provision, how it is funded and how learning opportunities are devised, accredited and evaluated partly depend on the education and training policies that have been created and implemented. These policies are written on a grand scale, such as those devised by government and on a smaller, local level by individual institutions, course teams and individual tutors and trainers. Policies, too, can be seen to be part of a much wider strategy based upon political ideology (see Hillier and Jameson, 2003; Fawbert, 2003; Hillier, 2006; Avis, 2010).

Structures and processes in lifelong learning policy

A policy history

If you are interested in the history of education, then I suggest you read Roger Fieldhouse's book on the history of British education (Fieldhouse, 1996), and Hyland and Merrill (2003) for a helpful summary of the history of education and training in post-compulsory education. Frank Coffield's inaugural lecture at the Institute of Education provides a critical analysis of lifelong learning (see www.ioe.ac.uk). Education and training provision is strongly linked to the social and political context of any country. It is mainly funded by government and, therefore, subject to the ideas of the time about who should be educated and trained, in what way and for what purposes.

I want to start with the 1980s, where Britain was faced, as were many European countries, with an immense problem of unemployment. There were huge numbers of young people and adults without jobs. Those with low basic skills levels and few or no qualifications were far more likely to be unemployed. This led government policy-makers to create wave upon wave of initiatives to try to reduce unemployment by the creation of training programmes. Underlying the policy was the notion that to be economically successful and thereby have full employment, people needed to have the skills, knowledge and qualifications to work. The resulting abbreviations and acronyms have become a testimony to the problems and trial solutions of the 1980s. These include YOPS (Youth Opportunities Scheme), TOPS (Training Opportunities Scheme), YTS (Youth Training Scheme), ET (Employment Training), CPVE (Certificate in Pre-vocational Education). For those who were unemployed, a number of initiatives were created to encourage them to gain work and qualifications in a relevant occupational area. The government's 'quango' (quasi-autonomous non-government organization) responsible for employment and training matters was the Manpower Services Commission (MSC), created in 1974. It supported the creation of training opportunities, primarily for those unemployed but also for those in employment. The MSC changed its name four times subsequently (Training Education and Employment Development (TEED), The Training Commission and the Training Agency (TA)). By the time it was known as the TA, it had become absorbed into the Department of Employment (DoE). The initiatives to foster training and employment drew heavily on the provision offered in both further and adult education institutions, as well as on the increasing number of private training organizations and voluntary organizations. By 1995, the Department for Education and Science (DES) merged with the Department of Employment to become the Department for Education and Employment (DfEE), signalling how much education and training was linked to employment issues in government policy. The Department was subsequently changed at the start of Labour's second term of office to become the Department for Education and Skills (DfES). This ministry then became divided into two: a Department for Children, Schools and Families (DCSF) and a Department for Innovation, Universities and Skills (DIUS). Within 18 months of the latter's creation, it became renamed as the Department for Business, Innovation and Skills (BIS). Further Education found itself being overseen by two government departments, as its provision for 14–19-year-olds came under DCSF and adults within BIS. With the election in May 2010 of a Coalition government, the DCSF has now become the Department for Education (DfE). Readers will understand why any book written about English government struggles to keep up to date with the changing structure. Readers from overseas as well as from the UK will continue to need updates through social networking and electronic dissemination!

An international dimension

It is important to recognize that many challenges facing the UK are also experienced worldwide. Given its membership of the European Union (EU), the UK is particularly influenced by policies and strategies with a European focus. In 2000, the Lisbon Strategy for the European Commission stated its goal that Europe would be 'the most competitive and dynamic knowledge-based economy in the world, capable of sustainable economic growth with more and better jobs, and social cohesion (EU, 2000). The Organisation for Economic Co-operation and Development (OECD) provides a wealth of data and analysis on how its member countries are faring on a variety of indicators in relation to such goals. Its annual *Education at a Glance* is a rich source of information (OECD, 2009). The Inquiry into the Future for Lifelong Learning (IFLL) also provides analysis of how well the UK is doing by taking data from Eurostat, the statistical arm of the EU, as well as national data from the UK Commission for Employment and Skills (UKCES) and the Office for National Statistics (ONS). These analyses help inform national government about how much more they need to do to ensure that their countries are performing well. The UK has slipped its position in the past few years, partly because other countries are investing heavily in education and training.

The major policies of the last decade

To help understand the way in which current structures have come to exist, and provision is made for people to learn, I want to discuss the major government White Papers and legislation over the past two decades. It is always difficult to decide where to start, as invariably any one policy draws upon an existing policy framework, and usually attempts to address the deep-seated, intransigent issues that previous policies have attempted to deal with. However, the reason you are working in the field, and are paid to do so, or volunteer to do so, stems from the provision that is available for you to work in, and this exists because providers are funded, and have responsibilities towards the learners, the staff and the funders. All of these aspects can be contextualized within the policy framework of the current and previous governments.

The government agenda for lifelong learning

One of the influences on policy-making for lifelong learning in England has been the increasing interest in education and training of adults by the EU. In 1995, a White Paper was produced on Education and Training by the EU, and in 1996 the education ministers from the countries of the OECD adopted a 'lifelong learning for all' policy framework (OECD, 2001, p. 9). Key components of this policy include the acknowledgement of different forms of learning such as informal learning, accreditation of learning, developing foundations for learning and resourcing learning. Linked strongly to these areas is a commitment to access and equity.

The key to understanding the New Labour government agenda for lifelong learning which was developing in the late 1990s can be found in the Green Paper *The Learning Age* (DfEE, 1998). Here, the government outlined its commitment to lifelong learning through a strategy of developing skills and knowledge for economic competitiveness and for social inclusion. It argued that there was a tripartite relationship with individuals, employers and education and training providers. It recognized the need to fund learning and that this should happen through the funding of provision by government, with the additional support from employers and from individuals. *The Learning Age* contained a series of recommendations including improving the basic skills of adults so that they can be economically active, unitization of qualifications, standards and inspection of provision and for regional and local collaboration.

The Learning Age did not arise from a vacuum. In the preceding autumn (1997) the National Advisory Group for Continuing Education and Lifelong Learning (NAGCELL), led by Professor Bob Fryer, reported on lifelong learning, *Learning for the 21st Century* (the Fryer Report). Here, emphasis was placed on the social exclusion of adults linked with the lack of formal education and training, and on the desperate need to find ways to enable them to participate in learning. At the same time, Helena Kennedy reported on widening participation in further education with *Learning Works: Widening Participation in Further Education*. One of the most insistent statements made in the Kennedy Report echoes today: 'If at first you don't succeed, you don't succeed' (Kennedy, 1997, p. 21). Kennedy acknowledged the important role that further education plays in providing a second chance for people to learn successfully who had previously failed in the school system. Together, the Kennedy and Fryer Reports provided evidence that to increase participation in learning by those groups who had so far not been involved required more than government exhortations. There needed to be a serious transformation in the way learning opportunities were devised, managed, funded and provided. The subsequent report on the basic skills needs of adults by Moser (1999), *Improving Literacy and Numeracy*, and a second report by NAGCELL (1999), *Creating Learning Cultures: Next Steps in Achieving the Learning Age*, continued to explore the action required to ensure that lifelong learning becomes a reality for the many people who so far have not participated in any formal learning activities.

To create an infrastructure that would implement the vision of *The Learning Age*, the government produced a further White Paper in 1999, *Learning to Succeed*. This outlined proposals to provide more effectively for both young people and adults by creating a new Learning and Skills Council (LSC). The White Paper began the strategy for rationalizing post-16 education and training through the creation of a national and regional Skills Councils. The Learning and Skills Act received Royal Assent in 2000. The core of the framework was to build a 'new culture of learning and aspiration which will underpin national competitiveness and personal prosperity, encourage creativity and innovation and help build a more cohesive society' (DfEE, 1999, p. 13).

The Learning and Skills Act

The Learning and Skills Act came into force in April 2001. The key features of the Learning and Skills Act concerned the funding and planning of post-16 education and training but exclude higher education. The National Learning and Skills Council (LSC), the biggest quango in the country, was created. It was a Non-Departmental Public Body, with responsibility for planning and allocation of nearly £9 billion of public money for over 7 million learners. The LSC was responsible for the funding, planning and quality assurance of the following areas of education and training:

- Further education sector colleges
- School Sixth Forms
- Work-based training for young people
- Workforce development
- Adult and Community Learning
- Information, advice and guidance for adults
- Education business links.

Connexions was created to provide an integrated youth support service. The responsibility for work-based learning for adults was transferred to the Employment Service, in order to provide a more integrated service of support for unemployed adults. This National LSC was a bold development in the government's strategy to ensure that all those over the age of compulsory schooling can have access to, and benefit from, education and training opportunities.

The council had a number of key priorities including:

- to deliver the vision of *The Learning Age* by fostering a culture and commitment to learning through partnership working, and to fulfil the duty to encourage participation in learning;
- to make a contribution to the economy in terms of productivity, competitiveness through updating of skills;
- to increase the basic skills of adults and young people
- to raise standards in post-16 learning and ensure excellence in teaching and training;
- to draw up an equal opportunities strategy and action plan with targets and performance indicators to tackle underrepresentation and underachievement;
- to build a single organization with a cohesive structure, common culture and common goals and objectives.

Success for all

In 2002, the DfES launched its strategy to build upon its earlier work in *Learning to Succeed*. The three main purposes were to create opportunities for everyone to develop their learning, to enable people to realize their potential, and to achieve excellence in standards of education and levels of skills (DfES, 2002). From these ambitious goals stemmed more policy documents and initiatives. Among these was the setting up of the Post-16 Standards Unit, with a remit to improve standards in teaching. The strategic aims of the Standards Unit focused on 'Putting teaching, training and learning at the heart of what we do' through developing leaders, teachers, trainers and support staff of the future. This strategy worked alongside the other LSC aims of developing a framework for quality and success (DfES, 2004b). The Standards Unit became subsumed within another quango – the Quality Improvement Agency (QIA) which no longer exists but has been replaced by the Learning and Skills Improvement Service (LSIS).

Young people in colleges

During this period, a notable change in the profile of learners in further education occurred. This followed from 14–16-year-olds being given opportunities to participate in vocational learning at further education colleges under a programme called Increased Flexibility (IF). Many young people who had been disaffected with schools flourished in the more 'adult' environment (Harkin, 2006). However, the changing nature of the learners meant that staff in the colleges needed to adapt their teaching to a much younger (and often less well behaved!) group.

The extension of learning opportunities to school aged children has had a profound influence on the activities and policies of the further education system. A key government policy which then became of importance to the learning and skills system was its Every Child Matters (ECM) policy. This policy arose from cases of severe child abuse leading to the death of a little girl, Victoria Climbie. The policy was aimed to ensuring all children were safe and well and that all agencies and organizations who dealt with young children were required to follow the requirements laid down through ECM. Now that young people of school age were learning in further education colleges, the ECM requirements also applied there. Interestingly, a new development will change the landscape again with a change to the school leaving age known as Raising the Participation Age (RPA) to 18 years by 2013. This interesting twist to policies affecting our sector is that from 2013, we will no longer have a post-compulsory group of young learners in college aged 16 and that virtually all the 14–19 provision in colleges will be part of compulsory education.

Structural reform of the learning and skills system

Raising expectations

The discourse of 'success' seen in the earlier White Papers of the New Labour government were succeeded by the discourse of improvement. The term 'raising' became part of subsequent White Papers. A 2006 White Paper *Further Education: Raising Skills, Improving Life Chances* (DfES, 2006) contained a number of measures including streamlining the then LSC, granting powers for further education colleges to award Foundation Degrees and begin to streamline delivery within the system. It also required young people to remain in education or training until they reached the age of 18. This issue is primarily aimed at dealing with the large percentage of young people who are not in any form of education, employment or training, known as NEET young people. This group is often described as being the 'lost generation', a term stemming from the late 1990s but sadly very much applied now. The UK has the fourth highest levels of NEET young people aged 18–24 in the OECD countries and a large proportion of this group are those who are of school age – almost 15 per cent of 16- to 24-year-olds in England in 2009 (DCSF, 2010; *Guardian*, 25 February 2010; Besley, 2009a).

In 2008, the government published a White Paper which heralded a huge change in the Lifelong Learning system. Titled *Raising Expectations: Enabling the System to Deliver*, the White Paper set out structural changes including the creation of two funding agencies and the abolition of the LSC, and requiring that the local authorities would be responsible for commission education for a 16–19-year-olds. This was a bold step by the two ministries responsible for further education.

The Apprenticeships, Skills, Children and Learning Act (2009)

The Apprenticeships, Skills, Children and Learning Act gained royal assent in April 2009. This Act provided a statutory framework for apprenticeships and introduced a new right to request time off from work for training. It transferred responsibility for funding of 16–18-year-olds to the local authorities and provided for adults through a new Skills Funding Agency (SFA). The Agency oversees a 'new demand-led approach to adult education and training', which is supported by strengthened advice and support services for adults and employers in the form of a new Adult Advice and Careers Service (AACS), the National Employer Service and the National Apprenticeship Service. Another agency, the Young People's Learning Agency (YPLA) was established to fund learners aged 14–19. The primary purpose of the YPLA is to support and enable local authorities to carry out their new responsibilities by providing national frameworks to support planning and commissioning, ensuring coherence of commissioning plans, managing the national funding formula, and providing strategic data and analysis.

The Act also established a new regulatory body for qualifications (Ofqual). Ofqual was established in interim form in April 2008, and took on the regulatory functions of the Qualifications and Curriculum Authority (QCA). The Act provides for the set up of Ofqual on a formal basis, equipping it with new powers.

The QCA was set to evolve into the Qualifications and Curriculum Development Agency (QCDA), which would be responsible for developing and advising ministers on the curriculum and related qualifications. The Agency would also have developed and have certain delivery roles in relation to national curriculum and Early Years Foundation Stage assessments. However, the new Coalition government announced that QCDA would be abolished and at the time of writing, it is not clear what will replace it.

Skills for Life

There is one other strategy that has had particular influence on the changing shape of life-long learning provision in England, and that is the Skills for Life strategy (SK4L). The strategy was created, following a survey of basic skills through the International Adult Literacy Survey (IALS), which included the UK in its survey in 1998. As a result of the survey, the government asked Sir Claus Moser to report on an inquiry into the level of basic skills of adults in the UK. The report makes sobering reading. Research indicated that at least 20 per cent of adults in the country have low levels of basic skills, so that they could not read simple instructions or calculate a simple arithmetic sum.

This low level of basic skills is linked to many indices of poverty, poor housing, poor health and unemployment. For example, in 2008 there were 4.2 million people of working age without qualifications, of which 1.9 million were inactive and 250,000 unemployed. Those with lower literacy skills had an employment rate of 55 per cent compared with 75 per cent for those with good skills (DIUS, 2008, p. 59). That is not to say that all people who have difficulty with literacy are poor, or that all poor people must have low literacy and numeracy levels. However, there is evidence that low levels of basic skills prevent people from being economically successful and can lead to social exclusion, thus creating a downward spiral which is hard to stop.

As with the other reports, Moser identified that action was needed, both in terms of creating learning opportunities for people which would be more accessible than previous attempts, to resource learning opportunities and to ensure that those who create, deliver and manage the programmes are qualified and supported to do so. The DfES created the Adult Basic Skills and Strategy Unit (ABSSU) to oversee the implementation of the recommendations which later became the Skills for Life Strategy Unit. The new strategy, *Skills for Life* (2001), reflected the agenda of the New Labour government and supported provision including the learndirect initiative, family learning projects, union-funded programmes, quality standards in basic skills provision, accreditation and training for basic skills teachers and organizers and in qualifications in basic skills for learners. There was hardly any form of education and training for adults which did not address developing the basic skills of the participants somewhere in their activities. There were government targets for adults to gain basic skills qualifications. By 2004, 750,000 adults were expected to have gained an equivalent Level 2 qualification in basic skills, 1.5 million by 2007 and 2.25 million adults by 2010. These targets were met and since then, the government agenda has changed its focus to functional skills for young people (Hughes and Schwab, 2010).

Skills for Life was not only directed at learners. In addition to the national curriculum for learners, there was a new set of standards for practitioners, underpinning qualifications at Levels 3 and 4. These standards for literacy, numeracy and ESOL included subject-specific knowledge in addition to the more generic issues of teaching and learning, as outlined by the LLUK standards. Many of you reading this book will be working towards the basic skills standards in addition to the generic LLUK standards.

The DfES funded a national research and development centre (NRDC) to help underpin knowledge about how best to help adults acquire basic skills, and this has been particularly active in working with practitioners as researchers, as well as setting up a number of research activities. The NRDC continues to provide a range of resources developed through research and through collaboration with practitioners in the field (see www.nrdc.org.uk).

Informal Adult Learning

What about the learning that takes place outside of formal institutions? Should this be supported by government? This question led to a consultation led by DIUS on Informal Adult Learning titled *Informal Adult Learning – Shaping the Way Ahead* which recognized that people learn in a number of ways, not least through the use of technology, informal networks and even in the workplace through sharing ideas and practices with their peers. As a result of the consultation, the New Labour government declared its continuing support for informal learning through a commitment to 'facilitate and stimulate self-organised learning by securing better access to public and private spaces so that groups of learners can pursue their interests and passions' (DIUS, 2009) but subsequent events in relation to cuts in public expenditure by the new Coalition government have called into question how much support will be forthcoming.

Commission for Inquiry into Lifelong Learning

In 2008, NIACE commissioned an Inquiry into the Future for Lifelong Learning, led by Sir David Watson and directed by Professor Tom Schuller and Jenny Williams. It took evidence from a myriad sources including practitioners, managers, researchers in the field as well as commission numerous research activities. The report *Learning through Life* was published in September 2009 (Schuller and Watson, 2009). Its main recommendation was that there were key weaknesses in the current system and that a more systematic approach was required including rebalancing the focus from high expenditure on children and young people to a small but significant increase in expenditure on older people. The commission suggested that there were four stages in the life-course: 18–24, 25–49, 50–74 and 75 plus. The report particularly noted the changing demographic profile of the population (in England but effectively, this holds true for most OECD countries). It was suggested that the 24–59 age group has the most responsibility for work, families and caring. Older people are increasingly willing and able to work and enjoy leisure activities and their interest in learning needs support. This learning, though, is unlikely to lead to qualifications and indeed, most would not wish to gain these. The most important aspect of the report is that it promotes the notion of entitlement – that is all adults should be entitled to learning provision and opportunities and a national framework to support this is required. It is not clear how far these bold proposals have made a difference to policy-makers, particularly in a time of recession and deep cuts in public expenditure. It is clear, though, that the most vulnerable provision lies in the adult and informal learning component of the Lifelong Learning system. A campaign to support this learning, Campaigning Alliance for Lifelong Learning (CALL) is a necessary balance to this situation. Even in formal provision, a survey by the Association of Colleges (AoC) suggested there had been a 16 per cent cut in adult learning budgets (Besley, 2010a).

Changing processes in the learning and skills system

Having identified the main policy initiatives of the New Labour government years, I want to discuss the processes that result from provision in the sector, namely, accrediting learning, funding and ensuring quality. The first major area of change within the structures and systems of the sector that policies have addressed is the qualification system. It is unlikely that any of you reading this book will have escaped the influence of the changing qualification framework, as you will either be taking or have taken programmes that lead to qualifications, and you are likely to be working with learners who are also working towards some form of accreditation of their learning.

The changing qualification system

In England in 1970, secondary school pupils could gain a General Certificate of Education at Ordinary level (GCE 'O' level) qualification in a variety of subjects; the most popular included mathematics, English language, English literature, foreign language, physics, chemistry, biology, history and geography. A lower qualification, Certificate of Secondary Education (CSE), had been introduced to enable those who would not gain an 'O' level to leave school with a qualification in the subjects chosen. A small percentage of young people stayed on at school and studied Advanced level ('A' levels), usually in three subjects. If they decided to continue to study at university or polytechnic, they were part of about 7 per cent of the population to do so. If young people decided to gain a vocational qualification, they could take National Certificates and Diplomas such as the Higher National Certificate (HNC) or Higher National Diploma (HND). Other qualifications were available, for example, in typing, validated by the Royal Society of Arts (RSA), an awarding body. The other main awarding body, City and Guilds, offered awards in more technical and craft-oriented subjects such as plumbing, bricklaying and mechanics. Awarding bodies were independent institutions that had been set up to foster the development of skills and knowledge in vocational subjects and award qualifications in those subject areas. During the 1980s, these bodies both grew and proliferated. Professional bodies, such as the chartered institutes, also award qualifications.

In 1981, a Government White Paper, *A New Training Initiative: A Programme for Action* (DoE, 1981), addressed the need to increase the level of skill in the working population. It set the scene for a number of changes to the provision of education and training and the types of qualification on offer. The government created the National Council for Vocational Qualifications (NCVQ) in 1986. This was in addition to government agencies which over-saw teaching qualifications of school teachers, such as the SCAA (Schools Curriculum and Assessment Authority) and the examination boards which were responsible for GCSE (General Certificate of Secondary Education) (GCE 'O' level and CSE were combined) and 'A' level qualifications. In 1997, the government created a single body to oversee the develop-ment and quality of the qualifications framework in England drawing together the NCVQ and SCAA, known as the Qualifications and Curriculum Authority (QCA). By 1986, National Vocational Qualifications (NVQs) could be gained not only by attending a course at a college or training organization, but by accrediting competences that people already had. NVQs were industry-specific and had been devised to meet standards set by a 'lead body' for any particular industry. At the same time, there was growing concern that the more academic qualifications did not meet the changing demands of employers and so more General National Vocational Qualifications (GNVQs) were introduced to enable young people to gain knowledge and understanding of vocational areas, such as tourism and leisure, business and administration. GNVQs were comparatively short lived and replaced in 2007 by new Diplomas (see below).

The Qualifications and Curriculum Development Agency (QCDA) was set up in 2009 to oversee the Qualifications and Credit Framework (QCF), an important component of the Vocational Qualifications Reform Programme. This programme is an important plank in the government's National Skills Strategy Skills for Growth which aimed to improve training to adults and develop a simple, streamlined qualification system which would be responsive to employer needs (see below). However, at the time of writing QCDA is being closed as part of the cutbacks in response to the huge budget deficit in England.

The national qualifications framework

The number of qualifications available today in the UK is both immense and almost uni-versally perceived as confusing. From 1986 when the first NVQs were introduced, attempts to rationalize the qualification framework have grappled with the problem of achieving equivalence. The first step towards achieving this was by devising a taxonomy of qualifica-tions according to level. This classification system is shown in Figure 2.3.

The first level is the equivalent of pre-GCSE qualifications. Level 2 is the equivalent of a GCSE, Level 3 the equivalent of 'A' levels, and Levels 4 and 5 the equivalent of higher education levels. There is less correspondence between NVQ Levels 4 and 5 and the higher education degree levels of Bachelor, Masters and Doctorate (see Figure 2.4). In theory, any qualification, that is, say, at Level 3, would require the breadth and depth of an 'A' Level, Advanced Certificate of Vocational Education (ACVE) (formerly GNVQ Advanced),

Level of qualification	General		Vocationally related	Occupational
5	Foundation Degrees/HNDs/HNCs			Level 5 NVQ
4				Level 4 NVQ
3 advanced level	A level	Free-standing units Level 3	Vocational A levels BTEC Diplomas Higher Diplomas Advanced Apprenticeships	Level 3 NVQ
2 intermediate level	GCSE grade A*–C	Free-standing units Level 2	Intermediate Vocational GCSEs Intermediate Diplomas BTEC First Young Apprenticeships	Level 2 NVQ
1 foundation level	GCSE grade D–G	Free-standing units Level 1	Foundation	Level 1 NVQ
Entry level	Certificate of (educational) achievement			

Figure 2.3 A taxonomy of qualifications according to level. See www.qcda.gov.uk/

Diploma or NVQ Level 3. In reality, it is quite difficult to state that the qualifications are equivalent, because the content and the way in which learning is assessed vary so much. For example, in a NVQ Level 3 in Learning and Development Practice, candidates must demonstrate that they have the skills and knowledge to undertake any part of the training cycle. Indeed, some of you may be working towards this qualification now. Can you see where this form of professional development has any similarity to, say, Chemistry 'A' level? Yet, if we are to ensure that people can continue their learning both vertically through a qualification systems and more importantly horizontally, then we do need to have some way of working out if one particular qualification has a certain depth in its subject area that equates to a very different qualification in a totally unrelated subject area. If job specifications require a specific level of qualification, it is important that the qualification frameworks help employers and job seekers to demonstrate that their particular qualifications fit the criteria. The level and the subject of the qualification need to be clearly defined. This also helps people who can already demonstrate that they have knowledge and skill through the accreditation of their prior experiential learning, APEL.

The Open College Network comprises a number of regional bodies that credit programmes of learning, primarily in adult and further education. It was set up to recognize the learning that takes in non-accredited programmes and have a primary aim of widening participation in learning. With Open College credits, the programme is devised by the college and if it meets the criteria of the awarding body, in this case National Open College

4	Certificate	C level	Certificates of Higher Education
5	Intermediate	I level	Foundation Degrees, ordinary (Bachelors) degrees, Diplomas of Higher Education and other higher diplomas
6	Honours	H level	Bachelors degrees with Honours, Graduate Certificates and Graduate Diplomas
7	Masters	M level	Masters degrees, Postgraduate Certificates and Postgraduate Diplomas
8	Doctoral	D level	Doctorates

Figure 2.4 Higher education qualifications framework. See www.qcda.gov.uk

Network (NOCN), then the learners will gain credit once they have completed certain activities throughout the programme.

Another development was the accreditation of Key Skills. The Key Skills Awards were specific units that could be taken at Levels 1–4. There were six key skills. A core of three: communication, working with number, information technology, and a wider set of three: problem solving, working in teams, and improving own learning and performance. Many programmes integrated the skills into the main curriculum, although learners could gain separate key skills awards and these could count towards entry to higher education. Basic Skills for adults had a set of qualifications following from the creation of a national curriculum. These followed the current framework, with qualifications at entry Levels 1, 2 and 3, and Levels 1 and 2. However, these skills have now been replaced by functional skills. Readers may well agree with Chris Humphries, the Chief Executive of UKCES when he argued

> Over the years, we've had core skills, key skills, functional skills, generic skills, soft skills, hard skills – what we seem to do every couple of years is change the name, as though to convince ourselves that we've done the job and can move onto a new one. The reality is that those employability skills, as you might call them, haven't really changed that much over the 15 years or so since the CBI and TUC first advocated them. If you look back at the original 'core skills' of communication, application, numbers, ICT, working with others, self-development, problem solving, it looks remarkably like the list employers will give you today. (Humphries, 2008, p. 13)

One outcome of all these policies was a new curriculum introduced into schools and colleges in September 2000. Curriculum 2000 was an attempt to bring together the academic and vocational qualifications that were previously seen to divide learners into two groups: 'those who can think and those who can do'. Pupils in sixth forms and students in further education provision were encouraged to study both 'A' levels and 'AS' levels (the approximate equivalent of the first year of an 'A' level), so that they begin with up to five subjects in their first year of study and, having taken the 'AS' level in these, choose which to study to 'A' level. 'AS' levels were intended to provide vertical, rather than horizontal, routes to accreditation. Vocational GCSEs replaced GNVQs at the foundation and intermediate stages in

2002. Vocational 'A' levels replaced the Advanced GNVQs. People could take a combination of vocational 'A' levels, 'AS' levels, 'A' levels, NVQs, Key Skills Awards and Open College Credits.

Critics and commentators of the post-16 curriculum argued for a 'unitized' system, where people could gain credit from whatever source and move more coherently through the maze of qualifications on offer. The unitized curriculum was first suggested by Geoff Stanton, then director of the FEU (Further Education Unit) (Stanton, 1982). These ideas have been implemented in Scotland and Wales (see Hodgson, 2000) and influenced plans for coherent provision of learning opportunities in England. The body responsible for overseeing the accreditation framework, QCA, introduced a Framework for Achievement which enabled learners to build up units towards qualifications which fit into a simple credit-rated system. There were common level indicators, with a range of core, optional and elective units which can be drawn upon to become awards, certificates, diplomas with agreed subject and sector classifications.

A directive developed by previous governments and which continues today set targets for the level of qualifications held by the population. One of these is the National Learning Targets for England and Wales, which replace the earlier National Education and Training Targets (NETTs). These targets specify what percentage of a section of the population should hold qualifications at certain levels. The government set Public Service Agreement Targets (PSAs) for adults which included by 2011 that 79 per cent of working age adults should have a Level 2 qualification, 56 per cent have a Level 3 and 36 per cent to be qualified to Level 4. In 2009, 75 per cent adults possessed a Level 2 qualification, which is fairly near the government target, 55 per cent were qualified to at least Level 3 and 35 per cent to Level 4 (BIS, 2009a). In 2009, 236,400 people gained their first Level 1 or above literacy qualification and 44,000 people gained a first entry-level numeracy qualification. However, 6.1 million people still have qualifications below Level 2 and a further 4.6 million people have no qualifications meaning 24.4 per cent of the population aged between 19 and 64 have a Level 2 qualification or under including no qualifications at all. This statistic reinforced the government drive to improve qualification levels among the working population and is a continuing challenge for the new Coalition government (Leitch, 2006; DIUS, 2008; Dataservice, 2010).

September Guarantee

In December 2009 there were 952,000 16–24-year-olds officially out of work. Both the previous and current government are keen to do all that they can to help the young people find work or engage in education and training. One of the steps taken was to create a September Guarantee which guarantees a place in education or training at the end of the school year. This has just been developed to include an entry to employment place for 16- and 17-year-olds who are not in education, employment or training. Claimants of job seekers allowance (benefit for unemployed people) will be able to move to this scheme after six months on benefit. There is also a Graduate Guarantee to help access to training, internship or self-employment for graduates who are still unemployed after six months (Besley, 2010c).

14–19 Curriculum Reform

In 2004 a Working Group chaired by Mike Tomlinson reported on the curriculum and qualifications for 14–19-year-olds and made a series of recommendations aimed at addressing the issues of status, equity and usefulness of qualifications currently gained by young people (and actually, by many adults too). The proposed new Diploma framework contained four levels, entry, foundation, intermediate and advanced, each mapped against existing national qualifications from entry-level certificates through to 'A' levels and NVQ Level 3. There would be specific subjects or areas of learning and a prescribed core of generic skills, knowledge and experience common to all programmes. The main thrust of the report argued for the current qualifications to be incorporated within a Diploma framework. The proposals recommended a change in the coursework requirements for GCSEs, and more teacher-led assessment than the current mix of external examinations, both modular and summative. Sadly, the recommendations were not fully implemented but a new form of Diploma was introduced in 2008 and A levels retained their distinct status.

There are currently 14 vocationally oriented diplomas and a further three in science, languages and humanities were planned (and subsequently dropped by the new Coalition government). Diplomas are provided by consortia of colleges and employers. Pilot diplomas and a quality assurance process titled Gateway was introduced to check that consortia wishing to offer Diplomas were ready to do so. From a slow start, there has been an increase in Diplomas being offered and by 2010 there were 314 consortia approved to offer Diplomas. In each local authority there are 14–19 Partnerships which are strategic bodies responsible for the 14 to 19 entitlement in their area. These partnerships map local needs and oversee the consortia delivery. By Autumn 2008, Ofsted reported that the partnerships were well established and collaboration was effective (Besley, 2009b, p. 9).

The Diplomas comprise a subject specialist component, personal learning and thinking skills (PLTS), work experience and a requirement to achieve functional skills. Learners are also required to complete a project. There are three levels: Foundation which is broadly equivalent to four GCSEs, Higher which is broadly equivalent to five or six GCSEs and Advanced which is broadly equivalent to three A levels. A Progression Diploma enables learners to take the equivalent of two A levels. The Higher and Progression Diplomas qualify as entrance qualifications for study in higher education.

Despite the wide range of qualifications, the traditional 'A' level continues to be perceived by employers, learners and parents alike as the 'gold standard'. AS/A level qualifications were high on the government agenda, partly fuelled by accusations of 'dumbing-down' of standards, and also by the fact that it is increasingly difficult to distinguish between applicants for places at prestigious universities or oversubscribed courses, as many are now achieving three or more 'A' levels with grade A. There were some unfortunate incidents with awarding bodies over examination results, and in 2002, the then Secretary of State for Education, Estelle Morris, resigned partly over problems with the 'A' level assessments and publicly disagreed with Sir William Stubbs, then chair of the QCA (who lost his job over the same issue!). Ann Hodgson and Ken Spours have written extensively about qualifications, particularly for 14–19-year-olds in their work for the Nuffield Review of 14–19 qualifications (Nuffield, 2008). This review of 14–19 Education and Training, England and Wales has critically analysed the changing qualification framework for young people and the review contains a number of Issues Papers addressing the implementation of the Diplomas and changes to the A level qualifications (Nuffield, 2008). There is evidence that many schools are continuing to use BTEC and OCR (Oxford Cambridge and RSA Examinations) National Diplomas rather than invest in Diplomas as the former are seen to be more manageable (Dunford, 2010).

Are you beginning to feel confused? Well, one of the consequences of government policies over the past two decades to ensure that people are able and qualified to work has been that there is a proliferation of qualifications (Hillier, 1999; Ward, 1997). This has created a 'jungle' (a phrase first coined by Sir Keith Joseph), where potential learners have no idea of the value of the qualifications, where employers are unsure of what the qualifications are and where educational providers continually revise their programmes to respond to new initiatives and ideas. Most recently, David Willets the new Minister for Universities and Science has spoken out against the continual interference with vocational qualifications and has stated that

> Governments have been able to mess around with vocational qualifications without any campaign in the media to protect them, And as a result, we have let down generations of young people who can find that their vocational qualifications are not valued by employers. I am a believer in rigour and excellence in vocational qualifications just as much as in academic ones . . . the new Qualifications and Credit Framework must not weaken them. (Willets, 2010)

The Qualifications and Credit Framework

The QCF is a framework where each qualification is composed of units. Each unit has a credit value and one credit represents ten hours of work. Each unit and qualification has a level from Entry level to Level 8. Every qualification in QCF is made at Award, Certificate or Diploma. Awards are between 1 and 12 credits, Certificates between 13 and 36 credits and Diplomas 37 credits or more. There is a Personal Learning Record (PLR) to record the achievements and this is also meant to help learners manage their own learning. There is a Managing Information Across Partners (MIAP) record so that individuals can move between providers without losing record of their credit. There are Rules of Combination (RoC), Routes to Achievement (RtA) to help in the process of credit accumulation and transfer. Each learner has a unique learning number (ULN) so that at any time, an individual will have a record of their own achievement to date and providers will be able to track them through the system. The PLR is fully operational in September 2010. The full QCF is due to be operation by the beginning of 2011.

A vocational focus

What about those who do not wish to pursue academic study but wish to work instead? One of the attempts to encourage young people to gain vocational skills was to enrol them on a Modern Apprenticeship (MA). Originally designed for young people aged 16 to 25, new Young Apprenticeships for 14–16-year-olds were available from September 2004 in some sectors such as engineering, business administration and the arts and creative industries. For those not yet ready or able to begin an apprenticeship, there was the Entry to Employment (E2E) programme, primarily designed to help people reach NVQ Level 2, as a route towards MAs. A key strand of New Labour government was aimed at skills and work-based learning seen through government reports such as the *National Skills Task Force: Towards a National Skills Agenda* (DfEE, 1999), *Tackling the Adult Skills Gap* (DfEE, 2000), *21st Century Skills: Realising Our Potential* (DfES, 2003a), *Skills: Getting on in Business, Getting on at Work* (DfES, 2005), *Further Education: Raising Skills, Improving Life Chances* (DfES, 2006). Here the government was keen to be

> leading the world in skills development, with virtually all young people staying on to age 19 and half going on to HE; all adults having the support they need to up-skill and re-skill throughout life; all employers seeing skills as key to their success (DfES, 2006, p. 4).

A major plank of government policy in relation to skills and employment stemmed from a report by Lord Leitch in 2006. Leitch argued that there was

- too little investment by employers in their employees
- too little responsibility taken by individuals for their own learning
- a qualification system divorced from the needs of the modern workplace
- a welfare system not meeting the needs of people in a fast-changing economy

(Leitch, para 21)

Using comparative statistics available mainly from the Organisation for Economic Co-operation and Development (OECD), Leitch argued that 'our nation's skills are not world class' (2006, p. 1). We have a strange 'spikey' profile in comparison to OECD countries in our low, medium and high skills. We rank 17th out of 30 countries on low skills, 20th on intermediate and 11th on high skills.

In response to the Leitch review, the New Labour government endorsed the targets Leitch had set for 2020. However, the economic downturn followed hard on the heels of the report and by December 2008, a DIUS Select Committee examined the implementation of the skills policy and found it wanting. Employers had identified how hard it was to make sense of the skills system (some notably describing it as a 'pig's breakfast' or 'dog's dinner') and there was concern over the mismatch between needs of employers and what was offered through the government's Train to Gain initiative. A further concern, long raised by Alison Woolf was how 'you cannot automatically assume that just because somebody has another qualification, they become more productive' (Innovation, Universities, Science and Skills Committee, 2010).

Skills Investment Strategy

In November 2009 the New Labour government published a White Paper titled *Skills for Growth: The National Skills Strategy* along with an analytical paper *Skills Investment Strategy 2010–11*. These papers strengthened the support for apprenticeships, Skills for Life and continued to highlight how the UK compared unfavourably with Europe (primarily Germany) and the USA. All arrangements put in place by this past government are subject to scrutiny by the current Coalition government but one glimmer of hope is that David Willets remains convinced of the need to support learning in the further education sector and additionally understands that the vocational qualifications system needs to be left alone and not tinkered with. A worrying trend, though, even in the past government's figures, is a decline in funding for adult learners (see BIS, 2009b, p. 12, and Thompson, 2009, p. 10).

Foundation Degrees

In 2000 the government recognized that there was a need to provide better learning opportunities for people who may already be in work at an 'advanced technical practitioner' level, the equivalent of the first two years of a full-time degree. They created a new award, the Foundation Degree (FD), and encouraged further education colleges to work with higher education institutions to provide work-based learning at this level. This new award blurred the boundary between further and higher education even further, and was a key component of a White Paper on higher education (DfES, 2003a). The FDs are intended to contribute to government target set by David Blunkett in 2000, which argued for 50 per cent of young people aged 30 and under to have experienced some form of learning in higher education by the year 2010, much of which could be achieved by collaboration between further and higher education. By 2007, there were nearly 30,000 FD students (HEFCE, 2007). This target has now been changed to incorporate wider forms of learning and to reflect the fact that the changing opportunities to learn outside higher education, particularly in further education render the target meaningless in its original definition. Evaluations of Foundation Degrees (Brennan and Gosling, 2004; Hillier and Rawnsley, 2008; Reeve et al., 2007; Edmond et al., 2009) provide examples of practice along with a critique of how well these degrees have been established.

By now, you will be gaining a picture of how policy influences the way in which provision is made for learners. This provision needs to be funded, and in many ways, a funding regime is a powerful determinant of the kinds of provision that are available.

Funding learning: funding learners

The wide variety of learning providers partly reflects the idea of a market for adult learning. Just as we can choose to buy our food from different supermarkets, and even go to certain ones for particular items, so we can decide to attend different institutions for different learning purposes. This includes deciding to go on holiday and attending short talks by local experts, searching the internet for a particular topic of interest, and deciding to attend an evening class to learn a foreign language. Each learning opportunity is funded and the cost to the individual will vary according to the way in which the funding mechanism works.

We know that children can be educated 'for free' by the state and this is largely paid from general taxation and local council taxes. Adults may or may not pay fees for their learning, depending on whether they will be gaining a qualification or not. A typical evening class in a local authority adult and community learning institution may be funded from a variety of sources, including the local authority, the SFA, department of social services and health service, and the local business community, and each source provides different levels of subsidy.

The funding mechanism in the Learning and Skills System

As with the previous funding mechanism of the Further Education Funding Council (FEFC) and the Learning and Skills Council (LSC), institutions were given funds for the learning opportunities they provide. The funding partly covered overheads including staff costs, building and accommodation, resources and activities such as marketing and recruitment. However, not all the funds came from the funding agencies, so institutions have to make decisions about raising income, often through fees for the learners. There were many rules about what provision would be funded, and how many learners could be funded. However, simply put, there was a funding tariff so that some types of programmes, such as English and other classroom-based subjects, were given a lower rate of funding than a science- or engineering-based subject which required expensive accommodation and equipment. There were different rates for levels of qualification, and for different lengths of programme. Most two-year, full-time programmes were funded more generously than most ten-week ones. The funding formula continues to be a national methodology which comprises a standard learner number multiplied by the national funding rate, provider factor and additional learning support.

Colleges, sixth forms and adult and community learning institutions were asked to make plans. This involved identifying what programmes of learning would be offered, and numbers of learners. As a result of this strategic planning, the local authority could then agree a level of funding. The policy initiatives have been described by Statz and Wright (2004) as a significant departure from previous supply-led strategies to a demand-led system. This plan-led, performance-led way of funding using a business cycle contrasted with the previous regime, where colleges were asked to make annual returns, and on the basis of this were given funding according to numbers of learners and how many were retained throughout their programmes, and how many achieved the qualification for which they were enrolled. If insufficient learners were recruited, or stayed on programme and gained a qualification, the funds were 'clawed back', making institutions very aware of retaining the learners they did recruit. To assist with a widening participation agenda, funds were available to 'reward' institutions which drew learners from previously underrepresented areas, including those who lived in a postcode area which was seen to be more 'deprived' than an affluent area. Funds were also available to support people with learning and physical disabilities and other specified disadvantages.

Following the government White Paper *Raising Expectations*, changes to the structure of funding were introduced into the Learning and Skills System. In April 2010, a new funding regime was introduced. There were two sources of funding for learners in the Learning and Skills System – the Young People's Learning Agency (YPLA) and the Skills Funding Agency (SFA). The YPLA is an agency of the DCSF and the SFA is an agency of BIS.

The SFA's role is to fund and regulate adult further education and skills training in England. It supports a variety of services including Train to Gain, the National Employer Service, the National Apprenticeship Service and the Adult Advancement and Careers Service, as well as funding colleges and working with Regional Development Agencies (RDAs) and Local Authorities. The SFA will manage relationships with colleges and providers through a national single account management system. At the start, the SFA will be responsible for £4 billion funds which will be routed to providers. An important feature of the SFA is a remit to ensure coherence within the Learning and Skills System. The SFA claims that its mission is to

> Ensure that people and businesses can access the skills training they need to succeed in playing their part in society and in growing England's economy. (Skills Funding Agency, 2010)

Given the diverse nature of provision, learners and professionals who work in the system, this is going to be a tall but very necessary order.

The second strand of funding for the Learning and Skills System involves 14–19-year-olds and this funding stream will operate from the YPLA. The YPLA 'champions young people' by providing financial support to young learners, funds Academies and supports local authorities in fulfilling their new duties in commissioning education and training for all 16–19-year-old learners in England. In many ways, this is a return to an original scheme whereby further education colleges were controlled by their local education authorities but now, the funding is still centrally controlled but effectively dispersed through the local identification of need and appropriate provision. The funding will be allocated through a National Funding Formula and may well serve to end the 10 per cent funding gap that existed between sixth forms in schools and those in colleges. Local authorities will have to ensure that such provision is effective on a regional basis involving them in collaboration with schools, colleges, work-based providers as well as by taking account of provision across neighbouring authorities.

Foundation Learning (FL) is one tier of provision that will be funded by the SFA *and* YPLA. This level of learning covers learning at Entry level and Level 1 for young people and adults. The learning programmes within FL draw upon qualifications in the QCF and include functional skills qualifications, personal and social development and subject and vocational qualifications.

The LAs have therefore now acquired a commissioner role for provision in the Learning and Skills System. For 2010/2011, £8.2 billion was being invested for the education and training of young people aged 16–19. At the time of writing, there is doubt over whether the YPLA will continue to exist. This is due to the Coalition government needing to make huge savings to fund the national deficit and cutting quangos are a source of income savings. Given the likelihood of the current funding formula changing, it is important to keep abreast of the funding regime by following information on the agency websites or through contact with your managers at your institution. The net effect, though, of a funding regime is that learners become important in relation to the funding they 'draw down' and you will find that you and your colleagues are exhorted to keep the learners you do have and ensure that they achieve their learning goals and qualifications successfully in the timescale originally planned.

Funding the National Skills Strategy

In the government strategy, *21st Century Skills: Realising Our Potential* (DfES, 2003a), a decision was made to directly fund Level 2 qualifications for any young person or adult who has not already gained one. In other words, the learner does not have to pay a fee. Those studying for Level 3 qualifications or higher do pay. Employers are expected to support the cost of their employees' attendance at colleges, rather than through subsidies from the funding mechanism. Train to Gain was an initiative developed to provide subsidies to employers to help them support training for their employees. This initiative drew many criticisms, particularly as it was used by some employers who would have paid to train their employees anyway.

One way to encourage people to learn is through the equivalent of grants. Education Maintenance Allowances (EMAs) are aimed at 16–18-year-olds on a means-tested basis so that they can afford to stay on at school or college rather than try to find work. Young people have to show that they are attending college and most colleges have devised procedures to ensure that young people remain in their lessons by only signing off attendance at the end of the session! EMAs have been successful in increasing participation rates of targeted young people, and is a step on the way to stop the damaging drop-out culture that some young people (particularly young men and people from poorer communities) experience (see, for example, *Guardian*, 6 April 2010).

Sector Skills Councils (SSCs) were created to work within their vocational areas to foster employer engagement. It is the responsibility of the Regional Development Agencies (RDAs) to help raise the demand for skills from employers. Other agencies currently engaged with adults and their learning include UKCES which advises BIS on current skills and future skills needs, monitors the employment and skills system, research in further education and skills and manages the Sector Skills Councils. At the time of writing, there is doubt over the future of RDAs.

A consequence of the funding strategy may well be the reduction and closure of traditional adult education programmes, and an increase in fees for programmes that do not lead to the priority areas of basic skills, ICT or Level 2 qualifications. Even though the current catchphrase is 'demand-led' provision, some demands will not be satisfied through the funding available. If anything, the success of the previous LSC in drawing in more learners overall means that funds are not able to cover all their learning demands, a huge irony and embarrassment and a significant dilemma for government.

One of the more interesting consequences of the funding mechanism is the way in which colleges have behaved over the last decade in response to the rules of funding. There has been a huge reduction in the average level of funding (ALF), with convergence between colleges which had historically been more generously funded by their LAs and those with very poor units of resource. Colleges now teach more students for less money per head. They began to compete with each other under the original funding regime of the FEFC, but subsequently collaborated over provision, as the LSC funding and planning regime took effect. With the new SFA and YPLA funding regime, colleges and all providers will need to collaborate in response to the commissioning role of the local authorities.

Colleges have employed marketing directors to recruit more and different learners. If the learners are to stay and derive benefit from their decision to enrol on a programme of study, then the provision needs to be fit for purpose, in other words, be of high quality. A mass of information about the sector exists, from monitoring exercises, management information and the inspection process. Originally the FEFC, and subsequently the LSC published annual performance indicators for the sector based on the information required from colleges. There are data on, for example, recruitment, retention and achievement. Benchmarks have been created for these showing what the national average is for certain indicators. Each college can now find whether it is meeting national benchmarks for any subject area. As the funding follows the student, it is in a college's interest to recruit as many students as possible up to a certain agreed level, and to ensure that they stay on course and gain the qualification they signed up for.

At the time of writing, a new funding mechanism is being proposed which arguably simplifies the methodology in the Education and Skills system (fe.fundingreview@bis,gov. luk). There are also swingeing cuts being made across the public sector and the AoC believes that thousands of staff will lose their jobs given a 16 per cent cut in funding for adult learning in particular (Basic Skills Bulletin, June 2010). Given that colleges provide education and training for 3 million people every year and that of these, only three-quarters of a million are young people, it is clear that cuts to the system has profound knock-on effects for thousands of adults who are doing their best to gain knowledge and skills to help them lead successful lives.

If we consider the need to be accountable for the funding which we receive from the public purse, as well as from individuals who pay to undertake programmes, the next question we must ask is how well are the programmes run? Do we know that people are getting 'value for money'? To help ensure that there is accountability within the system which is monitored and evaluated, the government uses a system of inspection.

Assuring quality: the inspection regime

Most colleges now have quality assurance managers to ensure that they meet both Ofsted inspection requirements and awarding body criteria. There are now many more managers in the colleges but the structure is 'flatter' with full-time members of staff often responsible for large areas of the curriculum. There has been a casualization of staff, so that more teaching staff are now employed on temporary contracts. There has been an increasing reliance on temporary staff to deliver large parts of the curriculum, who often held responsibility for whole programmes. By 2009, LLUK figures showed that over a third of staff employed in the sector are part-time and the proportion of teaching staff has declined over the past five years in relation to support. Of a total of 268,310 staff, 82,211 were on casual or fixed term contracts (LLUK, 2010). The sector has a decreasing core of full-time and fractional staff and a significant proportion of hourly paid and agency staff (Bailey and Ainley, 2000, p. 45, in Gray and Griffin, 2000; Hillier and Jameson, 2004, 2006; LLUK, 2010).

The inspection of provision is undertaken by Ofsted. The model of inspection has changed over the past few years and has moved towards providers' own quality improvement self-analysis. A database called Excalibur was created in 2004 containing examples of college good practice. There are five different categories of resources: Building Better Practice, Good Practice Examples, Learner-Centred Self-Assessment, Professional Discussion Tools and Actions for Quality Improvement. These resources accompany all Ofsted reports and a taxonomy of issues found across inspections.

Ofsted inspections create huge disturbance in college and institutional provision. Everyone supports the need to assure quality but the hugely bureaucratic nature of the inspection regimes has taken its toll on the health and well-being of college managers and tutors alike. As each cycle of inspection develops, college managers acquire knowledge of how best to organize their information to meet the evidence requirements. There is an increasing move towards 'lighter touch' inspections for colleges which have been awarded 'outstanding' in their inspections. Resources continue to be devoted to those areas that are found to be of concern and which do not achieve the necessary minimum of a category 3 (satisfactory). Such provision is reinspected within a year. You will not escape the impact of a college inspection and all the procedures that are in place to assure quality (record keeping of how learners are being given opportunities to learn, feedback, progression, etc.) are part of your own professional role.

Initiatives which put the learner at the centre

With a system in place, funded and inspected, the next aim of government policy that I wish to address is its intention to put 'learners at the centre of all we do'. This is being achieved by a number of initiatives, and government legislation that happens to affect the Learning and Skills System. I will start with the legislation on disability, as an example of working towards inclusivity, and how important it is that we are aware of legislation which affects every aspect of public life, and its implications on our own professional practice. I will then describe some of the ways in which new initiatives are leading the way in new forms of learning, for new groups of people.

Widening the agenda: inclusive learning

As the name suggests, inclusive learning is a term designed to address the need to ensure that people can have access to further education and training, despite any learning or physical disability that they may have. To have a grand aim like that is no use unless there are adequate resources, in terms of qualified staff, teaching and learning resources and buildings that can accommodate people who may find it difficult to learn in more traditional ways.

In the Tomlinson Report on Inclusive Learning (1996), the committee was keen to embrace good practice in teaching and learning, not just for those people who may have a learning difficulty or physical disability (LDD), but for all people, 'an approach which . . . represents the best approach to learning and teaching yet articulated' (1996, p. 4). The report has, therefore, been influential in promoting a learner-centred approach to further education and training which goes beyond the original remit of addressing the needs of people with three years learning difficulties or physical disabilities. The newer term for this approach is 'personalized learning'.

A key tenet of the report was that students with any learning difficulty or physical disability should not be seen as having problems, that is, a deficit model, but to focus on what institutions could do to respond to their individual requirements. This approach would ensure that people were not labelled, but that the institution would have facilities to enable all people to learn to the best of their abilities. The report was timely, as the Disability Discrimination Act came into force in 1995 and, although not legislating for learners at that time, did make sure that those who work in further education must also have full access to employment, regardless of any disability that they may have. Today, any establishment must ensure that people have access to its facilities, and this includes access for workers, learners, clients, patients or customers, depending on the nature of the organization and its business (Part 3, Disability Discrimination

Act 1995, brought into effect October 2004). Implementing the requirements of the Disability Discrimination Act has had far-reaching consequences for educational establishments, with capital expenditure requirements to ensure buildings are accessible, as well as identification of appropriate accommodation, learning resources and provision of staff suitably qualified and skilled to support learners. All institutions will have a policy relating to Equality and Diversity and institutional support may include childcare facilities, timetabling to take account of access on ground floors as well as additional learning support through additional staff.

Centres for Excellence

Centres for Vocational Excellence and Innovation

An initiative to foster good practice within further education provision was the Centres for Vocational Excellence and Innovation (CoVEs). Funds were made available to encourage colleges to specialize in certain subject areas, to widen the participation of people who would not normally engage in learning activities provided by colleges and to foster the learndirect initiative. The centres specialized in offering specific skills training. Sadly, this initiative has now come to an end but in some colleges, the work of the CoVEs has continued through the networks and partnerships they created.

Centres for Excellence in Teacher Training

Building on the success of CoVEs, the previous government dedicated funds to promoting excellence in the training of staff who worked in the Learning and Skills System. These Centres for Excellence in Teacher Training (CETTs) were set up as consortia of providers of professional development, usually a higher education institution with its partner colleges. Their funding has also just come to an end but there is a small amount of money left to help support the network of providers, managed by LSIS. The CETTs created a number of initiatives and resources to support staff in the sector and their websites contain numerous ideas for teaching and the support of professional development.

Academies

The New Labour government created a policy to develop Academies to replace failing schools. Academies are publicly funded independent schools. The new Coalition government has embraced this policy and gone one stage further – to enable all outstanding schools (as defined by Ofsted inspections) to have a fast track to become Academies. The Academies Bill received Royal Assent on 27 July 2010. Academies retain a sixth form and, therefore, begin to effect the provision of existing sixth-form colleges and further education colleges in some areas. There are critics of this policy who are concerned that Academies will further widen the gap between young people who remain in state schools (see www.education.gov.uk/academies/whatareacademies).

Aimhigher

One of the activities to widen participation involves schools, further and higher education institutions working together to encourage people from underrepresented groups to participate in higher education, known as Aimhigher. This initiative was originally designed to address the New Labour government's target that by 2010, 50 per cent of young people under 30 would have participated in higher education. The Higher Education Funding Council for England (HEFCE) has eight national schemes funding the Aimhigher initiative and funding covers activities on subregional and regional levels, attempting to provide cohesion of provision. One scheme, for example, is attempting to do this through football, and involves contact with professional and ex-footballers with staff and students from further and higher education. Aimhigher is part of a further initiative, Partnerships for Progression (P4P), again involving collaborations between further and higher education institutions. The funding for Aimhigher ceases in 2011 and at the time of writing, it is not clear what the new Coalition government plans for this activity.

Advice and guidance

Reading through the plethora of initiatives, you may be wondering how anyone can possibly make sensible decisions about what programme of learning to apply for. One of the services arising from the creation of policies to foster learning for young people and adults was Connexions, which combined careers advice and guidance services, youth, legal and health services to make a 'one-stop shop'. Again, the idea is to 'join up' the various agencies involved in helping people to make sensible choices about their learning and careers. As noted in Chapter 3, finding out what people need to know and helping them to identify the most appropriate learning programme, as well as helping them make sensible decisions about the world of work, is a crucial part of the teaching and learning arena. The Information, Advice and Guidance (IAG) service now has a National Policy Framework, published in 2003. In 2004 the IAG was integrated with UfI. Connexions plays an important role in working with young disaffected people, a group now called NEET (not in education, employment or training). A new Adult Advancement and Careers Service is being launched in summer 2010 which will provide a service to all adults by telephone, online and face to face. There will be targeted support for adults facing specific barriers to progress (see www.icg-uk.org.uk).

But will people participate?

So far, I have shown that policies direct the education and training provision for young people and adults. The latest policy initiatives focus on encouraging people to participate fully in society through work, civic life and through lifelong learning. Your role in this is clearly at the 'chalk face' where you work with people who wish to learn. However, you may have begun to wonder whether the policies which heavily influence where you work, how you are paid and what you are asked to provide do achieve their goals of encouraging all adults to participate in learning opportunities. Just how difficult it is to foster the learning culture can be seen from the NIACE National Adult Participation in Learning Survey (NALS) (Aldridge and Tuckett, 2010). Participation is highest among those from the top socio-economic groups and also high among younger learners. In 2010, 43 per cent of those surveyed stated they had participated in some form of learning but there were still 31 per cent who claimed they had done no learning since leaving initial education. This large percentage of adults surveyed who had not engaged in any learning activity stated this was through lack of time, lack of funds or childcare commitments, and some simply did not want to do so. We must be very careful with such a survey. Those who did participate may have interpreted learning as that associated with formal learning. I do not believe that adults 'learn nothing' in recent years, but they may not think that what they have learned 'counts'. However, it is clear that simply providing learning opportunities is not going to encourage certain people to participate.

Smith and Spurling (1999) provided a detailed account of the NALS and an analysis of what needs to be done to foster lifelong learning. They summarize the problem succinctly:

> the number of lifelong learners actively learning today is likely to be small, perhaps very small: and there is a sizeable body of non-learners who are doing very little learning after initial education, if any at all. These people have in effect switched off from learning – or they have been switched off. (p. 21)

Despite the government's vision for further education and lifelong learning, backed by generous funding, the sector may not achieve its ambitious targets. Twining (2001) raised doubts that even with increasing provision, people will wish to come forward.

> My next doubt is whether there really are so many people out there who want to learn and in particular who want to learn in college, or on-line. There are other things they want to do with their time and with their money. You can make people attend a class but you cannot make them learn. (Twining, 2001, p. 9)

The challenge for those of us who work in developing learning provision for young people and adults is to find ways to foster an interest in learning for a much wider group of people, while at the same time respecting an individual's decision not to participate. Frank Coffield (1999) argues cogently for this when he reminds us that

> There is a large hole in the heart of the Government's policies for lifelong learning . . . plans are afoot to create a new culture of lifelong learning without either any theory of learning or a recognition that a new *social* theory of learning is required . . . a *social* theory of learning argues that learning is located in social participation and dialogue as well as in the heads of individuals. (p. 493, italics in original)

Coffield continues to champion the lifelong learning sector even though he criticizes government for having made the system a 'curious mixture of advances and regressions'. He is not convinced that the government can turn what he calls a disorganized but pivotal sector into a learning system but suggests it can be done (Coffield, inaugural lecture 2006). Those of you reading this book have an important part to play in helping ensure that we focus on the important (people and their learning).

Charts and structures

I once downloaded a chart of all organizations involved in supporting employees from the National Audit Office in November 2008 which had been used in the Innovation, Universities, Science and Skills Committee report on the Leitch Report to take to Australia to explain to vocational educators and trainers what our system was like (BIS, 2009a). It was so complex that I couldn't even begin to tell them what was going on. A similar chart was devised by Frank Coffield (2006, p. 9) and used by James Avis in his discussion of systems theory and further education (Avis, 2009). It would be a good idea to have a blank template which can be completed on a regular basis just to reflect the current state of play – and possibly capture a history of failed quangos and abortive attempts to help adults in this country learn in formal settings. Apparently, quangos have a new name – arms length bodies or ALBs. I suggest you write the names in pencil – much easier to erase!

It is difficult to write a chapter on government policy in education and training which can remain current and I suggest that one of the many responsibilities we have as practitioners is to try to keep up to date with the key developments in our field, including those at national and international policy level. It is a good idea to consult government publications, and the commentaries on developments in the national press, particularly in The *Times Education Supplement* and the *Times Higher Education Supplement*, the Tuesday *Guardian* and the Thursday *Independent*. You can also consult websites of the DfE, BIS and other agencies, which are listed in Chapter 10.

A test of any policy is to search for evidence of the intended outcomes and also for any unintended consequences of that policy. You may find that you can see the policies in operation at a very local level in your institution. You may even be participating yourself as a learner, or finding out about learning opportunities in your area through learndirect.

This chapter has examined the lifelong learning policy of the government, particularly in the past five years. This policy steer is very much geared towards a more coherent overview of provision, but reflects the different patterns required to meet the varied learning needs of the population. You may like to reflect on how well the policy has been implemented and whether its goals have, indeed, begun to be achieved. Your role, as a practitioner, may not seem central to the grand plans of government, but it is because you work in the post-compulsory sector that you are part of this ever-changing provision.

What does all this mean for a teacher in post-compulsory education?

How are you affected by the policies above? How does the funding of your programmes affect what you do? How does your work fit into the qualifications framework? Obviously, as a teacher or trainer, the places and spaces in which you work are inextricably linked to the kinds of provision that are funded, by the learners that are targeted to attend, by the outcomes, particularly in qualification terms, that you are asked to help them work towards.

Not only is the range of learning programmes that you may be asked to work with varied, so are the people that you will work with. You may have old and young learners in the same group, and almost certainly they will have a range of abilities, motivations and personalities. You may have people who have never studied in a formal institution alongside those who have taken a class for the past 20 years. You may have people who have many qualifications sitting next to people with none. You may be asked to work with people who have learning difficulties. You may be asked to work with people who are no longer working but who wish to keep their minds and bodies active. There are people who want to know about the demands of a new lifestyle, such as new parents, parents with adolescent children, people with relatives who have developed a range of physical or mental disabilities.

What you do have is people who, for whatever reason, are hoping to learn about the subject you are going to teach. The following chapters now address how to reflect on the *practice* of teaching to enable you to facilitate the learning of young people and adults.

Further reading and information

Further reading

There are a number of networks and publications which support knowledge of the Lifelong Learning system. I suggest you keep up to date through the following:

Adults Learning, published by NIACE
The Basic Skills Bulletins – these three separate bulletins cover literacy, numeracy and the 14–19 qualifications published by Circa (basicskills@circaworld.com)
Inside Evidence, published by LSIS.

You can also download a number of reports from government websites given at the end of this chapter (see Useful websites).

Ainley, P. and Bailey, B. (1997) *The Business of Learning: Staff and Student Experiences of Further Education in the 1990s.* London: Cassell.
Aldridge, F. and Tuckett, A. (2010) *The NIACE Survey on Adult Participation in Learning 2010.* Leicester: NIACE.
Basic Skills Bulletin (2010) 'Cuts to higher and further education', *Basic Skills Bulletin*, Issue 84 June 2010. Cambridge: Circa, p. 10.

Besley, S. (2004) *Policy Briefing What's Going On? A–Z Guide to Developments in the World of Education and Training for the Period: Jan–July 2004.* London: Edexcel.

Besley, S. (2009a) 'A postscript to the GCSE results 2009', *Policy Watch*, 1 September 2009. London: Edexcel.

Besley, S. (2009b) 'Who does what in the 14–19 system', *Policy Watch*, April 2009. London: Edexcel.

Besley, S. (2010a) 'Keeping track of what happened in education in February 2010', *Policy Watch*, 26 February 2010. London: Edexcel.

Besley, S. (2010b) 'Meeting the needs of young people during the recession and beyond', *14–19 Learning and Skills Bulletin*, Issue 11 Spring 2010. Cambridge: Circa.

Besley, S. (2010c) *Policy Watch Priorities and Investment for 16–19 Provision for 2010/11.* London: Edexcel.

Brennan, L. and Gosling, D. (2004) *Making Foundation Degrees Work.* Brentwood: SEEC.

Coffield, F. (2006) 'Running ever faster down the wrong road: an alternative future for education and skills inaugural lecture'. London: Institute of Education (www.ioe.ac.uk/schools/leid/lss/FCInauguralLectureDec06.doc) accessed July 2010.

Dataservice (2010) *First Release Post-16 Education & Skills: Learner Participation, Outcomes and Level of Highest Qualification Held* (www.thedataservice.org.uk/statistics) accessed June 2010.

Department for Business, Innovation and Skills (2009a) *Skills for Growth: The National Skills Strategy.* London: Stationery Office.

Department for Business, Innovation and Skills (2009b) *Skills Investment Strategy 2010–11.* London: Stationery Office.

Department for Children, Schools and Families, Department for Innovation, Universities and Skills (2008) *Raising Expectations: Enabling the System to Deliver.* London: Stationery Office.

Department for Innovation, Universities and Skills (2009) (http://webarchive.nationalarchives.gov.uk/+/http://www.dius.gov.uk/learningrevolution)

Dunford, J. (2010) 'The 14–19 agenda for the new government', *14–19 Learning and Skills Bulletin*, Issue 12 Summer 2010. Cambridge: Circa, pp. 2–3.

Edmond, N., Fuller, A., Hillier, Y., Ingram, R., Little, B., Reeve, F. and Webb, S. (2009) 'Symposium: really useful qualifications and learning? Exploring the policy effects of new sub-bachelors degree qualifications', Scutrea Annual Conference, July 2009, Robinson College, University of Cambridge.

European Union (2000) *The Lisbon Agenda.* Brussels: EU.

Fawbert, F. (ed.) (2003) *Teaching in Post-Compulsory Education: Learning, Skills and Standards.* London: Continuum.

Guardian (2009) (www.guardian.co.uk/education/2010/feb/25/further-education-colleges) accessed 17 August 2010.

Guardian (2010) (www.guardian.co.uk/education/2010/apr/06/ema-educational-allowance-abused-rich)

Harkin, J. (2006) 'Treated like adults: 14–16 year olds in further education' (www.informaworld.com/smpp/title~db=all~content=t716100718) *Research in Post-Compulsory Education*, 11, 3, pp. 319–39.

Higher Education Funding Council for England (HEFCE) (2007) *Foundation Degrees, Key Statistics 2001–02 to 2006–07.* Bristol: HEFCE.

Hillier, Y. (2006) *All You Ever Wanted to Know about FE Policy.* London: Continuum.

Hillier, Y. and Jameson, J. (2003) *Empowering Researchers in Further Education.* Stoke-on-Trent: Trentham Books.

Hillier, Y. and Jameson, J. (2004) *The Ragged Trousered Philanthropists.* London: LSDA.

Hillier, Y. and Jameson, J. (2006) *Managing the Ragged Trousered Philanthropists* London: LSDA.

Hillier, Y. and Rawnsley, T. (2008) 'Engaging employers', *Higher Education Review*, 40, 2, pp. 47–62.

Hughes, N. and Schwab, I. (2010) *Teaching Adult Literacy: Principles and Practice* London: National Research and Development Centre for Adult Literacy and Numeracy.

Humphries, C. (2008) 'Slow train coming', *Adults Learning*, 19, 10, pp. 12–13.

Innovation, Universities, Science and Skills Committee (2010) *First Report Re-skilling for Recovery: After Leitch, Implementing Skills and Training Policies* (www.publications.parliament.uk/pa/cm200809/cmselect/cmdius/48/4802 .htm) published 16 January 2010.

Mayo, M. (2005) *Global Citizens: Social Movements and the Challenge of Globalization* London: Zed Books.

Mayo, M. and Thompson, J. (1996) *Adult Learning, Critical Intelligence and Social Change.* Leicester: National Institute of Adult and Continuing Education.

National Institute for Adult and Continuing Education (2009) *National Inquiry into Lifelong Learning.* Leicester: NIACE.

Nuffield (2008a) *The New 14–19 Diplomas Issues Paper 1* (www.nuffieldfoundation.org/14-19review) accessed June 2010.

Nuffield (2008b) *The Nuffield Review of 14–19 Education and Training* (www.nuffieldfoundation.org/14-19review) accessed June 2010.

Organisation for Economic Co-operation and Development (2009) *Education at a Glance.* Paris: OECD.

Reeve, F., Gallacher, J. and Ingram, R. (2007) 'A comparative study of work-based learning within Higher Nationals in Scotland and Foundation Degrees in England: contrast, complexity, continuity', *Journal of Education and Work*, 20, 4, pp. 305–18.

Schuller, T. and Watson, D. (2009) *Learning through Life: Inquiry into the Future for Lifelong Learning.* Leicester: NIACE.

Schuller, T. and Williams, J. (2010) 'Rebalancing the system', *Adults Learning* 21, 2, pp. 8–11.

Stanton, G. (1982) *A Basis for Choice.* Bristol: Further Education Unit.

Statz, C. and Wright, S. (2004) *Emerging Policy for Vocational Learning in England: Will It Lead to a Better System?* London: Learning and Skills Research Centre.

Taubman, D. (2010) 'Skills for life faces an uncertain future', *Basic Skills Bulletin*, April 2010. Cambridge: Basic Skills Bulletin.

Thompson, A. (2009) 'New strategy, same old story', *Adults Learning*, 21, 4, pp. 9–10.

Willets, D. (2010) 'First keynote speech as Minister for Universities and Science', University of Birmingham, 20 May 2010 (www.bis.gov.uk/news/speeches/david-willets-keynote-speech) accessed June 2010.

Useful websites

Adult Learning Providers (ALP) (www.learningproviders.org.uk)

Basic Skills Bulletin (also 14–19 Learning and Skills Bulletin and Numeracy Bulletin) (basicskills@circaworld.com)

City and Guilds (www.cityandguilds.com)

Department for Business, Innovation and Skills (BIS) (www.bis.gov.uk)

Department for Education (DfE) (www.dfe.gov.uk)

Edexcel (www.edexcel.co.uk)

FE online (www.feonline.co.uk)

Institute for Learning (www.ifl.ac.uk)

Learning and Skills Improvement Service (LSIS) (www.lsis.org.uk)

Learning and Skills Network (LSN) (www.lsnlearning.org.uk)

Learning and Skills Research Network (LSRN) (www.lsrn.org.uk)

Lifelong Learning UK (LLUK) (ww.lluk.org)

National Institute for Adult and Continuing Education (NIACE) (www.niace.org.uk)

National Research and Development Centre in Adult Literacy, Numeracy and ESOL (NRDC) (www.nrdc.org.uk)

Ofsted (www.ofsted.gov.uk)

Research and Practice in Adult Literacy (RaPAL) (www.literacy.lancaster.ac.uk/rapal)

University for Industry (UfI) (www.ufi.com)

Part 2
The Practice of Reflective Teaching

Who are Your Learners? 3

> **A new programme for learners**
>
> Sunil has been asked to develop a new course in 'Return to Study' as part of a summer school being held by his local further education college. He has been given access to accommodation in the new learning resource centre, which is equipped with an interactive whiteboard and laptops with a variety of multimedia facilities. The centre can accommodate up to 20 learners. There is an area for group work, with a data projector, interactive whiteboard (IWB) and a large monitor as well as more traditional resources including a flip-chart. Sunil has seen the prospectus advertisement for this course, which is primarily aimed at recruiting people who have not participated in learning at the college before. Fliers will be sent to local supermarkets, doctors' surgeries, health centres and schools in the relevant residential areas which have been identified by postcode as a target for widening participation.

It is clear from this situation that there is a host of unknowns. Sunil will not necessarily have met any of the people from the residential area before, as they have generally not come to the college. He has not worked in the learning resource centre as it has only just been created. He does not know the equipment well and has not run a Return to Study programme based in such a 'high tech' environment. Sunil does, however, have a lot of experience of running Access programmes. He does know about the importance of establishing what the learner hopes to gain from such programmes. He understands about the importance of creating a welcoming and safe environment, where diffident people can begin to learn and gain confidence.

How can he develop a programme which will be successful? One of the first activities he must do is to develop a clear set of aims and objectives for the programme. Yet can he do this if he has not met the learners and does not know what they need to know in order to return to study? This is where his past experience is so useful. Are there some core activities that can be used with all new learners? Could one of his aims include an analysis of their learning requirements as part of the programme? Even before Sunil meets his learners, he has numerous decisions to make about the learning they will undertake.

This chapter will discuss identification of learning requirements, diagnostic testing, Accreditation of Prior Learning and Accreditation of Prior Experiential Learning (APL/APEL), meeting awarding body requirements, initial assessment, individual learning styles, and giving educational advice and guidance. Although they are dealt with separately, it is impossible to undertake each in isolation. It is difficult to plan and deliver a learning programme if you are not sure what sort of learners you have and what they individually and as a group will need.

To know what your learners' learning requirements are, you need to do the following:

- Find out what your learners have already learned and what they hope to learn next.
- Find out if your learners have any specific learning requirements; for example, due to a physical disability, dyslexia or in terms of needing programmes which fit in with childcare or other caring responsibilities.
- Find out what your learners can actually do; that is, check that their current level of skill and knowledge is sufficient to meet the demands of their proposed learning programme.
- Ensure that your learners have all the information they need to make an informed judgement about their next learning programme.

Starting out – prerequisites for a new programme of learning

People decide to participate in formal learning activities for many reasons. Once they have decided to engage in a course or activity, they must then enrol. In some institutions, they can enrol by telephone or e-mail, and the only information about any learner that a tutor will have is the learner's receipt number. This is particularly true for adult education centres funded by local education authorities. In further education colleges, a more developed process of enrolment takes place, where learners are often interviewed prior to placement and where there is a learning agreement formed (a requirement of the funding agencies, see Chapter 2). Trainees who participate in government-sponsored employment programmes, are given in-depth interviews to establish their training requirements. The more elaborate the entry system to learning is, the more information will be available upon which tutors can base their programme planning.

For many courses of study which are at NVQ Level 2 or above (see Chapter 2), learners need a previous level of knowledge and skill. This is not necessarily in the subject area they are about to study, but in terms of their key, or functional skills. If they are about to study a Diploma in travel and tourism, for example, they will need to be able to communicate effectively, orally and in writing. They will need to have a level of appreciation of number and they will need to be computer literate, so that they can both produce work and interrogate data and information contained in spreadsheets and databases. One of the major difficulties in further education is that the learners' functional skills at the beginning of the programme may not be at the level required to study successfully (Martinez, 2000). Therefore, early on in the process, before study begins, diagnostic analysis of learners' capabilities is important. Many further education colleges use the skills test, for example, developed by the Basic Skills Agency (BSA), in literacy and numeracy. However, while this may identify the level of learners' functional skills, it is of no use if nothing is done subsequently to enable them to address their skills requirements, or if the programmes do not adequately identify what skills are required in order to successfully achieve the qualification. For example, a college may use a diagnostic test to look at learners' spelling. Yet many courses require note-taking, reading, comprehension and structured report-writing. Identification of spelling ability alone does not indicate if learners are able to carry out all the other activities. As these are necessary at the very beginning of the course, people with lower levels of literacy or functional skills will find themselves struggling at the outset.

Often, the diagnostic test helps to identify the appropriate level of study a learner should pursue. For vocational qualifications, learners may be advised to take an intermediate level rather than the higher-level qualification if their current level of functional skills is low. They may be advised to study an alternative subject area, if their first choice will be too demanding for their particular level of skill. Educational guidance is a key aspect of the pre-entry process and is covered in a later section of this chapter.

In many cases, provision is now made for learners to work on their functional skills in addition to their primary course of study. Funding is available for this, and early identification of need and use of the additional learning resources appears to enable learners to stay on course and achieve their qualification (Martinez, 2000). However, not all learning provision will have additional resources to help your learners progress, particularly, if they have not undertaken a diagnostic test or are not working towards a particular level of qualification. You will then need to find out about additional opportunities for your learners, perhaps in a different setting; and, of course, your learners may not be in a position to undertake additional learning. The role of educational guidance is particularly helpful at this stage.

What will your learners be learning?

One of the important areas to consider when planning a programme of study is what exactly you will require your learners to do in order to learn. Will they need to write notes? Will they need to use numbers and make calculations? Will they need to make written and oral presentations? Will they need to use a computer and, if so, do they need to know how to use a particular program? Do they need to have a level of background knowledge in the subject? If they are learning a language, what level must they have reached? Will they be required to draw or paint? Will they require practical skills which they can apply in such vocational subjects as catering, construction or electronics?

With some of these questions, the possession of a previous qualification may provide the necessary information. Yet in many cases, the qualification may have been gained a long time ago. Language classes are a case in point, where provision is sometimes made for people who have a 'rusty' 'O' level. They are not complete beginners but they will have forgotten quite a lot. Just to complicate matters, people forget different things, may have covered different things, language is dynamic and certain phrases are no longer in use. Deciding what your learners should learn is not as straightforward as it may seem.

How can you find out what your learners already know and can do? How can you ensure that they are about to enrol on an appropriate programme of learning? Where there is an opportunity for pre-entry guidance, if you are a course tutor, you may be involved in interviewing your own potential learners. What does this involve?

Pre-entry guidance

Pre-entry guidance may be an established practice in your institution. You may be given a proforma where you ask learners about their current levels of qualification, and where you check that these match the entry requirements of the programme of learning. This activity may be undertaken by a programme director, or by individual members of a team. It is important that all potential learners be given enough information for them to decide if the programme they are interested in is going to be appropriate. There are three aspects to educational guidance: information, advice and guidance. Information is simply that which is publicly available and tells a potential learner what a programme of study is offering, its aims, objectives and learning outcomes, what previous qualifications and experience are required, what the cost will be, the timing of the programme, and any additional costs – materials, for example. The more information is available, the more a potential learner can make an informed decision about whether to join the programme. Advice is more detailed and involves decision-making based on the information. Guidance is a process where the potential learner is enabled to consider not only a range of learning opportunities, but where a more in-depth analysis of their learning requirements can take place.

The plethora of qualifications available in further education, and the expanding curriculum on offer in adult education and community centres, requires complex decision-making on the part of the learner. Learners often seek advice about which courses to take and at what level they should study. Information about programmes is used to help make a decision. For example, a potential learner may have been away from any formal learning for a few years while working and then bringing up a young family. The qualifications gained previously may be different from those available today. Deciding if those qualifications are still current and valid requires more than simply ticking boxes on a pre-entry checklist. Staff who provide educational advice must, therefore, know quite a lot about the programmes on offer, what the entry requirements are, what previous level of experience is needed, and be able to help potential learners identify their current knowledge, experience and qualifications.

Nearly 20 years before, the Unit for the Development of Adult Continuing Education (UDACE, 1986) stated that the primary purpose of educational guidance is to improve the match between learning opportunities and the needs and interests of learners and potential learners. Finding the appropriate learning opportunity does not necessarily involve a formal learning programme. Educational guidance should be 'without prejudice' and should have the interest of the learner at its centre. In many educational institutions, particularly those in further education, the advice and guidance offered provide learners with information based on what is available at the institution and not what is available elsewhere. There is a tension, therefore, between ensuring that the needs of the learner are paramount and encouraging the learner to study at that particular institution. There are codes of practice used by career and educational guidance practitioners which specify clearly that the client's needs are at the core of the process. In 1994, the National Advisory Council for Careers and Educational Guidance (NACCEG) was formed. This body helped to establish a set of quality standards for all organizations providing guidance. Since then, a set of standards was devised by the then lead body for advice, guidance, counselling and psychotherapy which has been used to develop NVQ qualifications. These developments provide the quality framework for educational assessment and guidance. It has been recognized that teachers and tutors undertake educational guidance as part of their many responsibilities and such standards are immensely helpful in providing a code of practice for those who do not have educational guidance as their primary role.

There are generic guidance standards created by the Guidance Council (2001). These were developed for those working in specific contexts, such as career advisers working with young people, and for those who work with adults. The core code of practice is contextualized to fit with the particular requirements of any client group. Thus, Section A of the standards is known as Adult Impartial Quality Standards. One of the criteria relates to systems which provide information to clients. This information must be clearly understood by the user group, materials must not discriminate unfairly: for example, there should be printed, audiovisual and software programmes that ensure people with any disability can have the same information but in a different format. One of the main features of the guidance standards is that the core of information must be free from bias. This criterion is particularly difficult to meet if guidance workers are located in a further education institution which has to recruit as many learners as possible. Payne (1996) particularly asks whether it is possible to be completely impartial and suggests that it is possible, within a certain boundary, like that of giving guidance in a college setting, to work in the interests of the client, providing it is acknowledged that the information will not cover every possible option in the country.

Often, educational guidance becomes part of personal guidance and vocational guidance. Someone who is seeking advice about what to do for a career and how to incorporate this into such a life change as parenthood will obviously wish to decide on appropriate educational choices based on their personal and vocational aspirations.

The process of giving educational guidance involves four stages:

1. Evaluating a client's personal, vocational and educational development.
2. Identifying learning needs and choosing appropriate ways to meet these, taking account of their personal circumstances and the current availability of educational opportunities.
3. Undertaking the programme of learning.
4. Reviewing and assessing the learning achieved and identifying further goals.

Pre-entry guidance can cover any or all aspects of these four stages: it is primarily a process. Some learners will only undertake the first part of this process with professionally qualified guidance staff; others will make use of the guidance facilities throughout their time at an educational institution, or indeed after.

It is difficult, sometimes, for learners to know what they could undertake, simply because they are unaware of the opportunities. In other cases, people are deterred from learning at particular institutions because of their previous negative learning experiences at school or college. Guidance which is removed from the institution and perhaps inhabits 'neutral territory' is more likely to encourage those who are diffident about learning as adults. Some colleges now provide 'one-stop shops' for potential learners in city centres, where they can drop in for information and advice, and make appointments for further guidance. Such centres may provide detailed guidance activities, including diagnostic or psychometric tests to help learners make informed decisions about what to study. As discussed in Chapter 2, a new service, the Adult Advice and Careers Service (AACS) has been set up following the Apprenticeships, Skills, Children and Learning Act to take forward a strengthened advice and support service for adults and employers.

University for industry/learndirect

As noted in Chapter 2, there is a strong push by the UK government to encourage people to return to learning throughout their adult lives. One of the important developments arising from this directive is the establishment of the University for Industry (UfI) with learndirect – an information service and provider of courses for potential learners. This links to a range of educational information services and educational institutions, putting learners in touch with professional educational guidance opportunities and directly with educational institutions. The telephone helpline has trained advisers to help people decide what they want to learn and how they can do this. There is a learndirect website which can help people find the course they want, by conducting a simple search online. By 2009, celebrating its tenth anniversary, UfI announced there had been 2.6 million people taking 7.5 million courses, the majority doing so to help gain employment, a qualification or change direction in their careers.

Acknowledging previous learning and achievements of learners

In competence-based programmes, it is possible for your learners to gain exemption for their previous qualifications or experience. The process by which such previous experience is accredited is called Accreditation of Prior Learning (APL) or Accreditation of Prior Experiential Learning (APEL). With APL, learners are asked to bring forward accreditation from previous units in NVQs or equivalent qualifications. If, for example, a mature learner had started an NVQ in Care but had to leave the programme to move house, then her units gained so far would be brought forward when she returns to the NVQ in her new college a year later. With APL, there is a set process used by many learning institutions which involves the learner making the claim for previous knowledge and qualifications, which is then verified by the programme director in the new institution. In some further education colleges, there are staff who provide an APL service across the whole range of programmes on offer. They are generalist advisers who are responsible for ensuring that potential learners do gain credit for what they have already achieved in the past. There has been an increase in the use of National Records of Achievement (NROAs), particularly for younger learners entering the post-compulsory sector. Here, initial assessment will take account of the profile each individual brings and may not necessarily involve taking any diagnostic tests (see Figure 3.1).

Trainers in Management	
Central asessment centre	
NVQ UNIT INITIAL ASSESSMENT	

Candidate Name:	Olive Bachmayer
Qualification/Level:	NVQ 5
Unit/Element No:	Unit 6
Unit Title:	Enhance productive working relationships

Unit/element	**ADVICE AND GUIDANCE**
6	**Do you currently do this? Have you evidence of doing this in the past? Provide example.** I lead a team of trainers who are responsible for providing induction for all new staff joining the organisation, and in house training as requested from the departments. This means that I have team meetings weekly. I also meet regularly with the departmental heads so that I also am part of the decision making process about training needs. As the departments are all different, I need to ensure that my team produces relevant training but that they work together coherently. I do this by ensuring that in each team meeting, they have room to report back what is going on in their departments and to discuss any problems that arise. We then try to share ideas so that the individual trainers do not feel isolated. In my previous job, I was responsible for a team of front line staff. It was important that they had up to date information about new procedures, especially as the system was being computerised. So again, I had to ensure that they felt they knew what was going on and could have a say in it. See my minutes from the team meetings (ref File A, p22) **Relevant Qualifications** NVQ Level 3 Administration (June 2002) NVQ Level 4 Training and Development (July 2003)

Assessor:	Date:

Figure 3.1 Example APL assessment

With APEL, potential learners are asked to look at their previous experience, not necessarily gained through study, to match it against the programme specification. For example, many parents who have spent time bringing up young children have a wealth of experience including managing people, managing time, managing finance, developing negotiation skills, acquiring first-aid knowledge and developing experience in preschool education. These skills and knowledge can be used to create a portfolio of evidence against entry criteria, for example, an Access programme, or an introduction to management programme. The process required here is more time-consuming because most people do not easily recognize the skills and knowledge they already possess, and 'translating' this into evidence to meet educational requirements is in itself a skill.

Staff who work with APEL often find themselves offering educational advice and guidance, itself a highly skilled and professional activity. However, where potential learners are dealt with by programme staff, then they will need to know when to refer their learners for specialist advice and guidance. In colleges of further education, there is usually a guidance service to potential learners. Advisers for trainees on New Deal programmes, too, find that they will need to refer their trainees to a variety of specialist agencies. In traditional adult education and community provision, there is less specialist advice, but the situation is changing, partly as the system itself becomes more complex and partly because there is more recognition of the important role of educational advice and guidance for adults.

APEL process

- Learner makes an appointment with an APL/APEL adviser.
- The adviser asks the learner to complete a short form which provides details of the learners' educational and training history, schools attended, subjects studied, qualifications gained (if any), any training received either during employment or as part of government-sponsored training programmes.
- The adviser asks the learner to describe some of the tasks and responsibilities experienced while in work, or while caring for a family, elderly relatives, and the like.
- Any additional activities, such as voluntary work, helping with school trips, organizing school fetes or taking part in club committees are noted.
- The adviser then begins the process of matching the range of skills and knowledge that the learner has developed as a result of the activities listed, with the requirements of the learning programme. The learner may join a group to work on the identification of activities and the production of the way in which these match the criteria. A portfolio of evidence will be built, including examples such as letters written, posters produced or notes from committee meetings.

How does this work in practice?

Let us consider Judith, who wishes to enrol on an introduction to management programme. She has been caring for a young family for the past ten years. She left school with only one RSA qualification in typing, and worked in an office for barely a year before starting her family. Judith feels that she has a lot to do before she can find a 'decent job'. During the interview with her adviser, it transpires that Judith has been a staunch member of the local preschool club. She helps organize the summer outing, helps organize their stall for the 'autumn fair' and every week helps out with the refreshments. At home, she is responsible for keeping the family budget and bank account and ensures that her partner looks after the children on a regular basis so that she can take part in her weekly swimming lessons.

Judith comes along to three sessions at the local college. She is asked to spend one week keeping a record of all the things she does. When she brings this to the next session, the tutor works with her to translate these activities into management criteria. The adviser helps Judith list the activity, what she is responsible for and how this fits the criteria for the management award in the form of a grid. Judith is then asked to think of the different things she does throughout the year. This time, she is asked to try and match these to the criteria for herself. She is asked to bring along some examples of her work with the tots club.

When these activities are translated into roles and responsibilities, it is clear that Judith is already managing people (her partner and children), finance (family budget, tots club, petty cash for refreshments), activities (organizing summer trip and autumn fair stall) and resources (food and clothing for the family, refreshments for the tots club, items for the autumn fair). There are gaps, of course, and this is what Judith needs to learn about at the college. However, by undertaking this process, Judith realizes that she has a lot of management experience – she just was not paid for it!

Key skills/transferable skills/generic skills

Particularly for learners in further education or employment training, there is a requirement to develop key skills. As discussed in Chapter 2, key skills are specific skills which can be evidenced at four levels and which are now incorporated into the post-compulsory curriculum. In some colleges, learners will work on their key skills separately from any programme content. In others, their work on key skills will be integral. Even where they do work separately on developing their key skills, any programme content will incorporate some aspects of this, because, of course, key skills are integral. For example, consider the key skills involved in writing a business report on the use of mobile phones. There will be key skills of communication in obtaining information from a variety of sources and setting out the information clearly in the report. There will be key skills in the use of numbers where data is interrogated and synthesized in the form of charts and graphs in the report. There will be key skills in the use of information technology in the presentation of the report, including text and graphs. If the report had been written as a result of a group project, then key skills in working with people would have been used. Finally, individual learners would have identified their own learning requirements before beginning the project and created evidence of their learning. They will, therefore, have met some of the key skills in identifying their own learning. The extent to which they meet these key skills requirements depends on the level required by the project itself and their own capacity at the outset to meet these requirements. If your learners are required to demonstrate their key skills in addition to any other programme specification, then when you plan your curriculum and individual sessions, you will need to ensure that you have both identified the particular skills they will be using and developing, and identified ways for them to evidence these.

There is growing evidence that the generic nature of key skills does not necessarily transfer across specific situations (Livingston et al., 2004). However, generic skills, which to a certain extent subsume key skills, is a highly contested term, and most research does not agree on a specific definition of any of these terms. Furthermore, the merger of basic skills with key skills to form functional skills is a development that is still being trialled at the time of writing. You will need to keep abreast of developments, as by the time you read this, there will be further changes to the system following introduction of Diplomas which contain the personal learning and thinking skills (PLTS) as well as the functional skills noted above.

Meeting awarding body requirements

If you are teaching on an accredited programme, then one of the things you must plan for is how to meet the awarding body syllabus and assessment requirements. You will be planning how your learners will gain their necessary knowledge and skill to meet the awarding body requirements. You must provide the appropriate assessment activities that are considered to be valid by the awarding body. Chapter 8 discusses assessment in more detail. With the increasing accreditation of all programmes, meeting the requirements is necessary in the planning phase and must be considered as integral to the learning programme. In all these programmes, a key element is to assess what the learners can already do and enable them to provide evidence of this for the award. Some of your initial assessment will, therefore, be of what your learners have achieved in the past through APL or APEL. You may also consider their current levels of knowledge and skill to identify which units and elements can be met now and any gaps to fill to meet the full award.

Initial assessment of learners' needs

Identifying learning needs can, therefore, take place through national initiatives such as learndirect, locally through college educational guidance centres and at programme level prior to enrolment. What can individual tutors do to find out about their learners' needs?

There is a variety of activities that can be undertaken to help you establish what their current level of skill and knowledge is. With languages, some centres use a self-diagnostic process where learners indicate what they are familiar with and what they will need to learn. In music, dance and drama, learners may be asked to audition and demonstrate an aspect of their performing ability. In basic skills, learners may be given the Basic Skills Agency (BSA) test, or given an interview where they discuss aspects of literacy or numeracy in which they feel competent, and aspects where they know they need help.

Not all pre-entry guidance and initial assessment is conducted on such a formal basis. In the past, sixth-form colleges and adult education centres have provided a more informal approach. In the case of sixth-form colleges, a system of pastoral care is used extensively, and learners are given guidance about their current abilities and what subjects to choose through tutorial programmes. This has the advantage that the tutors responsible are well aware of the curriculum on offer. However, it does mean that often more in-depth guidance is less available. In adult education centres, the guidance available has been less centralized and more likely to rely on centre co-ordinators or programme co-ordinators who may not be able to advise across all areas of the curriculum.

For many teachers and trainers, there is no pre-entry guidance for their learners. Learners will join the programme with a range of abilities, none of which has been identified prior to enrolment. This means that during the first meetings, you will need to quickly identify the level of the learners' knowledge and skill. This is one of the most important parts of the planning process. Too often, tutors are so keen to get started on the teaching and learning aspect, that they do not take enough time to fully establish their learners' learning needs. There is a tension between ensuring that learners enjoy their very first session and leave with a sense of accomplishment and desire to learn more, and of finding out in that session what their current level is. Many learners feel cheated if they have to wait until the second session to 'do something' because the first has been spent doing a 'round robin' of introductions and identification of what they want from the course.

Carrying out initial assessment and feedback to learners

So far I have discussed the main features which could be identified about your learners: their current skills and knowledge, their learning style and their reasons for wanting to take up learning opportunities. How do you go about carrying out initial assessments, and how do you feed back to your learners what these assessments show?

This is a really important aspect of the learning process. Very often, particularly where learners are enrolling on accredited programmes, they need to know at the outset if there are any areas that they should be working on immediately so that they can fully participate and benefit from the programme. If they are already qualified or have units towards a full award, then they need to know what units they have still to cover and achieve. Finally, there will be circumstances where their chosen programme is not going to be most appropriate for them, and they will need to be carefully counselled so that they can make an informed choice about alternatives.

So how should one use an initial assessment? As mentioned before, diagnostic assessment is used to identify current level of skills and knowledge and any gaps. Great care must be used with such assessment activities. Many potential learners will feel highly threatened by being asked to undertake a diagnostic assessment. If they have poor experiences of learning, or are anxious about failure, then they will not only be affected by their emotional response to the test, but they may not wish to pursue the learning programme at all. Therefore, when asking potential learners to undergo any initial assessment, it is important that the reason for undertaking this is explained carefully to the learner, and an opportunity given for the learner to ask questions. What happens to the results? Are these kept confidentially and, if so, who will know the outcome?

How should an initial assessment be performed? Where there are large numbers of people to be enrolled at the start of a learning programme, this can create enormous pressure on guidance services or programme co-ordinators. Your college may have set times when potential learners are asked to attend for their diagnostic or initial assessment. It may be conducted under conditions similar to exams, where groups of people undertake the assessment sitting in classrooms or halls. This may be particularly threatening to people who are hesitant about studying in formal settings. There may be a system of individual interviews during which the assessment activity is conducted. The important aspect of conducting initial assessment is that it should be carried out in the same way for all learners. Otherwise, the results obtained may vary not only because of the differences in people's ability but also because of the different conditions under which they undertook the assessment. With the increase in interactive computer programs, more learners are being asked to undertake an initial assessment electronically. This has the advantage that the conditions are the same and the results very quickly created. Profiles of groups of learners can be obtained and recorded against future progress. However, people who are unfamiliar with using computers may feel disadvantaged, although they may feel that the activity is not like taking a traditional test. The diagnostic tests for literacy and numeracy attempt to set people at their ease by giving them examples with the correct answers to work through before taking the diagnostic test. There are always going to be people who feel threatened or who are disadvantaged by taking assessment tests, an issue which will be explored fully in Chapter 8.

One way to find out about your learners' current level of knowledge and skill is to ask them to engage in activities which cover an aspect of the content but which demonstrate their current abilities. For example, in practical classes like drawing and needlecraft, learners can be given a task to complete which will necessitate using a range of skills. The tutor can observe how each learner is managing, can examine the finished product and can establish the areas to concentrate on in the following sessions. It helps if these initial tasks are not intimidating and rather fun, so that learners who are nervous will not feel threatened, and people who are confident will feel challenged.

In language classes, learners can be asked to engage in conversations between pairs, establishing information about themselves. This same activity can be used for a variety of programmes which can be loosely described as self-development.

In technology classes, learners may be asked to set up a database or spreadsheet if they already use such facilities, or be given easy to follow instructions so that they can begin to work autonomously. Many people have some knowledge about some aspects of using computers. They often arrive with tremendous expectations of the tutor and the course, and can be easily frustrated if there are problems with the hardware and software, or if the pace of the programme does not allow them to develop from their current level of knowledge and skill.

Tutors and trainers who work in the fitness field require information about people's medical history, not only because it is a health and safety requirement to do so, but also that they can ensure that they find appropriate activities if someone cannot fully participate. The questionnaires given to learners can provide the opportunity to ask what their hopes are. For example, one person may wish to lose weight through exercise. Another may wish to train for a fun-run. Another may wish to regain her shape after pregnancy. Someone with back problems will need to use alternative exercises in some activities. Knowing that one person has a goal of running a race in a few weeks will enable the tutor to identify appropriate levels of activity which are likely to be more demanding than for the mother trying to regain her shape after pregnancy (unless she, too, is a marathon runner!).

Having established what your learners can do, what are their own objectives for taking the course? If you have participated in teacher training, you may have been asked to state at the outset what you thought your strengths and weaknesses were, what you wanted to develop and what you hoped to achieve during the programme. You may have been given a profile against which you judged yourself now and against which you will judge yourself when you have completed the course. You may find that a similar process can be used with your own learners.

Individual learning styles

People not only have different levels of experience and knowledge relevant to the programme they are embarking on, they also have different ways of learning and preferences. Have you noticed from previous teaching experiences or learning experiences that some learners really enjoy a particular session while others do not? Some learners may say that a particular tutor is a good teacher whereas another learner may say the reverse. Why should two people in the same learning environment develop such different views? One of the reasons could be that the form of learning activities offered does not suit their preferred style of learning. If you are a visitor to a city and you need directions to a park, what do you do? Do you wander around using your sense of direction and finally stumble upon the right place? Do you go to a petrol station and buy a local map? Do you stop a stranger on the street and ask for directions? Do you need to see a visual representation before you can make sense of the directions, or can you follow directions from someone's verbal instructions? All of these preferences indicate your preferred way of acquiring new information. Acquiring information so that you can find a park in an unfamiliar city is not exactly the same as learning, but it does help us to consider just how different we are in the way we receive information. This means that when you have a group of people who have come together to learn something, then they are likely to be different in the way they prefer to do this. Some people like to have information written down so that they can read it later. Others need to talk it through before they feel that they have fully taken it in. Another group of people may prefer to act upon the information before they feel sure that they have 'got it'. Finding out about your learners' preferred learning style will help you to provide a variety of learning experiences.

How can you find out about learning styles? One of the most influential developments in learning style has come from ideas about experiential learning. According to Kolb (1984), people learn from their experiences. He described a model of experiential learning in the form of a circle, where individuals may experience a particular situation – for example, getting on and standing up on a windsurfing board. They could then reflect on their observation about what was happening at the time, and thus begin to think through their experience and feelings at the time. This would lead to more abstract conceptualization, for example, deciding that there were specific actions that would enable them to stay up rather than fall off at each attempt. Having thought through this far, they could then experiment next time they try to windsurf. This would lead to them having another experience upon which to reflect and develop theories about what they have done so that they can further test and refine their ideas.

Now one of the difficulties with a model like this is that people assume that there is one point to 'get on' the circle and go round. In fact, people are thinking and experiencing all the time, and often test out ideas without fully articulating them. As Chapter 1 discussed in detail, people have implicit theories which they do not articulate very often. This does not prevent them using these theories constantly.

Kolb's experiential learning cycle has had a profound influence on training practices in particular. However, I want to issue a 'health warning'. Just because we have experiences does not mean we learn from them. Just because we can reflect on an experience does not mean we subsequently generalize from this and further test out our ideas. The cycle has come to stand for 'fact', when it is still a theory about how people learn. As I discussed in Chapter 1, theories must be tested to see how well they stand up to scrutiny. One of the difficulties with Kolb and subsequent proponents is that their models have not been tested sufficiently. An examination of the research on learning styles conducted by Coffield, Moseley, Hall and Ecclestone (2004) has demonstrated how complex and pervasive the use of learning styles is

Figure 3.2 Four types of preference

in the Learning and Skills Sector. They conclude that we simply do not know the costs and benefits of using learning styles, or even exactly how these are being used throughout the sector. Chapter 5 discusses these important issues further.

Kolb's theory has been extended to develop a model which states that people have preferences for one of the points on the circle. For example, it is said that some people like to jump straight in and try out things straight away: they are uncomfortable with thinking about the experience. Others are reluctant to try out activities before they have had a chance to fully explore what this means. Kolb's experiential learning cycle has, therefore, led to the identification of four types of preference, based on a position on a grid which has an axis of feeling and thinking in one direction, and doing and watching in the other (see Figure 3.2).

1. An *accommodator* is someone who learns best by doing and feeling. This person tends to rush in with answers to questions and, although works well with other people and likes variety and excitement, will rarely plan.
2. A *diverger* likes to undergo experiences and reflect upon them. This person is often very creative and can see connections between different topics but is often less good at detail.

3. A *converger* prefers thinking and doing. This person is particularly good at setting goals and making plans but is less able to see alternatives and may not be a good team worker.
4. An *assimilator* prefers watching and thinking. This person organizes facts very well and works alone well but often needs a lot of information before starting work.

If you have a group of individuals who represent these different styles, then you will need to think about how to ensure they learn well. An important consideration, too, is how to help them develop the aspects they are less developed in. There is a complex interaction between individual learning styles and the type of subject being learned. For example, numerical subjects may appeal to certain people because they can think reflectively and work on problems alone. Pottery and drawing may appeal to others because they can undertake the creative experience and reflect on them as they progress.

A further development from Kolb's learning styles has been the use of a questionnaire to ascertain people's preferred learning style. Honey and Mumford (1992) devised an 80-item questionnaire with statements with which people either agree or disagree. For example, there are statements such as 'I often throw caution to the wind' or 'I like to reach a decision carefully after weighing up many alternatives.' Once the questionnaires are completed, they are scored against four categories. These are based upon Kolb's initial set, but they have been renamed as:

- activist
- reflector
- theorist
- pragmatist.

A high score against one of the categories shows that they have a strong preference or learning style. Honey and Mumford recommend that once people have identified their preferred learning style, they should then try to match their learning experiences to their preferred style. If you are primarily an activist, then you are more likely to learn successfully through active experiences. Reflectors are more likely to learn through observation, theorists will fare better with intellectual examination, and pragmatists will require practical experiences.

With any preference, the other categories may be present to varying degrees. Some people score fairly equally across all four categories; some may have two clear preferences. It is, therefore, important not to assume that all people have a definite learning style based upon one preference. Here are some of the characteristics for each learning style, according to Honey and Mumford. Remember, these categories should not be taken as an absolute statement of how people behave, or that the descriptions will fit everyone exactly.

- *Activists* tend to enjoy immediate experiences and will become involved in any new activity with an open mind. They tend to act first and think about the consequences later. They thrive on new experiences. This means they may become quickly bored and may also be less able to deal with longer-term consolidation.

- *Reflectors* are unlikely to jump into activities straight away. They prefer to collect information and think things through before coming to conclusions. This can mean that they delay making decisions. They are thoughtful and listen to others, which can look as though they have a low profile in group work. However, when they do act, it is after consideration of others' perspectives as well as their own.
- *Theorists* tend to think in a logical, almost vertical way. They are often perfectionists and try to fit everything into a rational order. They like to analyse and synthesize ideas. They are, therefore, quite detached and prefer rational objectivity to subjectivity and ambiguity. Theorists will reject anything that does not fit in with their 'mental set'.
- *Pragmatists* will try out ideas and theories to see if they work. They like to experiment and are very keen to put into practice ideas they have gained recently. They, like activists, are keen to act quickly and they do not enjoy discussions which are more open-ended. They are always looking for a better way and feel that if something works then it is good.

From these descriptions, it is clear that anyone with a clear preference is going to find alternative approaches difficult to deal with. Why should we believe that someone scoring highly as an activist would not be able to critically examine the philosophical tenets of Plato's *Republic?* Why would we think that a theorist could not cope with being asked to implement a new assessment strategy without discussing its advantages and disadvantages first? Could a pragmatist wait until a new assessment strategy had been fully examined prior to testing it in the learning situation? Every learning situation requires elements of all these learning styles. The important issue, therefore, is not simply to match learning activities with people's preferred learning style, but to enable them to develop the other aspects which are not so clearly present, so that they will be able to learn effectively, regardless of the activity.

Learning styles are just one way to identify people's preferences in the learning situation. Stella Cottrell (1999) has a particularly interesting alternative to the Honey and Mumford categories. She calls them:

- the diver
- the dreamer
- the logician
- the searchlight.

What sorts of areas will people with particular preferences need to develop?

- *Activists* (the divers) need to work on their creative thinking, reflecting and planning. They may need to improve their ability to listen to others and to work with them. They probably will need to increase their interest in a topic so that they can work for longer periods.
- *Reflectors* (the dreamers) need to develop their ability to participate in group activities. They will need to develop their ability to set priorities and make decisions. This will involve them in taking risks and also require them to take responsibility for themselves.

- *Theorists* (the logicians) have to work on their creative and lateral thinking, and develop an ability to work with others, including being sensitive to different ideas and approaches proposed by their peers. They will also need to develop skills of personal reflection.
- *Pragmatists* (the searchlights) need to work on their analytical and critical thinking, to develop memory for detail and to develop an ability to categorize and select from a range of interesting topics.

How do you find out what sort of preferences your learners have? It is often not feasible to provide each potential learner with the Honey and Mumford Learning Styles Questionnaire. However, if learning styles have such potential for affecting how people learn, then clearly it is important to devise ways to help you and your learners understand their learning styles. One possible way is to ask them to think about different situations and state which activities they prefer. You could create your own inventory that you use with your learners, either before they join your programme or fairly early on. For example, here are some ideas that you may wish to explore about yourself. Remember, you, too, are a learner and have your own preferences.

- Do you prefer to work alone or with others?
- Does information make more sense if you hear, see, or speak about it?
- Do you need to do something practically, or do you prefer to watch and listen?
- Can you work with different pieces of information or do you need to have things presented one at a time?
- Do you prefer to have a structure to your learning activities or would you rather set your own agenda?
- Do you need to have feedback often or are you happy to decide for yourself how well you are doing?

Not everyone will be able to specify what they prefer to do, particularly if they are thinking about their learning experiences from a long time ago in primary school. It is not necessary to have identified everything about a person's learning style before working with them in the learning programme. In many cases, particularly where your learners are engaged on a lengthy process which will involve them in reflecting on their learning as part of the assessed outcomes, then it is better to allow the discussion on their learning style to evolve as they go through the programme's activities.

Alternative ways of establishing people's different approaches to learning include looking at personality, particularly the Myers Briggs Personality Inventory (1993) which has recently been discussed in relation to the learning styles categories of Honey and Mumford.

Caution

Remember, if you do use learning styles questionnaires, there is a danger that people may accept their 'label' which has been almost predetermined for them. With all of these ideas, try not to believe that your learners will fit into categories based on the individual learning styles, otherwise you will restrict what activities you offer, or make judgements on behalf of your learners without consulting them. Great care must be taken not to reify ideas about people's preferences. When we reify an idea, we make it become a 'thing' rather than a belief or theory. In other words, we must ensure that we do not use the categories to place people in 'boxes' and expect them to behave consistently in one particular way. There is evidence that people do change their learning styles over time; and of course, we must take care when considering the immense cultural differences between people in our groups.

As noted earlier, Coffield and colleagues have strong reservations about the claims made for learning styles, and they go so far as to claim

> It must be emphasised that this review has failed to find substantial, uncontested and hard empirical evidence that matching the learning styles of learner and tutor improves the attainment of the learner significantly. (Coffield et al., 2004, p. 41)

Matching learners' current levels of knowledge and skill with the demands of the learning programme

Not only do we need to think about our learners' preferences and learning styles, but we also need to consider what sort of learning activities our programme demands. If you are involved in developing learners' practical skills, then there will be many cases where you do require your learners to try out activities, possibly without endless discussion beforehand. On the other hand, if your learning programme involves a lot of reading of texts and discussion, then it is unlikely that you are going to be devising practical activities without the need for discussion and exploration of the meaning of the texts. It helps to know what type of learning is required for the specific discipline or content. Too often, when learning styles are mentioned, it is divorced from the context in which they will be applied. In any context for learning you will need to identify the skills that your learners require. Where your learners must read and carefully consider complex concepts, then their ability to think critically and possibly reflectively will be an important capability that can be extended during the programme. Where your discipline requires analytical thought and logic, again, learning styles, particularly the theoretical aspects, will be an advantage. It is not the case that all learners opt for disciplines and subjects that have a close correspondence with their learning styles, particularly where they have to select from certain programme constraints or meet awarding body or curriculum criteria. When you have analysed what your own learning programme is about and the type of learning and skills required by your learners, then you can establish a learning inventory that most meets the requirements of your learners. This is important information for planning your programme and individual sessions. Once you know what your learners want to learn, how much they have learned already, what they have to learn to meet awarding body requirements, then you can begin to plan effectively. Chapter 4 discusses fully how to set about creating aims, objectives and learning outcomes for your programme of learning.

Special considerations

So far, we have discussed identifying the learning needs of your learners in terms of their hopes and aspirations, the content of the programme and any external awarding body requirements. In any group of learners, you will find some have particular requirements if they are to learn successfully. An obvious example is if you have a learner who is physically disabled. If you have learners who hear with difficulty and use hearing aids, then it is important to consider their particular learning needs when you plan your sessions. If you intend to present all your information orally, they will become very tired. If you are presenting visual information, and your learners need to read your lips to fully 'hear' the information, then they cannot look at a screen and watch you at the same time. You will need to plan additional time so that people can read what is on screen or on handouts before you start talking. If you have people who do not see well, you will need to ensure that you read aloud information that is presented visually. If you are planning to use demonstrations with your learners gathered around you, those with mobility problems, including arthritis, may not be able to stand for long. Can you plan your demonstrations in shorter phases, or provide opportunities for people to sit rather than stand?

If your learners have learning difficulties, then again, how will you incorporate their particular requirements into your sessions? Will you need to offer many opportunities to reinforce a learning activity? If so, what can you do to avoid simply repeating the same thing over and over again? If some of your learners have dyslexia, are you able to accommodate their particular needs? You may find that when you get to know your learners, you have to undertake research into their disabilities so that you are able to meet their requirements fully and sensitively. This is where your skills of reflection are important. Can you see where your current practice is not enabling learning for some people? What assumptions have you made about how to work with your learners that perhaps can be challenged?

I recall working with a group of people who had severe hearing impairments: some relied upon lip-reading and others used the loop system during their classroom sessions. I was so used to looking around individuals in a group to establish eye contact when showing a slide on the overhead projector, that I often turned my face away from individuals in the group. This meant that they were unable to read my lips and, therefore, missed out on much of what I was saying. Even though I thought I was speaking slowly, my pace was too fast. I realized that I needed to plan my sessions differently, allowing far more time for any visual item I used so that learners could read this and then look at me before I started talking. I had to alter my preferred style of delivery so that I faced the people who most needed to see my lips.

I found it incredibly difficult the following term working with a blind learner, who needed almost the reverse of everything I had just developed!

Making an initial assessment of your learners' needs is not something that you will do once. You will find that you must continually assess their needs, identifying how much learning they have undertaken, perhaps what activities they have successfully completed and, therefore, deciding what you can do next. It is a bit like a central heating feedback mechanism, which continually monitors the temperature in a room and takes action by switching on or off as required. The gauge is constantly in use, even if the boiler isn't.

The 14–16-year-old groups

Nowadays, following the initiative for vocational learning for 14–19-year-olds, young people who would normally only learn in schools are being offered opportunities to study in further education colleges as noted in Chapter 2. Although most of my suggestions are aimed at working with adults, there are huge challenges facing tutors who will be working with 14–16-year-olds in particular. There is current research aimed at identifying how best to accommodate their specific learning needs within what is essentially an adult learning context, and emerging findings suggest that the young people favour further education because it treats them as adults (see Harkin, 2006). I will not, therefore, be addressing their learning needs separately throughout the following chapters, but remind readers that this group of people are by their very nature not yet fully mature, and often exhibit behaviour which can be challenging, as well as requiring different approaches to ensure that they engage in learning activities.

After the initial assessment, what next?

After you have undertaken an initial assessment of your learners, what will you do with this information? Are there other colleagues who need this information too? In some colleges, the initial diagnostic test is undertaken centrally by staff in learning resources and this is passed to programme directors. If you are a part-time tutor, do you have this information? Knowing that each of your learners has got a particular score on a diagnostic test is of no use unless you construct your learning programme in such a way that the learners can progress. It may be that you identify that they require additional learning activities, to develop their key skills or language skills. You may decide that you can develop extension exercises that they can work on independently.

Once the assessment has been conducted and the result obtained, what will happen to this information? In some further education colleges, where there are central guidance and learning support centres which undertake the test, the results are passed to programme co-ordinators who then discuss with the learner what additional learning support (if any) is required. All learners who undertook programmes funded by the FEFC were required to

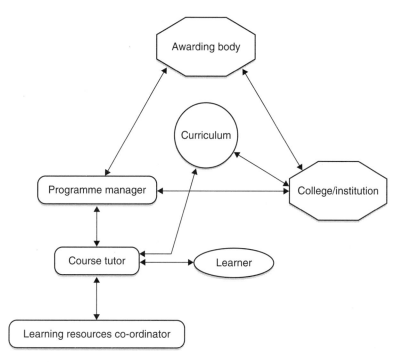

Figure 3.3 Relationships in the initial assessment of learners' needs

have a learning agreement which stated what programme they were taking and what learning support they needed. This requirement may continue under the current LSC provision.

The process of initial assessment of learners' needs is not one that is conducted in isolation. To assess potential learners' abilities and identify gaps, match their profiles to programme requirements and ensure that all the learning support required is available, involves a variety of activities and liaison with numerous colleagues. Figure 3.3 shows this complexity.

It is very important to identify specific support for learners who have either a learning or physical disability. Any institution funded by the funding agencies can claim additional funding to provide the support required. This may include interpreters or note-takers for people who are deaf or hearing-impaired, care assistants for people who are physically disabled, classroom assistants for people with learning difficulties, modified computers, and other learning resources. As noted in Chapter 2, the Tomlinson Report had clear recommendations to ensure that all people can participate fully in learning programmes.

Not only should the results of any initial assessment be passed to programme co-ordinators or tutors: individuals should also be informed of their result. This is an extremely sensitive activity to undertake, particularly where the results indicate that the individual may not yet be ready to join a particular learning programme, or who will need additional learning activities to be able to meet the entry requirements. It is vital that people do not feel that they have failed even before they embark on a learning programme. Yet if they are not aware that they have to develop particular skills and knowledge to enable them to cope with the programme, they will ultimately find difficulty during their studies. This whole process requires great skill and is something that educational guidance professionals are equipped to deal with.

Giving feedback

Not every learning programme has the resources of a qualified guidance worker to discuss initial assessment outcomes with learners. What are the main principles involved in giving feedback to learners, in this case about their initial assessment? McNair (1996) outlines the principles which form the ethical framework for practice of guidance and learner support as follows:

- learner centredness
- confidentiality
- impartiality
- equal opportunities
- accessibility.

What does this mean in practice? Many of us as children will have experienced receiving 'marks' for our work which are called out by the teacher in front of the rest of the class. Our experiences may have ranged from surprise, pure joy and relief, to disappointment, shame or anger. Giving feedback to our learners is a vital component of the way in which we can facilitate their learning. If we give information which is perceived by them to be evidence of failure, they may lose any motivation to continue. If we give them information which is not detailed enough, we may not help them identify whether they are ready to join the learning programme, or if they need to take certain steps to ensure that they can benefit from the programme they have chosen. We have to find a way to achieve a delicate balance between 'telling it how it is' without putting people off, or giving them a false sense of security. It may feel daunting to achieve this balance, and of course, gaining experience of giving feedback does help. The following guidelines offer a way to give feedback.

If we have the opportunity to sit down and discuss with each learner the result of any initial diagnostic assessment we have conducted, then it is usually better to start by asking the learners to state what they think they can do, already know, or need to do to be able to participate in the learning programme. Then we can give the feedback based on what the diagnostic activity has revealed. All the time, it is important to focus on the knowledge, skills and affective aspects of the learning situation, rather than to make statements that can be taken as criticism of the person concerned. For example, if we say 'The results show that you have remembered many of the verbs and nouns for ordering a meal in French, but your tenses are a bit mixed up', this is focusing on the grammar. If we had said 'You aren't very good at tenses', we are making a personal criticism.

Remember to give positive feedback, especially at the beginning and end of your conversation. People have a dreadful tendency to focus on the negative aspects and it is important to recognize what they have already achieved.

If feedback is given in written format, or electronically, it is even more important to be specific about what has been demonstrated or achieved and what needs to be done. You will not be able to read the 'body language' of your learners. Written feedback often comes across as more harsh, possibly because there is no 'softening' with the use of tone of voice. Remember, too, that your learners may have no idea about the educational meaning of some of your feedback, so, therefore, try to avoid jargon. With our example of a diagnostic test of someone's language level, they may have no idea what a subjunctive is (or at least have forgotten it). The whole point of initial assessment is to find out if people are ready for the next stage of their learning and what they also need to do to participate at that level. A learner-centred approach recognizes that the learner should be involved in the assessment and discussion of what is required, rather than be a passive recipient of some external test, with no follow-up discussion of the implications of the result.

Finally, feedback from initial assessment should be seen as a starting-point for further action. After an initial assessment process, we may know something more about our learners and their preferred ways of learning. We know more about what they can already do and how this matches the learning requirements of our programme. We are ready to work with them to facilitate their learning.

You will now be in a position to develop an individual learning profile (ILP) as a result of your initial assessment of your learners' current knowledge and skills. Increasingly, this is a requirement for many programmes of learning, and initial assessment will help you to develop a learning programme on the basis of this important information.

Conclusion

This chapter has discussed a vital part of any learning process – the initial assessment of learners' needs. Now that we have established what our learners already can do and what they need to do in order to successfully participate on a learning programme, we now must consider the learning programme itself, particularly preparing the necessary resources and content, and teaching and learning techniques.

You should now be able to analyse your own knowledge and skills against LLUK standards. You should be able to identify why they are necessary and how you would practise these criteria professionally.

LLUK standards

This chapter will help you work towards LLUK standards – Domain F: Access and Progression.

Further reading and information

Further reading

Briggs, Myers I. (1993) *Introduction to Type.* Oxford: Oxford Psychology Press.

Coffield, F., Moseley, D., Hall, E. and Ecclestone, K. (2004) *Should We Be Using Learning Styles? What Research Has to Say to Practice.* London: Learning and Skills Research Centre.

Cottrell, S. (1999) *The Study Skills Handbook.* Macmillan Study Guides. Basingstoke: Macmillan Press.

Crawford, M., Edwards, R. and Kydd, L. (1998) *Taking Issue: Debates in Guidance and Counselling in Learning.* London: Routledge/Open University Press.

Francis, M. and Gould, F. (2009) *Achieving Your PTLLS Award: A Practical Guide to Successful Teaching in the Lifelong Learning Sector.* London: Sage.

Guidance Council (2001) *Quality Standards.* Winchester: Guidance Council.

Harkin, J. (2006) 'Behaving like adults: meeting the needs of younger learners in further education' (www.lsnlearning.org.uk/search/Resource-35734.aspx) accessed August 2009.

Hawthorn, R. (1995) *First Steps: A Quality Standards Framework for Guidance Across All Sectors.* London: RSA.

Honey, P. and Mumford, A. (1992) *The Manual of Learning Styles.* Maidenhead: Peter Honey.

Hughes, N. and Schwab, I. (2010) *Teaching Adult Literacy: Principles and Practice.* Maidenhead: McGraw Hill/Open University Press.

Kolb, D. (1984) *Experiential Learning.* Englewood Cliffs, NJ: Prentice Hall.

McNair, S. (ed.) (1996) *Reflections from the Guidance and Learner Autonomy in Higher Education Programmes.* Moorfoot: DfEE.

Martinez, P. (2000) *Raising Achievement: A Guide to Successful Strategies.* London: DfEE/FEDA.

Petty, G. (2004) *Teaching Today: A Practical Guide* (3rd edn). Cheltenham: Nelson Thornes.

Useful websites

Functional skills support programme (www.lsneducation.org.uk/functionalskills)

Learning and Skills Improvement Service (LSIS) (www.lsis.org.uk)

Skills for Life (www.direct.gov.uk/en/EducationAndLearning/QualificationsExplained) (www.move-on.org.uk)

Planning a Learning Programme 4

When we know our subject well, it is comparatively easy to decide what we want to teach. A reflective teacher will devote much thought to deciding what people will learn. When we offer a programme of learning, either a one-year full-time course leading to a qualification, or a one-day workshop, we must ask ourselves the following questions:

- How do people learn?
- What kinds of things do they want to learn?
- What can we do to help them learn?
- How will we know that they have learned?

Could we learn from our experience and the learners' experiences when we offer this programme of learning again?

The first question, how people learn, is the subject of much debate. Our primary source of knowledge comes from learning theories, and in particular theories about how adults learn. Our second question relates to the 'What', that is, what content, what order, what knowledge, skills and attitudes can be acquired. Our third question relates to teaching and learning strategies and methods. Here we can consider activities for our learners as individuals and in groups. Our fourth question is all about assessment, and our fifth question about evaluation. This chapter will consider the 'How' and 'What' questions. Chapter 8 will examine issues of assessment and Chapter 9 issues of evaluation.

Our planning involves deciding how to work with the very different learners that we may have in our groups. An underpinning consideration for all these questions is who are our learners and what do *they* want to learn? We may have to think of the information, advice and guidance that our learners will require so that they are in the 'right place' for their studies. All of these issues are extremely complex, and most of these questions should be considered before we even meet our learners. Chapter 3 discussed how you can get to know your learners better. In this chapter, you will be able to apply this knowledge to your programme and session planning.

I shall begin with the theories of adult learning. There is a large literature on this subject, and I can only discuss the bare essentials and tenets of the main theories that are applied to the way in which adults learn. Further reading is recommended at the end of this chapter.

How do adults learn?

There are numerous factors which may influence how people learn: their ability, motivation, personality, attitude, age, previous experience of learning, life experiences, their physical well-being and the time available for learning. Some of these factors are determined at birth, and others influenced by the environment in which people live. If we are not sure how people learn, then our teaching remains more of an uninformed experiment. Although we may have an idea of what seems to work when we facilitate the learning of a group of individuals, we may be getting it right by chance.

It is important to remember, as discussed in Chapter 1, that our theories are not fully tested and complete: they are the best descriptions and explanations that we have so far. This means that when you read about theories of learning, they are not statements of fact as such. There is a danger that theories often become 'reified', in other words the ideas promoted are thought to exist in practice.

A second difficulty is that we do not know about all of the theoretical developments in the field of learning while we continue to practise. We, therefore, operate in a messy everyday situation, applying our own informal theories and continually finding new challenges in situations that we have not met before. If we are reflective, this need not be a depressing scenario: rather it is a challenge, a journey to find new ways of doing things and new ideas to add to our current repertoire.

Models of learning

There are many ways in which to categorize the theories of learning. They can be divided into those which deal with learning from a physiological stance, those that deal with learning from a psychological point of view, and those that deal with learning from a socio-political point of view. Within each of these three main categories there are numerous subdivisions. Table 4.1 outlines a selection of these theories.

It is not my intention to describe in detail each of the theories shown in Table 4.1: full discussions of these can be obtained from a variety of sources, which are listed at the end of this chapter. However, I do want to draw attention to one important distinction. Many of the theories discuss how learning *should* take place: they are predicated on a basic scientific assumption that if one does x then y will occur. Yet, as Brockbank and McGill (1998) cogently argue, 'there is no science or theory of learning which embraces all the activities involved in human learning' (p. 32).

Table 4.1 Principal models of learning

Models of learning			
Physiological	**Psychological**	**Sociological**	**Multidisciplinary**
Neurological	Behaviourist	Radical	Deep and surface
Chemical	Cognitive	Transformative	Experiential
	Humanist	Liberal	Andragogy
	Developmental	Human/social capital	Situated learning
	Psychoanalytical	Group dynamics	

The first set of theories is drawn primarily from the psychological group.

Physiological theories of learning

There has been much interest in identifying how people learn through the study of the physiology of the brain. This research has often stemmed from other related questions, for example, the work of Susan Greenfield (2000, 2008) on Alzheimers provides important clues into how memory works and, unfortunately, how it is lost through this terrible wasting process. Other work has focused on the influence of genes although the notion that our genetic make-up defines who we are and how we behave is challenged by the social and environmental theorists. This debate is often described as the 'nature versus nurture' debate. Yet it is clear that the brain, which ensures that our basic survival needs, our emotions and our thinking all function underpins how we learn and adapt to our environment. Recent research funded through the Teaching and Learning Research Programme (TLRP) has focused on education and neuroscience (see Howard-Jones, 2007) and this area continues to provide new and exciting glimpses into the fascinating world of our brains and how they function.

Psychological theories of learning

Behaviourism

In its simplest form, behaviourism is the study of the behavioural consequences of stimuli, and its beginning stems from the work of John Watson (1913). Watson wished to overcome the difficulties in explaining what goes on in people's minds through concentrating on what can be seen, that is, a person's behaviour. This theory reached its zenith through the work of B. F. Skinner (1938, 1959) and has subsequently been criticized by educators who feel that his work takes no account of human cognition and free will. Skinner's work drew upon his experiments with animals, usually pigeons or rats. If a pigeon was placed in a box (known as a Skinner box), and pecked at a key, food would follow. The pigeon would increase its pecking of that key, and the food would, therefore, always follow. The pigeon's behaviour was, then, shaped by the consequences of its action: more pecking resulted in more food. If the food was then withdrawn, the pigeon would not receive this 'reinforcement' and eventually the behaviour would decline and cease. Behaviourism is a complex theory of how behaviour is shaped by reinforcement. I recommend readers consult Tennant (1997) for full analysis.

It is not obvious how a pigeon in a Skinner box can tell us about adult learning. The following example of how behaviourist approaches are used in teaching will demonstrate how powerful and prevalent this theory is in education and training.

Making tea

Madge is learning how to make tea. She has learning difficulties and is at college one day a week. Her tutor, Frances, starts by showing her how to boil water in a kettle, put out cups, milk and sugar on a tray, warm the pot when the water has boiled, empty the pot and then place tea in it before pouring the boiled water in. Finally, she shows Madge how to wait a few minutes for the tea to 'brew' before pouring it into the cups. When it is Madge's turn, each step that Madge takes draws comments from the tutor. 'That's right, fill the water up to the level of cups you need.' 'Good, now what comes next?' 'That's right – don't forget to warm the pot.' 'Well done, you remembered that bit.' 'Good, now you have put the tea in.' 'Brilliant, a nice cup of tea for you and me.'

Throughout this example, Frances is reinforcing Madge's behaviour verbally. The process of making the tea has been broken down into discrete steps that Madge can perform. Every step can be reinforced so that it is more likely that Madge will remember and execute them next time.

One form of behaviourist approaches, the token economy, works on the principle that if people behave in ways prescribed for them by their guardians, then they can have certain rewards. For example, inmates of psychiatric institutions may earn their right to television time, or cigarettes, if they manage to control their tempers or other 'inappropriate' behaviour. Token economy is very effective, but the behaviour does not last once the token economy regime has stopped. As you may have begun to realize, there are issues of power operating in such situations, and the respect of the individual is not necessarily considered when devising ways to shape certain behaviours and deter others.

Competence-based forms of learning derive from behaviourist principles. If you want someone to do something in a particular way, then describing what that is and then shaping up their behaviour so that they do it will ensure that they have acquired the necessary skill. Unfortunately, describing what behaviour is required can become bogged down in such detail that it is hard to maintain an overall picture of what is being learned. Any of you who are dealing with NVQs will know only too well how many performance criteria (the 'How' of any performance required) there are to assess. There are numerous critics of competence-based learning (see, for example, Anley, 1993; Chown and Last, 1993; Hyland, 1994, 1998; Ecclestone, 1996, 1997) and many of these argue that competence-based learning is flawed because it draws so heavily upon behaviourist principles.

Why has behaviourism been so criticized? One of the difficulties is that once we know how to reinforce behaviour, we can become manipulative: the principles of behaviourism can be misapplied and used to manipulate people. It's worst application is in torture where people's behaviour is shaped through painful and disorienting which lead to 'confession' and submission. However, in competence-based programmes of learning, we are not forcing our learners so that they can learn certain skills! Behaviourism does not deserve the bad press it receives. We certainly shape the behaviour of young children constantly through behaviourist approaches but this does not mean that we automatically exclude their autonomy and individuality.

Neo-behaviourism

Neo-behaviourists have developed less stringent ideas of how we can analyse behaviour in terms of how it is reinforced. Gagné, in particular, has been influential in describing the *conditions* for learning, where the tutor has responsibility for designing and managing the learning process and also evaluating the learning outcomes of that process. He argues that it is by considering how events relate to each outcome that we can describe the conditions for their learning. To achieve this, we must first consider what type of learning is necessary. According to Gagné there are five types of human capability: skill, understanding, knowing facts, competence and transferability of skills, and developing attitudes. Here are some examples for each of these capabilities:

- skill, for example, threading a needle
- understanding, for example, Newton's laws of motion
- factual information, for example, events in history, descriptions of the natural world
- competence, for example, in finding new solutions to practical problems
- learning positive values, for example, respect and honesty.

We must first consider what type of capability we are trying to facilitate in our learners and then identify the conditions that will foster the development of that capability. As we acquire and develop these capabilities, we progress to the stage where 'cumulative learning results in the establishment of capabilities that make it possible for the individual to solve a great variety of novel problems' (Gagné, 1985, p. 137).

Cognitive approaches

Cognitive approaches are concerned with how people gain knowledge about the world. These approaches, therefore, deal with the aspects that behaviourism ignored, that is, the mind. Here the learner is the focus of the theory, not the task. Cognitive approaches incorporate ideas of intelligence and the psychometric tradition of using IQ tests. There is an assumption that once people become adult, their intelligence is less fluid and more stable or 'crystallized'. In childhood, thinking develops through a series of stages (Piaget, 1978) until adulthood, where people are able to use and develop abstract ideas.

Cognitive approaches are generally structuralist; in other words, there is an assumption that there are stages of development and then stability. There are many analogies used by cognitive theorists. One of the more prevalent is that of the computer, where people are seen to process information which has been 'input' into their brains. People do not simply receive the information but do something with it, thereby actively engaging with the initial stimulus. Learners do not necessarily learn what they are taught; rather they make sense of what they are taught and recreate or reframe this information to construct their own knowledge. The theory, therefore, acknowledges individual learner autonomy.

It is on the basis of this sense-making that theories of teaching have been derived. The major protagonists of cognitive theory are Bruner (1966), Ausubel and colleagues (1978) and Vygotsky (1962). All articulate the importance of the learners and how they organize knowledge. Vygotsky's work has led to the concept of scaffolding, whereby knowledge is gradually built up through the introduction of certain basic concepts that are then developed. It is easy to see this approach in mathematics and science, where learners need to be able to manipulate the basic arithmetic functions of addition and subtraction before they can begin to work with multiplication and division. Indeed, given that multiplication and division are more advanced ways to add and subtract, it would be extremely difficult to help someone multiply if they could not yet add.

A central figure in approaching this need to split knowledge and skills into smaller components is Benjamin Bloom who developed a taxonomy. He showed that lower order skills could be taught directly but that for a fully functional knowledge of a topic, learners would require thinking skills and need to be able to make connections. In his taxonomy, low order skills and lower 'cognitive demand' could be captured by asking people to describe or recall what they have just learned whereas with the high 'cognitive demand' and functional knowledge, people would need to be able to evaluate or make judgements, for example, about a historical event, a scientific experiment or educational policy. Petty (2004) provides a helpful explanation of Bloom's taxonomy.

Humanistic approaches

Humanistic psychology places the individual in the centre. It is a theory concerned with the 'self'. Maslow (1968) was the main protagonist of humanistic psychology, and he argued that there is a hierarchy of need by which argued are motivated. The lowest level consists of basic needs: food, water, shelter, warmth. This is followed by safety needs, then love and belongingness needs, self-esteem needs, and finally the need for self-actualization. Only when lower-level needs are satisfied can an individual become motivated to satisfy the higher level. The highest level can be seen to be a state of equilibrium, where people are making full use of their capabilities, are 'rooted' in self-knowledge and are in control of the direction of their lives. Applied to adult learning, Maslow's theory would predict that people who are hungry or thirsty are not likely to learn effectively because their energy will be directed to satisfying their basic needs. Adults will learn when they are motivated to reach the higher levels of the hierarchy because they will then be active participants in the learning situation. One can criticize this theory because we know that we can learn even if we are cold or hungry, and that our survival skills depend on our being able to learn when we are in extremely challenging situations.

In fact, as anyone familiar with Buddhism will know, the way to enlightenment is achieved by specifically eschewing physical comforts which Maslow argues must be satisfied before moving towards self-actualization. The model, then, is culturally bound, as argued by Urmi Joshi, a doctoral student at the University of Greenwich, School of Post Compulsory Education and Training, at her presentation on Foundation Degrees, Further and Higher Education Network meeting at the Society for Research in Higher Education (SRHE) in June 2004 (SRHE, 2004).

Carl Rogers was a clinical psychologist, like Maslow, whose theory proselytizes respect for an individual and the development of genuine feelings. For a tutor of adults, this means that we should be ourselves, and not try to develop a facade. We should have a warm regard for our learners, but accept our learners as individuals in their own right. We need to treat them with empathy; that is, to 'understand the learner's reactions from the inside' (Rogers, 1983, p. 129). Rogers' work has been particularly influential in group dynamics and the study of how people behave in group learning situations, covered more fully in Chapter 7.

Multidisciplinary theories of learning

Some theorists have developed what I call 'multidisciplinary' theories of adult learning. These theories, therefore, draw upon sociological ideas and the more 'pure' psychological theories. They take account of both the individual as an actor in the world and the world in which the individual lives.

Theories of adult learning: andragogy

The psychological theories covered so far could apply to any person, at any age. There are far more theories about learning by children and I do not intend to examine these. Many of these theories do not account well for the way *adults* learn. Adults are busy people, with experience gained from living through their transition from childhood to adulthood. When they join a programme of learning, they come with a foundation of knowledge, skills and attitude, including habits of learning acquired in the past. One theorist, Malcolm Knowles (1978, 1984), argued that the theory of how adults learn is different from that of children. The study of how children learn is called pedagogy, and Knowles coined the term 'andragogy' for the study of how adults learn.

Knowles applies a range of theories in his pragmatic approach to the facilitation of learning in adults. His main argument is that people are 'self-directed' and the role of the adult educator is to help adults to move from being the type of dependent learner from their childhood days to self-directed learners as adults. This means that people should be able to control and negotiate their own learning environment and goals. Knowles' ideas draw heavily upon the Rogerian notions of respect and empathy.

Experiential learning

The most influential theory in recent years for adult learning has been the experiential theory, particularly Kolb's learning cycle. Here it is shown as a cycle of learning from a concrete experience. As noted in Chapter 3 on learning styles, Kolb's cycle accounts for the way in which people can abstract generalizations from a concrete experience and devise ideas for future experimentation based on their reflections. Although experiential learning is often defined as learning by doing, it actually refers to the learning as a result of thinking about the doing.

Kolb's cycle has been adapted to take account of many of the criticisms of this earlier model. Cowan (1999) describes loops of learning, almost coiled like springs, where people do not simply have an experience, reflect on it, generalize about it and then start experimenting with their new ideas. He argues that people bring their experiences to any new learning situation and that not only is there reflection on the recent experience itself, but the assimilation of this into previous experience. Learners can then consolidate their reflections when they put their new learning into action, which thereby creates opportunities for them to gain new experiences which can be assimilated into their now previous experiences. He also shows how this form of learning is compatible with behaviourist approaches where learning is programmed, and with cognitive approaches where the more traditional approach of 'tell them what to do, getting them to do it and then remind them what they have done' helps learners develop cognitive abilities (Cowan, 1999, p. 41).

Deep and surface learning

Another theory of learning which is more overarching is that of deep and surface learning. Originally developed by Marton and Saljö, and Entwhistle (1997), this theory suggests people have different approaches to their learning. Those who take a surface approach simply want to 'pass the test' and do not develop strategies for permanent learning. Those who adopt a deep approach devise their own models from the information they have to learn. The approaches have been identified from higher education learners who initially were asked to read a passage and answer questions. Those who used a deep approach to their analysis of the passage created concepts and related these to emerging themes, whereas those who used a surface approach simply memorized disparate items. Further work by Marton, Hounsell and Entwhistle (1997) and Biggs (1999) has expanded the theory. Biggs developed a taxonomy of learning which identifies five levels of learning:

1. *Pre-structural:* no knowledge
2. *Unistructural:* limited knowledge about one aspect
3. *Multistructural:* knowledge about a number of aspects
4. *Relational:* knowledge about aspects related to each other
5. *Extended abstract:* knowledge about aspects synthesized to form hypotheses.

If we want our learners to make connections between different ideas or concepts, then we want them to be learning at the relational level of learning. If we simply want them to list a set of ideas, or characteristics, then we want them to perform at the multistructural level. If we want people to think critically and analytically about a topic, weighing up different ideas and creating a coherent argument for a point of view, then we are asking them to perform at an extended abstract level. Biggs argues that it is no good setting people tasks that will encourage them to adopt a surface approach to learning: they will simply remember at the time and then forget. Identifying tasks that encourage a deep approach to learning will be more effective in enabling them to apply their knowledge in future, as yet undefined, ways.

Situated learning

When we learn about something, it is not usually in a sterile environment. In fact, Lave and Wenger (1991) argued that we need to look at the context in which people learn to maximize the effectiveness of our teaching and facilitation of learning. They proposed that learning is situated within the social context. In other words, when people learn, they do so through acquiring the social knowledge within which they are situated. For example, apprentices acquire technical knowledge and skill but they do so by being steeped in a particular environment with taken-for-granted ways of working which they need to learn, even though these ways are not normally specified or articulated. Lave and Wenger, then, like Biggs, would argue that we need to think of learning in terms of its application in the real world, something which is far more complex than working at the unistructural level. New attempts to embed basic skills within a vocational curriculum, for example, would fit with the model of situated learning.

Lave and Wenger noted that we live in a number of communities which have their ways of doing things and proposed that as professionals we work in such a community of practice, in this case, of post-compulsory education. In fact, this is too broad a term and we actually belong to various communities, for example, we may belong to one that relates to our subject specialism, and another that relates to the kind of institution. Being a numeracy tutor would involve belonging to the functional skills community, to the numeracy and maths specialist community and quite likely, the further education, adult and community or work-based vocational community. These communities overlap and interrelate. Newcomers to a community of practice need to acquire the tacit knowledge about what they need to do and understand. You will be part of a community of practice as you undertake your professional development as Chapter 10 discusses.

Applying learning theories to our programme planning

So far, having introduced some of the learning theories available, I am sure you will be feeling quite swamped by the variety of ideas and descriptions of how people learn. Deciding what to teach partly depends on how you expect your learners to learn. Should we adopt one theory and direct all our practices towards working within one framework? Or is the eclectic approach better, where we take 'packages off the shelf' from the display of learning theories and use these at different points along the way? Of course, it is not that simple. When we are working with a group of adults, we can describe their learning in physiological terms, in psychological terms and in sociological terms. Any one activity can be analysed from a variety of standpoints. What we are aiming to do is to act both pragmatically and in the way described in Chapter 1 as *phronesis*. This means that we are continually striving to practise with insight.

How can these learning theories help us work with our learners? Here is an example:

Healthy living

Mukesh is working with a group of older learners who are following a 'healthy living' programme at their local community centre. The group members have not taken part in any formal education programme before, and only opted for the programme after much outreach work by the health visitor and housing action officer who works on their council estate. The aim of the programme is to encourage people to adopt healthier eating habits and to take exercise, therefore, reducing the risk of heart disease and obesity. It is a programme aimed at changing behaviour and attitudes.

How can the learning theories outlined above inform Mukesh in his programme planning and delivery? If we look at the psychological approaches, we can see that Mukesh could draw upon the principles of behaviourism to help him work towards behaviour change. He could shape people's behaviour by reinforcing the desirable aspects. This could be done, for example, by giving people tastes of 'healthy' food that perhaps they might not have eaten before, enabling them to enjoy the experience and making it more likely that they will try this again. By gradually reinforcing their consumption of certain foods, he is effectively shaping their behaviour. Now many readers may be feeling that this is much too close to a manipulative approach and, as previously mentioned, behaviourism has a very bad press in educational circles. However, if you analyse the number of times you encourage people through verbal behaviour, smiles, compliments, you can begin to see how much we use a behaviourist approach in our teaching. Making this explicit at least enables the tutor to plan how to introduce new ideas and concepts.

An alternative, but not mutually exclusive strategy, could be to adopt a cognitive approach. Here, the individuals in the group would be encouraged to think for themselves about their current lifestyle and what they should be doing to ensure that they reduce the risk of heart disease. They would need information about healthy foods, how exercise can reduce the risk, how much is necessary to be effective, foods that should be avoided. Then the individuals would need to devise their own diets and exercise regimes. The cognitive approach enables people to 'own' the process. However, even while this is developing, how Mukesh provides the information and how people are encouraged to accept it will still reside in a behaviourist model.

We can develop a purely cognitive approach to a more humanistic strategy. Here, principles of self-actualization (Maslow) and Rogerian notions of the ideal self come to the fore. If people want to be healthy, then they have to take responsibility for this themselves. They need to want to be healthy and to want to find ways to achieve this. They will want to challenge their previous eating habits and to introduce different foods and ways of cooking them. Here, the focus is on the individuals making active choices, not simply being forced to take ideas which have been imposed on them.

It is clear from a sociological perspective that there is a 'hidden curriculum' operating in the scenario. Healthy people use less resources from the health service. They may benefit psychologically (see Institute for Employment/NIACE, 2000). They will, therefore, not only 'cost less' in terms of health and social service provision, but they gain in terms of social capital (Field, 2000; Field and Schuller, 2000).

What will Mukesh actually *do?* Here is an example of a typical session:

- Introduction and time for questions from previous session, how the week has gone.
- Taking exercise – short presentation with video extracts showing people walking, swimming, jogging, using weights and in an exercise class.
- Discussion in small groups on what people have done in the past, what they do now and what they would like to try over the next five weeks.
- Break.
- Warm-up and cool-down exercises – group activity led by instructor from local gym.
- Presentation by community officer on resources available in the local area.
- Plans for the week.
- Close.

The rationale for this programme is one that starts with the individual learners' perspectives giving them an opportunity to share their experiences from the previous week. Each week has a task set which provides the group members with experience, so that they can actually practise what has been covered in the session. Here Mukesh is aiming to reinforce ideas through kinaesthetic experience and also provide an opportunity for individuals to develop cognitive strategies for themselves.

With the presentation, Mukesh is providing information and, again, reinforcing certain behaviours, showing examples of older people enjoying themselves; he is modelling behaviour and challenging taken-for-granted ideas about older people not being able to do certain activities.

Group discussion provides people with a chance to share their ideas. It reinforces the previous input because they will have been passively watching the video. The group discussion, therefore, again enables people to challenge what they have been thinking and also to air their own views, particularly if they may disagree with what they have just seen, or are reluctant to change their own lifestyle.

After the break (which is an extremely important part of the process, giving people a chance to chat informally, and, of course, satisfy a variety of fundamental bodily needs)

Mukesh has moved on to a practical activity. Once again, this reinforces the original ideas about exercise and what can be achieved. It also introduces safe practice, ensuring that people are not going to injure themselves if they suddenly launch into exercise after years of non-participation. He has brought along a colleague who is both qualified to teach exercise and who runs sessions in the community centre on a regular basis.

Finally, information for group members about what is on offer locally provides a follow-on to what is now a gentle nudge towards getting involved. By the end of the session, everyone would have seen examples of, heard about and taken part in exercise and aired their own views. The task for the week will reinforce this further, asking them to carry on the gentle warm-up and cool-down exercises through the week, and possibly trying out one of the many activities on offer locally.

What can adults learn about?

So far we have considered theories of how adults learn and why this is important when we plan any learning programme. We can now turn our attention to the 'What' our learners could be learning about. We need to identify what the content will be and how we will cover it. We have to consider the main aim and the objectives. These two terms alone account for much confusion, as any of you undertaking a teacher training course will know only too well!

Having established the learning needs of your learner group, you can plan more effectively for what is going to happen during the programme that you are offering. As there are so many different situations in which teaching and learning take place, I am going to define a programme as any planned learning activity which extends over a period of time and which contains a structure within which participants will be expected to achieve certain learning outcomes. Programmes can be delivered in a variety of ways; there may be weekly two-hour sessions in the evenings, a series of Saturday workshops, an intensive training course over a two-day period, a year-long vocational or academic course. It may involve learning at a college or community centre, learning at a college with work placements, learning entirely at the workplace, learning entirely through distance learning or web-based learning. The important theme which links all these differing forms of learning activity is that there has to be planning to ensure coherence and consistency. Castling (1996) offers a range of reasons why planning is important. It prevents rushed or hasty decisions, helps create a structure for complex content, provides a structure for teaching, assessment and evaluation, helps learners prepare for sessions in advance and helps identify necessary resources in advance.

What do you need to consider when planning? If we are to reflect on what we do when we plan, we can ask ourselves a number of questions: What am *I* trying to achieve? What are *my learners* going to achieve? How can I enable these two goals to be met? To do this, you will need to consider your learners, the programme, the resources available and your own responsibilities.

Learners

Adults come from immensely diverse backgrounds. They differ in age, sex, ethnicity and cultural background. They have differing previous learning experiences, reasons for doing the course and may have special learning requirements. Chapter 2 discussed how there are specific policies for being inclusive in adult learning, and Chapter 3 described how to identify such requirements through initial diagnostic testing and through guidance procedures. In Chapter 5, I identify how important it is to think of learning resources that can ensure that all learners can engage in a learning programme. In this chapter, we must now think about the programme itself, its content, structure and activities. Throughout, we must remember that we do not have a homogeneous group of people: they are all different.

How can you plan and execute a programme of learning for a group of learners with differing learning requirements? The method of working with people who have a mixed range of ability and need is currently known as 'differentiated learning'. In the past, it was known as mixed-level teaching. The issue here, and in subsequent chapters, is how to ensure that individuals within any group are having their learning needs addressed and given opportunities to acquire the skills and knowledge that they have signed up for.

Content planning

There is a variety of taxonomies of learning which help us consider what we are covering. Bloom's *Taxonomy* (1956) is very useful for identifying teaching objectives. He divided educational objectives into domains – cognitive and affective. These objectives are written in such a way that observable behaviour is defined. The more precisely the objectives are written, the more likely it is that the outcomes of learning will be observed and, therefore, assessed.

Defining subject knowledge: technical requirements and skills required

Gagné, we noted earlier, has proposed that we think about the *conditions* of learning. For Gagné, a learning occurrence

> takes place when the *stimulus situation* together with the contents of *memory* affect the learner in such a way that his or her *performance* changes from a time *before* being in that situation to a time *after* being in it. The *change in performance* is what leads to the conclusion that learning has occurred. (1985, p. 4)

Gagné argues that we should consider how events relate to each learning outcome so that we can describe the conditions for their learning. In this way, we can plan for learning, manage learning and create the conditions for learning. This means that for every capability there are external and internal conditions which are more favourable to their learning. For example, for intellectual skills, recall of prerequisite skills is the most important internal condition and the external condition is the guide to the combination of simpler skills, usually through verbal direction. For a cognitive skill, the favourable internal condition is recall of intellectual skills and the external condition is frequent practice of strategies. This is perhaps more easily shown through the idea of developing spelling strategies when learning to write. The more words that are learned and used, the more easily one can develop strategies for certain patterns of letters, and by practising these writing skills, individuals can further develop their cognitive abilities. For Hayes (1976), people can learn how to learn, which gives them a capability to deal with future events. Thus, as Gagné notes:

> cognitive strategies are a kind of human capability . . . there is increasing evidence that the kinds of cognitive strategies applicable to thinking and problem solving can be learned and that when learned they exhibit transfer to new problem situations of the same general sort. (1985, p. 151)

It is the acquisition of concepts that makes instruction possible.

> Typically, the learning of a topic or part of a course of study can be viewed as a hierarchy in which the most complex rules require the learning of simpler rules as prerequisites to efficient attainment . . . learning hierarchies imply that learning has a cumulative character in which the acquisition of specific rules establishes the possibility of transfer of learning in a number of more complex 'higher order' rules. (Gagné, 1985, p. 135)

What does this mean for our planning? It certainly helps us break down our content into what has become known as KSA (knowledge, skills and attitudes). How can we possibly help our learners learn if we do not know whether they require certain skills acquisition first before developing higher order skills? Do we understand how best to set the conditions for their learning? Gagné has been highly influential in helping us examine the kind of learning required and how best to facilitate this. His model is highly prescriptive and analytical, and may be partially responsible for the competence-based movement, where skills and knowledge are broken down into discrete 'chunks' and set into criteria against which learning can be assessed.

Incorporating individual levels of knowledge and skill

Lovell (1979) suggests that 'One of the oldest rules of teaching is that the teacher should take the learner from where he is to where the teacher wants him to be' (p. 140). Planning, therefore, not only must take into account the type of content, for example, logical, ordered or topic-based, but also how to accommodate people's existing levels of knowledge and skill. One aspect of this is knowledge construction. Here, in the planning stages, it is necessary to consider how each session can build upon previous sessions and upon individual learners' experiences and knowledge. Ausubel and colleagues (1978) offer a model of progressive differentiation and integrative reconciliation. This is where the most overarching principles of any discipline should be thought of as at the apex of a pyramidal structure, with detail being progressively differentiated lower down towards the base. The more general and inclusive ideas at the apex should be presented initially, with the more specific details following. For example, if a tutor is introducing fractions to a numeracy class, then the idea that fractions are parts of a whole is the general principle. Using fractions, particularly when finding fractions of fractions (i.e. multiplying fractions) is a more specific aspect of this. Not only should ideas be presented which are progressively differentiated, but they should also build upon what has gone before, therefore, integrating new ideas with existing ones. Integration is more coherent than using a simple explanation of a complex concept initially, then rejecting it later and replacing it with a more developed notion. I can remember being told in biology classes in my last years at school that what we had been taught about certain aspects of plant reproduction was totally inaccurate but that it had been good enough for a lower level of understanding. The teacher joked that we had been lied to. Although it was humorous at the time, on reflection, I would have preferred to have a development of concepts that became increasing specific rather than a heuristic approach that simply was untrue and had to be replaced by something else.

This problem of lack of integration can lead to conceptual confusion, where the learner may not realize that new concepts are in fact the same as older, less defined ones. When using progressive differentiation and integrative reconciliation, learners should be given opportunities to look for contrasts and similarities between the concepts they are developing and to apply these in their conceptual formation. This model can be applied in highly cognate subjects such as philosophy, where learners may be developing skills of analysis alongside concepts, for example, of ethics, and in skill-based subjects where developing a web page can draw upon increasingly specific notions of communication theory and design.

Now that we have identified that there is a variety of learning theories to inform our teaching and learning strategies, and that we can break down our content into manageable 'chunks', we are ready to think about planning a programme in more detail.

The learning programme

Here are some issues to consider when you plan your learning programme:

- *The pace:* should you find a medium pace and hope those who learn fast will not be bored and those who learn slowly can keep up?
- *The level:* easy to hard? Pitched at a middle level?
- *The sequencing of material:* will it be in a logical order? Will you place it chronologically?
- Will you use *themes* or *issues?* Will you cover a *number of procedures?* Will it be on a *need-to-know basis* (e.g. safety), will you need to *spiral,* that is, use the same skill but develop it in terms of complexity (e.g. listening skills in counselling at levels of complexity)?

Building in assessment and evaluation activities

How will you know that your learners are acquiring skills and knowledge during your programme? How will you know what they have learned by the end of your programme? A full discussion on assessment can be found in Chapter 8. It is vital that you plan how to build assessment activities into the learning programme. If you are running an accredited course, particularly those that depend on work-based assessments or simulations, then you must provide a number of opportunities for your learners to undertake assessed activities. Even in non-accredited programmes, activities which are assessed, even informally by yourself and the learners, provide an important opportunity to give feedback on how your learners are progressing.

Flexibility

Planning does not need to be a straitjacket. If I discover that a group of learners had not been able to work on an assignment which was due the following week, I may decide that it is better to delay my original planned session and provide them with an opportunity to discuss what is required for the assignment, what they are finding difficult and how they are going to tackle it. My planned session can take place at a more appropriate time.

More often, I may find that I was too ambitious in my plan and during a particular session realize that I will need to adapt my plan to take account of the different timescale. I may feel that the tangent learners are taking in their discussion is worth staying with as it is relevant to future areas of the curriculum. With this approach, we can have a carefully planned session and programme and the flexibility to change when required.

Aims

The first question we must ask, then, is what we want our learners to achieve; in other words, what are our aims for this programme and then what are the objectives for each session? What do we mean by aims and objectives? This is where metaphors are very useful. One way is to think of how the word 'aim' is used in sport. If you are an archer, you would take aim at a target and shoot your arrow, with the intention of hitting it as close to the middle as possible. You can see exactly what you are aiming for. Sometimes, the aim is not so clearly visible. If you are a walker aiming for a very nice pub at the end of the valley, you may take a path that winds up and down hills and valleys. You may not be able to see what you are aiming for when you start, but as you travel along the path you cross the streams and climb over the stiles, all of which are necessary for you to reach the pub.

When you set out a programme of learning, you are effectively beginning a journey and enabling your learners to travel along a path that you may have defined very carefully. You may have a programme of learning which does not require such a set route, particularly if you are involved in programmes which do not lead to any formal accreditation or qualification.

You may be involved with a programme where the learners define their own pathways and you are there to help facilitate their chosen journey. So planning not only does not have to be so defined that there is no opportunity to wander off the path or choose another, it may have to be the kind of planning that is done at the end of each day's travel.

However, sometimes we set aims that are so nebulous that it is quite difficult to see what we are heading for; and, more importantly, we will not know if we have got there. As John Cowan's grandmother said, 'If you don't know where you are going, any bus will do' (Cowan, 1999, p. 103).

Let's look at a few examples of aims.

Cooking for one
Aim: To introduce learners to methods, recipes and healthy eating for people who live alone.

Classical influences on Renaissance architecture
Aim: To introduce learners to the revivals and reinterpretations of classical antiquity in Renaissance architecture.

Return to learn
Aim: To enable learners to acquire study skills and confidence to continue studying for qualifications.

Counselling
Aim: To introduce participants to principles and practices of counselling skills: active listening, reflecting and empathy.

Using a database
Aim: To introduce participants to the applications of Microsoft Access.

What do you notice about these aims? They are very vague. They do not describe in enough detail exactly what will be covered (the content), how they will be covered (the process) and with what groups of learners (the social perspective). We need more information. We could introduce our learners to the principles of counselling, for example, in a number of ways. We need to break down our overall aim into smaller components, which are our *objectives*.

Objectives

Objectives are best described as the stepping-stones to achieving an aim. It is the 'How we are going to get there.' So in the example above, where the course aim is to introduce participants to the principles of counselling, our objectives may be that at the end of the course, everyone will be able to listen actively, reflect on what another person has said, summarize the main points from a person's narrative and use empathy with that person. Now these objectives do not specify how well this should be done, and we do not know how we will find out if someone is listening actively. Does it mean that she or he will nod throughout a person's presentation or does it mean that she or he won't nod off during it? How is a person empathetic and how will we know? There is a vital link here between setting aims and objectives and assessing learning outcomes. Planning what we hope our learners will achieve is inextricably linked to planning how we are going to find this out. With our more practical examples of using Microsoft Access, or cooking for one, the skills we hope our learners will acquire will be performed as they participate in the programme. If we ask our learners to create a file in Access, type in data, save it, print it and save the file, then they will be demonstrating their skills and knowledge about using Access in one activity. We must plan our sessions so that they can do all of these things, and there may be a logical order for covering this. It would be better to learn to save a file early on even if learners had not created one before, so that they do not lose their work!

Learning outcomes

If you are working on a vocational programme leading to NVQs, Diplomas or other competence-based awards, then your outcomes will be very clearly laid down in the standards being used. The best way to help identify what a learning outcome could be is to ask yourself 'What at the end of this session or programme will the participants be able to do?' The focus for a learning outcome is on the learner. The focus of aims and objectives is on what you are hoping to teach. There is no guarantee that just because you have aims and objectives your learners will learn anything. The advantage in trying to define learning outcomes for your programme is that you have to think of what your learners will have *achieved*, rather than what you have covered.

Weasel words

We should try to use clear language to define our aims, objectives and learning outcomes. If I say that my aim is to help you understand how to teach adults, and my objectives are to help you understand learners' needs, backgrounds and aspirations, and that by the time you have finished this chapter you will be able to define aims and objectives and learning outcomes, then I have created a set of words which are subject to immense variations in interpretation. When I say that I understand something, in this case that I understand my learners' needs, does this mean that I can tell you what they are, or that I know how it feels to have the same needs myself? The word 'understand' can mean many different things. However, if instead I say that I hope that you will be able to identify what your learners' needs, backgrounds and aspirations are, then you will be listing them, and by doing so I will know that you have found something out about your learners that will help you plan effectively.

Table 4.2 Useful verbs for defining learning outcomes

Knowledge	Skill	Attitude
Define	Assemble	Describe
Explain	Draw	Choose
List	Make	Explain
Solve	Perform	Indicate
State	Use	Verify

(© Sandy Alden)

Some people suggest that you should avoid words like 'understand' when writing aims, objectives and outcomes precisely because we cannot know what this means or share the same meaning. This viewpoint is often rejected by people who do not like working with competence-based programmes because they feel that they are not allowed those unquantifiable aspects of teaching and learning. For example, I may not be able to define what a good teacher is exactly, but I may recognize one when I observe a session. We talked earlier in Chapter 1 about implicit or tacit knowledge. I make judgements based partially on explicit criteria but also on my implicit ideas and theories. How will my learners know what is in my mind if I do not make it public? Learners do need to know what they are likely to achieve if they embark on a learning activity so that they can decide if the programme offers what they are hoping to learn.

Which words help us define learning aims, objectives and outcomes? Table 4.2 shows a sample adapted from a list compiled by Sandy Alden, at The City Lit. She suggests that some of the verbs are most useful when writing outcomes which relate to the knowledge that learners will acquire, and others are more useful when describing the skills that they will acquire.

As you can see, many of the words have a very practical nature. This is helpful when you are involved in teaching a practical subject such as bricklaying, cordon bleu cooking or badminton. We can see what someone is doing and how well they are doing it. It becomes more difficult when we consider more knowledge-based subjects such as history or philosophy. Can we see someone thinking analytically? We can hear their discussion which could be seen as an outcome of their thinking, but how well have they thought? Can we break down a course on Kant and Spinoza into meaningful chunks where we can state that each week the learners will learn to do something? Sometimes, we have to introduce many activities, possibly of the same kind, before learners learn how to think, or can apply their learning to a variety of situations.

When we look at our third example, where we are dealing with people's emotions, we have even more difficulty. Can we plan for people to challenge their taken-for-granted assumptions? Can we define how they should be assertive? This is a particularly sensitive issue when we consider the cultural backgrounds of our learners. A person who has been brought up to believe that it is rude to establish direct eye contact with someone in authority will not feel comfortable in doing so if it is seen to be a part of being assertive. We must take care to define our objectives and outcomes to allow for cultural differences. In this example, we can now apply words from Table 4.2 as follows:

> *Outcome:* Participants will be able to *explain* what is meant by active listening, *indicate* where they have demonstrated this in their practicum and *describe* how they have actively listened when dealing with colleagues.

For our fourth example we have a two-day workshop on how to use databases. We know that understanding a database is not a clear enough objective for us and our learning outcomes need to tell us what our learners will have learned and been able to demonstrate. We can now say that by the end of the two days they will have developed a database to meet a specification of the organization in which they work. They will be able to identify what fields are required, create the fields, identify what reports can be derived from the fields, input the data and interrogate the data to respond to specific enquiries from managers. They will not only be able to do this, but also be able to develop databases for future, as yet unknown, specifications. So they will have acquired a procedural knowledge, knowing how and knowing what (Ryle, 1949).

Session planning

Once we have established the overall aims, objectives and learning outcomes for our programme, we are now in a position to think about what will happen in each session. Some subject areas are quite progressive in nature, in the sense that certain skills and knowledge have to be acquired before someone can move on to the next stage. In numerical subjects, it is necessary to have the basic skills of computation before being able to work with fractions and decimals. Literature is an example where there may be underlying skills such as writing, reading and deducing information which can be refined over time, but the topics in which these skills are displayed and acquired do not need to be in a particular order.

When we start planning individual sessions, we need to ask how our planned activities are going to work towards achieving our final aims and outcomes. We need to think about the order in which we wish to do this, and how we are going to help our learners acquire and practise their skills, acquire knowledge and use it, and how they will develop views and attitudes from their new knowledge and skills. We also must consider how they will feel about the process of learning.

- Within any session, we need to think about the following:
- What are the aims and objectives?
- What teaching methods will be used?
- What resources are needed?
- What will the learners have learned by the end of the session?
- What opportunity exists for assessing the learning?
- How will the session be evaluated?

There is a variety of ways that you can devise a plan. Figure 4.1 is an example used by The City Lit. You will notice that it is broken down into sections: time, tutor activity, learner activity and resources. Very often, planning tends to focus on what the tutor is

```
                                     Session plan

Date 4 May                                Topic Vitamins

Aim  To introduce learners to the need for vitamins in a healthy diet
Outcomes  At the end of the session, learners will be able to name the main vitamins,
describe what each does and main sources in food

Time          Tutor activity           Learner activity        Resources
9.00          Question what foods       Write list of           Whiteboard
              eaten yesterday           foods
9.30          Presentation of chart     Listening               Chart, OHP
10.00         Group work set up         Form groups             Case studies
                                                                food labels
11.00         Plenary                   Presentation of         Whiteboard, OHP
                                        analysis of food
                                        discussion

Assessment of outcomes
Group presentation, discussion, written summary in coursework
```

Figure 4.1 Example of a session plan

doing. By defining what you and your learners are doing, the balance of tutor-led and learner-led activities can be established. Once you have constructed your plan, you will see how much time you have allowed for learners to participate and how much for your presentation of information or ideas. If your plan involves a presentation for one hour, a short break and another presentation, your learners will be passive for a long time and they may well fall asleep or get distracted. Planning is linked not only to what the learners are doing, but also to your choice of learning methods and teaching methods. A full discussion of teaching methods is found in Chapter 6. Here it is important to note that a variety of activities often aids concentration, particularly those which actively involve the learners.

Why do we need session plans?

Why write out session plans? Surely if people are organized and experienced, then they will know what they are going to do, how long it is likely to take and what resources they will require without having to write it all down. Those of you who work in further education know that you are required to keep session plans, not just because you may be observed by your line managers, curriculum managers and Ofsted inspectors, but also because it is part of the quality assurance process. Session plans can also be used by a substitute if you are suddenly unable to take the session yourself.

Session plans contain a deal of implicit knowledge. If I say that I am going to organize a game with my learners which I have devised myself, my session plan might just state

'Balloon game', what resources are needed and the time I think it is likely to take. A substitute tutor might not know what this game is and why I want to use it. However, if I have specified clearly in my session plan that the point of doing the game is so that learners will have developed negotiating skills, then my replacement tutor may have an alternative strategy to achieve this same outcome. If I did not have any written plan, then my replacement would have no idea what my learners should be achieving.

Having a written plan keeps you focused and is also useful if you 'lose your way'. Plans are very useful when you are teaching a new subject, or a group of learners with whom you are unfamiliar. Suppose your subject is hairdressing, and your college has been asked by a community organization to offer a short, five-session course to their members who have learning disabilities. You know your subject area very well, but you may not have had much experience of working with people who have a variety of learning disabilities. Your first plan may be in need of revision once you have met your group and discovered what they can do and what they need to learn, and the pace at which it is appropriate for them to undertake certain activities. Having a plan, then, can also help you identify adjustments more easily.

Differentiated learning

It is important to remember that when you are working with groups of learners, you need to ensure that you consider what each member is doing. The government has become very keen to support what is now known as personalized learning, or differentiation. Here, you are required to plan for the different levels of ability and individual requirements of each learner when you plan your session. You not only need to have specified what each person is going to be working on during that session, but you also need to think about how you will know that person is learning, that is, plan for assessment activities (discussed in Chapter 8).

You may, then, need to think about different activities within the same session. If you are teaching law, you may decide that having introduced a topic, for example, the Age Discrimination Act, you may ask one group of learners to work on a case study whereas another group which is working towards a higher grade of the award may be asked to undertake additional examination of case studies and prepare a synthesis. This is where the use of worksheets, and additional web-based sources and activities are really useful. The application of Biggs' taxonomy is also appropriate here, where you can distinguish between the levels of learning through the activities you use.

Negotiating with learners

When planning a programme and individual sessions, it is important to remember to involve your learners in the process. They may involve negotiating the timing of assignments or assessed activities, agreeing learner-led activities or the content itself. The level of negotiation depends on whether the programme is following a set syllabus or has to meet industry standards. Here the content is non-negotiable, but the way in which it is covered can be. Earlier we discussed the concept of andragogy, where adults are seen to have their own experiences and desires for the learning situation. We must take these into account when we plan how we will facilitate their learning.

What, in practice, can be negotiated, and how can it be done? One of the first activities that can be done with a new group of learners is to ask them to talk to their neighbours in pairs, exchanging a small amount of information about themselves: names, where they live or work, and what they are hoping to achieve from the programme. This information helps us to specify what can be covered in the timescale, and what can't be, or what is outside the scope of the programme. It helps to set the boundaries in terms of meeting the learners' expectations within the constraints of the programme offered. It is very important to recognize that people have varying expectations from any learning activity, and sometimes the expectations far exceed what can sensibly be achieved. By stating at the outset that certain areas cannot be dealt with, or that it is likely to take more time to develop particular knowledge and skills, learners will have a more realistic idea of the programme content and process.

A constant criticism of the standards and competence-based curriculum is that practitioners feel they have very little opportunity to negotiate with their learners because there is so much to cover in so little time. There is no doubt that programmes which have precise specification of standards and outcomes must be met for learners to successfully gain the qualification concerned but there is still scope within such programmes to discuss and agree what will be covered and how. It is too easy to accept the requirements of a programme as having to be taught in a mechanical or functional way without challenging how this can be done. The approach to teaching literacy, language and numeracy, for example, does not merely have to cover the functional requirements by teaching spelling, or punctuation or fractions without paying attention to the use to which such skills are put. The alternative social practice (Tett et al., 2006) is much more fulfilling and I would argue appropriate and does not need to be compromised simply because learners also need to cover a national curriculum in order to gain a specific qualification (see RaPAL for more information on this issue).

Negotiation of expectations and boundaries is an important aspect of any contract and is dealt with in Chapter 7 on how groups form and your role as facilitator.

Timing

It is not easy to estimate how long an activity will take. One way to think of timescale is to think of 'episodes'. Pollard (1997) suggests that a session can be thought of in terms of four episodes: beginnings, transitions, crises and endings. Although you do not want crises to occur, it is highly unlikely in any session that everything will go according to plan. There are interruptions for equipment not working, learners may disagree on a discussion point which developed into a heated argument, there may be a fire drill. These are unplanned situations which you simply cannot expect. However, as Chapter 5 discusses, it is best to consider alternatives when using any item of equipment. If you had planned a whole session around a DVD recording or website and discovered that it had not even been recorded for you, or the computer was not working and there was no replacement, then your whole session is wasted. If you plan to use a DVD or computer, think of an alternative activity 'just in case'.

Beginnings and endings

Beginnings are important. I have been a learner on an IT course where we all arrived at different times and switched our machines on and worked on tasksheets. When the tutor arrived, we all needed help. The tutor was swamped with demands and he could not even start the session with a greeting. Even if you do walk into a room full of busy learners, make sure that you have made a clear start to the session.

People need a sense of continuity from one session to another. Even if they are returning from a coffee break on a one-day workshop, there needs to be a time to gather thoughts and return to the matter at hand. The learners may have been discussing things after the earlier session and wish to raise further points or ask questions. It is important to recognize what has been happening earlier and to acknowledge that the next session has started.

One important requirement for beginnings when learners are in a well-established group is to allow time for 'settling down', sharing information about each other. People may be arriving after a stressful day at work or at home, they may have had a busy week, or they may have just returned from a holiday. They bring their feelings and experiences into the room with them and it is a good idea to allow time for them to put these to one side in readiness for their learning activities.

If it has been a while since the group last met, it is important to remind learners what had been covered in the previous session and allow time for questions or comments. This also helps to ensure that anyone who missed the previous session has an opportunity to hear what was covered, not a repeat of the whole session but to get a resume or brief idea. It reinforces some of the previous learning and 'sets the scene' for what is about to happen.

When the session is nearing its end, make time to draw thoughts together again. There may be time for reflection on what has been learned, to discuss plans for the following session, practical questions about assignments, finding resources. It is unsatisfying for people to drift away without a formal end. You can decide to make yourself available after the formal close for people who do want to stay on. A formal close to a session ensures that people who do need to leave on time can do so without worrying about when the session is actually ending!

Planning for individual learning

So far, I have discussed planning for a group of learners. Many of you will be working with individuals rather than whole groups, or will spend some of your time working with individuals when they are learning in a group. Most of the points in planning sessions have been discussed in relation to working with groups. In certain learning situations, you will be working with individuals, within a group such as those working in functional skills or study skills groups, or on a one-to-one basis, for example, in tutorials, guidance sessions or learning support sessions. You still need to consider the order in which you plan the content and delivery of your sessions. If you are working with individuals who are dropping in to a resource centre, or who each have an individual learning programme, then your need for planning in some ways is even greater, as you will need to track carefully what learners are doing each time they visit you, and you will not know when they will return. Here is selection from a typical adult basic skills group attending a two-hour session in a learning resource centre.

- Anne is a working mother with three children under 10 years old. She wants to help her children with their reading and homework.
- Gary has been unemployed for two years. He has difficulty spelling but can read a daily tabloid newspaper with ease. He wants to gain the Literacy Certificate at Level 1.
- Nikolaos is working temporarily as a security guard. He wants to improve his English language. He can read but has difficulty with grammar and spelling.
- Rajdeep is studying for a qualification in business. He needs help with study skills and particularly writing assignments.
- Camille works as a receptionist in a legal firm. She has been diagnosed as having dyslexia. She needs help with being able to take written messages.

Each learner has already had an in-depth interview with the Skills for Life co-ordinator. They have agreed their learning objectives for a ten-week term. They can attend the learning resource centre on any session they choose. This means that they might see up to five different tutors in any one week.

The learners each have a record of activities they have undertaken with comments from the tutors recommending further work. How can Phyllis, a tutor, plan for a session? She can look at the learners' records as they arrive for the session. She can set up the computers so that they can be used immediately. The resource centre will have a range of web-based and paper-based material that learners can be directed to. She will know which resources are appropriate for the different levels of basic skill.

Phyllis will need to plan time to work with each learner. She can do this in various ways. She may quickly 'start everyone off' with activities she found for each learner based on her analysis of their individual record. She can then decide when to introduce the group activity and when to introduce the individual work that arises from this. Finally, she will need to set aside time for learners to record their work covered in the session and to negotiate what they should work on next time they come along.

Throughout her plan, Phyllis will need to consider the time allowed for individual work, what each person will be doing, when, and to allow opportunities for negotiating content. Often, learners will arrive with something they have to deal with at home, a letter from school, a bill, a request for information. Phyllis will have to set aside time when she moves around the group for such spontaneous requests for help.

Phyllis can also plan for people to work together. She can decide that there may be a group activity with which all the learners can engage. This is where the idea of working with topics, themes or issues is useful. Often, there will be an item from the day's news that could be discussed. Learners could read this information from the daily paper and then write their own views. They could then discuss these in the group, thereby enabling those working towards the Literacy qualification to cover the units on speaking and listening. Although learners may have different goals, the way for them to achieve these may be by doing similar activities. For example, Camille, Rajdeep, Nikolaos and Gary all have difficulty spelling. They will need to learn strategies for spelling and the context in which they learn these can be shared. By writing a response to a controversial news item, they will be using their spelling strategies. Gary will count his work towards his Level 1 Certificate, Rajdeep will be refining his ability to structure a written assignment and Nikolaos will be able to concentrate on his use of grammar.

Planning resources

When thinking about the content, the learners who will be learning this content and how they will learn, it is important to include what resources are required. When planning any learning activity, you will also need to think about how you are going to present the ideas. We have already discussed the fact that learners have different learning styles. Some fare much better if they have plenty of visual illustrations: others prefer to receive information aurally. There is a range of audiovisual resources that you can use in a learning activity. These do not need to be state-of-the-art electronic materials like DVDs, CD-ROMs and web-based resources although these are freely available. Some of the best learning activities I have observed use simply the resources of people in the group. For example, in a session on identifying personal learning styles, I have seen a tutor suggest that the group tries out a group sculpture. Here, individuals place themselves in such a way as to spatially represent how they are feeling. One person might crouch down, another face away, another stand with arms outstretched. The only resources required are a room with open space and the people in the group.

In some situations, particular items of equipment are vital for the session to take place. If you are teaching how to use computers, the hardware must be in working order and the appropriate software loaded. If you are teaching photography, you will need access to a dark room, and lighting and screens. Certain subjects require specialist equipment and accommodation is provided in specialist rooms. Laboratory-based programmes have specific protocol for the ordering of equipment and it is important to check your items carefully before you start your session. I once saw a tutor get halfway through her practical demonstration before realizing she was missing a vital piece of equipment which meant that she had to abandon the experiment. Other subjects require tutors to supply their own equipment and resources. They may have to bring in a variety of everyday items for their session. For example, in drama, there may be sessions where learners learn to use household articles for improvised sketches. It is often said that an adult education tutor can be spotted by the length of her arms and by the boxes of equipment she carries around with her!

Planning project work

When thinking about aims, objectives and learning outcomes, it is sometimes useful to analyse a particular process into the knowledge, skills and attitudes that are needed for successful completion. This can then be set as a project for our learners to undertake. For example, suppose we have a group of learners studying for a Diploma in travel and tourism. We have set them a task which is to create a plan for taking a group of people with physical disabilities to a museum. First, they will need to know about the group members and what their particular requirements are for wheelchairs, mobility aids, if they require carers, and any dietary requirements. They will need to consider how to reach the museum by public transport, and how accessible this is. They will need to know about timetables and opening times for the museum. They will need to know what access facilities there are in the museum. Are there loops for people with hearing aids? Are there labels in braille for blind people? Will they need an interpreter for deaf people? They will need skills in organization: letters confirming the bookings, letters to the group members informing them of meeting time, what to bring with them, when they will return, contact numbers. They will need negotiating skills in making sure the group members' interests are met by the visit and to ensure that any guides they book are aware of the individual requirements of the group members. Importantly, they will need to know how to treat people with respect, to be aware of the dangers of patronizing such a group or to make assumptions about what they can and cannot do. They are also required to perform a risk assessment for health and safety considerations. This project, then, requires an enormous amount of knowledge, skill and attitude to be conducted successfully. Now that we have broken the project down into what we think our learners must know, then we can begin to ensure that they acquire the necessary knowledge and skills and develop the appropriate attitude to their planning. Once we have undertaken our audit, we can begin to plan for our sessions with them.

Project work creates great potential for finding alternative ways to meet particular criteria. It helps develop autonomy and, when undertaken in groups, the skills of working with people. If we decide we wish to use this process with our learners, then we must ensure that we provide support for them. Not all groups of people work together well, as Chapter 7 will show. Here, it is necessary to consider, at the planning stage, what will be offered to facilitate the group process. Will the learners be asked to choose their own groups or will you direct them? Will you allow time within your sessions for the groups to meet or will they have to do this outside of the formal sessions? Will you provide tutorial support during the sessions or outside of them? Will there be somewhere for the groups to meet or do they have to work within one room? There are all matters for consideration when planning project work.

Conclusion

We have considered how adults learn, how we can specify the learning outcomes for any programme and session, and how we can begin to plan the content. We have considered that our learners are individuals, with different strengths, needs and learning preferences. Once we have planned our session and its content, we must now move on to thinking about the different ways in which we can facilitate learning and how individuals will behave when they learn in groups.

LLUK standards

This chapter will help you work towards LLUK standards – Domain B: Learning and Teaching.

Further reading and information

Further reading

Ainley, P. (1993) *Class and Skill*. London: Cassell.

Armitage, A., Bryant, R., Dunnill, R., Hammersley, M., Hayes, D., Hudson, A. and Lawes, S. (1999) *Teaching and Training in Post-Compulsory Education*. Buckingham: Open University Press.

Biggs, J. (1999) *Teaching for Quality Learning in Higher Education*. Buckingham: SRHE/Open University Press.

Bloom, B. (1956) *Taxonomy of Educational Objectives*. London: Longman.

Briggs personality information (www.personalitypage.com.ENFJ.html)

Curzon, L. B. (1990) *Teaching in Further Education*. London: Cassell.

Entwhistle, N. and Ramsden, P. (1983) *Understanding Student Learning*. London: Routledge.

Frances, M. and Gould, J. (2009) *Achieving Your PTLLS Award*. London: Sage.

Gagné, R. (1985) *The Conditions of Learning*. New York: Holt, Rhinehart and Winston.

Greenfield, S. (2000) *The Human Brian: A Guided Tour*. London: Basic Books.

Greenfield, S. (2008) *The Quest for Identity in the 21st Century*. London: Sceptre.

Howard-Jones, P. (2007) *Neuroscience and Education: Issues and Opportunities A TLRP Commentary*. London: TLRP (www.tlrp.org.uk).

John, P. (1993) *Lesson Planning for Teachers.* London: Cassell.

Lave, E. and Wenger, E. (1991) *Situated Learning.* Cambridge: Cambridge University Press.

Marton, F. and Saljö, R. (1997) 'Approaches to learning', in F. Marton, D. Hounsell and N. J. Entwhistle (eds) *The Experience of Learning.* Edinburgh: Scottish Academic Press.

Petty, G. (2004) *Teaching Today: A Practical Guide* (3rd edn). Cheltenham: Nelson Thornes.

Pollard, A. (2008) *Reflective Teaching* (3rd edn). London: Continuum.

Schuller, T., Preson, J., Hammond, C., Brassett-Grundy, A. and Bynner, J. (2004) *The Benefits of Learning: The Impact of Education on Health, Family Life and Social Capital.* London: Routledge.

Tennant, M. (1997) *Psychology and Adult Learning* (2nd edn). London: Routledge.

Tett, L., Hamilton, M. and Hillier, Y. (2006) *Adult Literacy, Numeracy and Language: Policy, Research and Practice.* Maidenhead: McGraw Hill.

Useful websites

Equality and diversity (www.equalityhumanrights.com) (www.teachernet.gov.uk/wholeschool/equality/)

Inclusion (http://inclusion.ngfl.gov.uk)

RAPAL (www.literacy.lancs.ac.uk/rapal/)

www.lsn.org.uk – this site has information on a range of national guidance and publications including the Disability Discrimination Act

Developing Learning Resources

Resources for learning

Martin wants to explain about points of sail for his windsurfing class. The group is on the beach, having an hour of instruction before setting off to improve their skills in the beginners' windsurfing class. He knows that there is quite a lot to learn in terms of skill and technique, but one of the core pieces of information that his learners need is how the wind affects the sail and what to do to move the surfboard along the water. How can he effectively demonstrate this?

Martin is working with his group in the open air, and he cannot use any electrical equipment. He has a blackboard with different coloured pieces of chalk So he draws large, white, thick arrows to show the wind. He draws a triangular shape in red to show the sail. He uses blue to show the waterline. To show movement, he draws green lines to show where the board and sail would go as a result of the wind. He gradually builds up a series of pictures showing the triangular sail, different directions of wind and the resulting direction of travel.

Martin has another way to show the effect of wind. He has a model made from a wooden board, with a wooden dowel placed on a small piece of plasticine. The sail is made from cardboard. The sail can move around the wooden dowel. He can then demonstrate what happens if the sail changes direction across the wind and where the windsurfer would consequently be heading. He can show how to tack and gybe to help the windsurfer travel in the direction required.

The blackboard and model are examples of learning resources. They cannot, by themselves, ensure that people learn: they are usually artefacts that can support learning. They can be models, miniatures, simulated examples, visual examples, audio examples, web-based examples and even include people. The underlying feature of a learning resource is that it can be used to aid someone's learning.

What are learning resources and why do we need them?

Can you remember hearing stories when you were a small child? Sometimes, a picture was shown to illustrate part of the story. Sometimes, if there was no picture, there was a song, and sometimes everyone joined in and acted out the story. Every time a picture, song or activity was included, the content of the story was reinforced. This is exactly what we do when we use learning resources. We reinforce the content of a topic by showing examples, or providing opportunities to try things out. Learning does not happen in isolation. It is much more difficult to learn how to do something if there is no example. Have you ever tried following instructions for constructing a piece of furniture from a 'do-it-yourself' kit? Sometimes it is only the diagram that helps us work out exactly what should be done. (Although you may have watched someone struggling to assemble a piece of furniture without using the instructions only to realize how vital these are when there inevitably ends up being screws missing or parts that don't seem to fit together!) In the same way, the illustrations and examples that are provided for our learners often are the most effective resource for their learning.

If we reflect on what we do when we teach, we can probably think of many examples when we use resources, even though we may not have labelled these as such. Here are some of the main resources that are used:

- Textbooks
- Whiteboard
- Interactive whiteboard
- Flip-charts
- Handouts
- Visual slides
- Tape recordings
- Videos and DVDs
- Diagrams
- Overhead transparencies
- PowerPoint' slides
- Pre-prepared examples
- Models
- Examples showing stages of a process
- Real-life examples, including art galleries, buildings, even fields and woods
- Peers
- Websites.

Some of these resources are used primarily by us as teachers and trainers to demonstrate how to do something, or to illustrate a point we are making. They are used as *teaching* resources. Sometimes we use resources so that our learners can try something out, or see for themselves or learn by themselves. The resources are then being used as *learning* resources. Very often we use resources for teaching and, at the same time, our learners are using them for learning. The distinction is often blurred. Whether the resource being used is for teaching or learning is a secondary consideration, as long as we are aware of how we are using the resources and what we hope to achieve from them.

Using learning resources is inextricably linked with the plans we make for our sessions and the aims and objectives for our learners. We cannot think about using learning resources without thinking about our teaching and learning methods. We can use the resources in a variety of ways. Indeed, one of the results of reflecting on our use of resources may lead to far more creative uses of some quite traditional resources.

We must take care when we use resources that we do not decide on the resource before thinking about the content. For example, it is very easy to create a series of overhead transparency slides, or PowerPoint slides, and to assume that any presentation is best done by using these resources. If we stop and think, we may decide that there are other forms of presentation that we can use as well. I recently observed a presentation at a plenary session at a national conference where the presenter showed a series of photographs as part of the presentation. She asked us to think of how these scenes made us feel. It was far more effective than showing us a series of bullet points on a PowerPoint presentation. In fact I have recently begun to produce PowerPoint presentations which only contain pictures to illustrate complex ideas which has been effective in capturing people's attention but it may be because I also experiment with how these pictures and cartoons appear – I am particularly addicted to using the 'bouncing' entry animation!

Which resource?

So we must ask ourselves two questions: what do we want our learners to learn and, therefore, what is the best resource that we have to aid this learning? For example, suppose we want to discuss the way that colour is used in painting to create an impression of light. We could show this on a series of bullet points on a PowerPoint slide or transparency. We could ask our learners to read the chapter on use of light in a particular textbook. We could show our learners a series of slides. We could ask them to search the website of a particular art gallery. We could arrange a visit to an art gallery. All of these resources – PowerPoint presentations, overhead transparencies, slides, books, websites and galleries – are resources we can draw upon to illustrate the content of our topic. They are not mutually exclusive. In an art history course, we could decide to show a series of slides, then ask our learners to browse a website, and then set up a visit to a gallery to see the paintings we have chosen which illustrate how artists have used colour to show the effect of light. If, in addition, we ask our learners to do something about the slides they have seen – for example, examine them in groups to identify particular aspects of the portrayal of light by use of certain colour – then we are likely to reinforce more effectively the point we are making with the resources we are using.

Technology has evolved tremendously in the past decade. The Open University, for example, has a marvellous learning resource for the study of art, where paintings can be downloaded from particular websites, and juxtaposed against other paintings for comparison. This is something that showing a series of slides on a traditional projector cannot achieve. So the learning resource enables other points to be explored more visually than before, and particularly synchronously. In fact, this method can be used asynchronously, too, so that learners can revisit the sites in their own time and spend longer studying the paintings.

Graphics have been extensively developed in information technology. It is now possible to show maps and then illustrations of land features, or clips of weather patterns from a web-based presentation. Learners can graphically manipulate images and explore what happens if they change certain parameters. The resources of technology enable a far more interactive approach to learning about dynamic systems than from looking at a series of diagrams which try to capture a process. An added bonus of web technology is the opportunity to capture other presentations through 'podcasts' which can be replayed and even the main terrestrial television channels now have an opportunity to view programmes or listen to podcasts through their websites.

Not everyone has access to the internet. Even if you are lucky to have access at home, the college or institution where you work may not have enough computing resources for you to use with your learners on a regular basis. I think there is a danger that we will begin to feel both incompetent and threatened if we do not produce beautiful slides, 'whizzy' websites and musical interludes! I have seen some of the most effective teaching sessions when the simplest materials have been used. Sometimes, a computer is just not the most appropriate tool. I remember watching and participating in a microteaching session led by a tutor who teaches music, including an 'I can't sing' class. He had us all lined up facing the wall making a low humming noise. We then turned around and repeated the humming. The effect of feeling the vibrations in our chests, and the way that the wall reinforced this feeling, was particularly well demonstrated. All he needed was us and a wall!

Let us now look at how we can use learning resources. I shall concentrate on those that are more 'traditional' as these are still more widely available in learning institutions.

Whiteboard

The whiteboard has now largely replaced a blackboard. Whiteboards have surfaces that require the use of special marker pens. Always check that the pens you use have not dried out and that they will wipe away. I usually do this by making a little squiggle in the corner and wiping it a few seconds later. If I do inadvertently use the wrong pen, then I have only placed a small mark in the corner where it can't be seen.

A whiteboard can be used in a variety of ways: to write key points on, to show a mathematical formula or work through a mathematical problem. It can be used to draw diagrams. It can be used to capture points being made by the learners in the group. You can decide to write on the whiteboard before your learners arrive. You can divide the whiteboard into sections using different coloured pens and use each section for a different issue, or provide instructions in one section, information in another and leave the third to capture points made in a plenary at the end of the session.

There are some top tips for using a whiteboard, and top mistakes to avoid.

Top tips

- Do use colours that are visible from the back of the room.
- Try to write neatly and legibly.
- Do print using lower-case letters.
- Leave plenty of space between points that you are making.
- A variety of colours is both interesting and attractive.
- Use different colours to group ideas, make points or ask questions.

Top mistakes

- Writing too small.
- Colours illegible.
- Words written in capitals.
- Diagrams messy.
- Writing slants.
- Too much information in a small space.
- No structure to the content.

I want to say something about writing. Many people think that using capital letters is a good way to make sure that their writing is legible. In fact, capital letters are not helpful for the following reason. Most of the information that we need from reading comes from the parts of the words that 'go up and down'. If you think about a word like 'totally', our eye is drawn to the tops of the letters t, l (ascenders) and to the bottom of the letter y (descenders). If the word is printed in capitals, we do not have this level of information; all the letters are at the same level. So printing in capital letters is actually more difficult to read than using lower case. The same point is true of word-processed words. Remember that some of your learners may not see particularly well, or they may have difficulty in reading. If the language used is not their first, then it is very important that the writing is both clear and as easy to read as possible. Those of you who teach languages will be very aware of the necessity of showing both spelling and accentuation which is clear and unambiguous. (Some of us may remember how we tried to cover our poorly revised French by placing an accent straight up above certain letters in the forlorn hope that our teacher would give us the benefit of the doubt!)

Flip-charts

Flip-charts are often used in training sessions. They are stands which have a pad of large plain paper that can be written on with coloured felt pens (I learned recently while visiting in Australia and talking to VET practitioners that this paper is known as butcher's paper as it is the same material that was used to wrap meat in years gone by by butchers). Individual sheets can be taken from the pad which is held on a flip-chart stand and used by small groups. The sheets can then be displayed around the room. Flip-charts are, therefore, extremely useful in enabling learners to show what they have been talking about to the larger group (or plenary).

Flip-charts can be used to record a brainstorm session (see Chapter 6). They can contain pre-prepared lists, diagrams or instructions. They have an advantage over whiteboards in that they can be kept as a record. I have often used flip-charts to record learners' original goals and then bring them back at the end of a programme when we evaluate how well these goals have been achieved.

Flip-chart paper is great for drawing pictures and diagrams. As the paper is large, it often requires people to lean over tables together, or even stretch out on the floor. This creates much movement and, therefore, releases energy in the groups, in contrast to learners sitting passively while the tutor makes notes on the flip-chart.

As with any learning resource and activity, it is important to be specific about what you want your learners to do. Try asking for three main points from the small-group discussion which the group members decide they wish to share. Try asking groups to place their paper around the room as a 'picture gallery' for everyone to look at. It is quite difficult to appreciate what another group has done simply by looking at flip-charts, so make time to discuss these either informally over a break or more formally in a feedback session where group members can explain what the content on the flip-chart means.

As flip-charts are more 'spur of the moment' than prepared slides, you may find, as with writing on a whiteboard, that you have to stop and think how to spell words. It is surprising how often you find you cannot spell a well-known word once you are trying to write what people are saying quickly. You may be asking your learners, too, to write in public. Be sensitive about this, as some people may be very reluctant or unwilling to participate in an activity which requires them to write or draw in public.

Remember to write what your learners say, rather than change it to your own words. The use of whiteboard and flip-chart is potentially inclusive, as in most teaching and training situations you have the unelected power of control. If you take over and write your ideas, rather than theirs, there is no point in asking their opinion in the first place. Of course, you may negotiate, such as 'Do you mean x?' or 'So shall I say y?' when you write the words down. People do not speak coherently all the time, and they may be struggling to express what they are thinking. With many of these points about using language, the issue is about being sensitive and inclusive. Writing down people's own words and helping them to refine their thinking are ways to ensure that you are respecting them.

Top tips

- Do write legibly.
- Try to use different colours to show different points.
- Write in lower case (as with whiteboard).

Top mistakes

- Asking people to write down points of discussion on a flip-chart and then hearing the whole discussion reported back to the plenary group using as much time as the original discussion.
- Not making any comment on people's flip-charts.
- Unclear instructions about what should be recorded on the flip-chart.
- Messy diagrams.
- Illegible writing.

Some of the resources above do raise questions of sustainability, as the pens used and certainly the amount of paper consumed in brainstorming can be very resource intensive. Where possible, do try to reuse flip-chart paper and then recycle it and for preference, think of alternatives that won't consume so much paper which is also relatively expensive to buy.

Overhead projector

The overhead projector works on the principle of a light projector. There is a bulb which sends light through platen glass which is reflected by a mirror onto a screen. The distance of the projector from the screen can be moved, enabling images to be enlarged or diminished as required. The focusing of the image is done by a dial by the side of the mirror. Most people use overhead projectors to place transparencies which have either a diagram or text on them. It is possible to build up a picture using a series of transparencies that overlay – particularly useful if you are creating a model diagrammatically. This particular item of equipment has increasingly been replaced by data projectors but it is useful to know how to use them. They also work well when you are doing group work which requires people reporting back as they can create their feedback using a transparency and project this for the rest of the group to see. This is much harder to achieve if there are no other facilities available.

Top tips

- Do make sure you have checked the slide is placed centrally on the screen and is not upside down.
- Do make sure that your text is clearly written if not produced by word processor.
- Make sure that your text is large enough to be seen from the rear of the room.
- Do provide plenty of space around the text.
- Do use colour that is clearly visible.
- Turn the projector off when you are not specifically referring to a slide.

Top mistakes

- Too much text.
- Lettering too small.
- Colour not visible.
- Focus is fuzzy.
- Bullet points are unconnected.
- Not knowing how to focus.
- Pointing to the screen not the transparency.
- Not being able to find the 'On' switch.
- Leaving the projector on after you have finished using it.
- Standing in front of the learners' line of sight.

One of the most irritating things is when people using an overhead projector project a transparency on to the screen and start to talk without checking that it has been placed centrally or is focused properly. They then proceed to look at the screen and go and point to the image on the screen, thereby having their back to the group. This is *not* the way to use an overhead projector. The fabulous advantage of the overhead projector is that you can face your learners while you are making points which they can see on screen. You can use your finger or a pen to point to the particular item you are referring to on your transparency. This ensures that you can see and be seen by your learners. Those who need to watch your lips carefully because of hearing difficulties will, therefore, be able to gain as much information possible. If you turn your back they will not have these extra clues and, of course, your level of voice will be quieter.

Another irritant for learners is watching people try to focus the image without knowing how to do so. Always try to experiment before you have to show your slides to your learners. One way to do this is to place a set of keys on the glass plate and fiddle with the focus until you have an image that is both focused and large enough to be seen clearly from the back. The nearer the projector is to the screen, the smaller the image. It is much better to place the projector at a reasonable distance and to focus using the dial. Try to avoid standing between the overhead projector and the screen, where you will be blocking people's line of sight. You can often tell when you are doing this, as people will be craning their necks or shifting seats to try and see the screen.

Finally, do make sure that you familiarize yourself with where the spare bulb is kept. Most projectors have either a spare bulb under the glass plate which you can lift up, or they have two bulbs which are side by side. If one bulb blows, there is a switch on the front of the projector which you turn so that the other bulb comes on. Always check that you can work the projector before you use it. People have been seen to flounder in finding the 'On' switch, something that happens easily when you are trying to impress a crowded room of people! It certainly does give an impression that you do not know what you are doing and is bound to make you feel even more flustered than is necessary.

PowerPoint presentation

PowerPoint is a software which enables you to create slides and show these from a data projector connected to your computer (usually a laptop unless there is provision for computers in your classroom). There is a series of designs available to choose from, including a variety of colours and backgrounds. The text can be animated, so that it 'flows across' from right or left as part of the demonstration. People often create slides where the bullet points are listed one at a time while they speak. I have to say that I have really enjoyed playing around with colour schemes and different backgrounds when I use PowerPoint, but I am not sure that it has improved the *content* of what I am covering! I have also made many mistakes in creating text that cannot be seen through the background colour. It is not necessary to print out your slides if you have access to a data projector. However, if you have not printed out the version of your slides, and the hardware or software

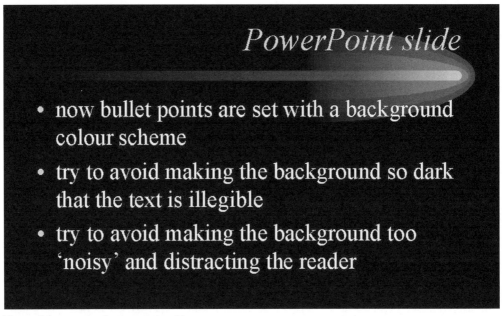

Figure 5.1 Example of a PowerPoint slide

lets you down, you do not have anything to show your learners. I have seen a variety of PowerPoint presentations – or rather, not seen them – because of difficulties with the hardware. A lot of time has been lost while people try to work out what is wrong, and the presenter has been both frustrated and embarrassed. Unless you are very confident about using the technology, or have good technical support on hand, I would advise you to produce these on handouts so that, if all else fails, you can at least share your ideas with your learners on paper. The handouts can be created so that there is room to write notes by the side of each slide. You can also write full script to be handed out as notes. Remember, with any form of slide, the content should indicate what is going to be said, rather than cover everything that will be said. This is why it helps to consider whether you need to have additional reading material for your learners; a series of bullet points can often be meaningless to your learners a few weeks after your presentation, whereas the notes will not.

Top tips

- Clear bullet points.
- Animation which illustrates a point.
- Animation which is timed to ensure the message is read easily.
- Background design which enables text to be seen clearly.
- Visual material is clear.

Top mistakes

- Too much content.
- Background colour which obscures the text.
- Too much 'noise': that is, visual material which detracts from the message.
- Animation which interferes with the message.
- Animation text which is shown too fast to read.
- Visual material is too small to be seen.

DVDs, audiotapes and podcasts

As there is an increase in use of multimedia technology, so the possibility of using this as a learning resource develops. In addition to short audiotapes and slide projectors we have DVDs and web-based materials such as podcasts. Once again, the first question we must ask ourselves is, what are we trying to achieve by using the particular medium? If we are teaching a course on the influence of gospel music on early twentieth-century classical music, then it is extremely helpful for our learners to *listen* to examples. We may also include clips of particular choirs performing, or orchestras playing. We must be careful that we do not use DVDs or videos without deciding what we want our learners to pay attention to. Short clips are actually better than playing a tape for half an hour and hoping that the learners will pick out the 'important' points. The same applies to using audiotapes. A short piece which can be replayed so that learners fully appreciate what they are being asked to hear is better than playing the whole piece. The excerpts are being used to illustrate, exemplify or even test the learners' ability to distinguish or identify certain sounds, or concepts.

As with any equipment, it is important to check that it is working before your learners arrive. Most machines have similar operating mechanisms, but there are always idiosyncrasies with which you may be unfamiliar. You also need time to find the position on the recording at which you wish to start.

Make sure everyone can see and hear clearly. If you have a large group of learners, then crowding around a small monitor is unlikely to be successful. If you do not have a large monitor, think of ways of structuring the session, for example, by dividing into two groups so that some learners can watch the clip while others work on a task, and then change the groups around.

Top tips

- Do ensure that you have chosen appropriate clips that can be shown in short periods of time.
- Do ensure that your learners know what they are listening to or watching for.
- Do discuss their impressions immediately after the recording has been played.

Top mistakes

- No prediscussion of the content and what to look or listen for.
- No indication of what is being covered, and why.
- No discussion of learning points arising from the recordings.
- Lengthy clips which create boredom.
- Poor quality sound or vision.

Models

Models really do come in all kinds of shapes and sizes. You may have a model of a hydraulic system for an engineering class. You may have a seam for a shirt. You may have a plastic atom that can be taken apart into its electrons and protons. You may have a cardboard stage with a scene from a play. All of these are models which are used to show how something works or a process that is taking place.

If you are planning on using models, then first make sure that they are an accurate representation of 'the real thing'. If they are very flimsy, you must take care with handling, and your learners may feel frustrated if they cannot examine by touch. On the other hand, if you have a model that is so robust that it does not capture the nature of the thing you are trying to illustrate, then your learners will not get the message either.

Make sure that your learners can see the model clearly and if it has movement, that you can point out what is happening. If you have parts that fit together, you obviously need to ensure that the parts do not get lost and, of course, that you know how to put it together properly!

Models are good for reinforcing the kinaesthetic aspect of learning, in other words that which involves physical motion and sensations. If people can *touch* your model and use it, they will remember more than from merely looking at it. If they have to put pieces together, they will have had to concentrate on both the physical feeling and the process of construction. Remember that learning can be broken down into small steps. Models are particularly useful for demonstrating the small steps, or for helping delineate a complex concept.

Top tips

- Use models that are accurate representations.
- Make sure the models are in good working condition.
- Make sure that they can be easily seen, heard and manipulated.

Top mistakes

- Complex parts that cannot be seen or heard easily.
- Parts that become lost or are difficult to assemble.
- No obvious connection with the 'real thing'.

Handouts

Handouts are usually paper-based resources. They cover a diverse range of learning resources. They can be a set of notes to accompany a presentation or lecture. They can be copies of the overhead slides. They can be worksheets which require learners to undertake certain activities. They can be photocopies of an article from a journal or a newspaper clipping. The number of possible ways to use handouts is immense. Using handouts is probably the most common resource and it is easy to become lazy when using them. A major pitfall is that they are used solely as a teaching tool and never as a *learning* resource.

First, consider why you are planning to use handouts. Do your learners need notes because they have to undertake further work or reading at home? Can they download your notes from a website, rather than rely on your photocopies? Do they really need every copy of your slides, or can they write their own notes? Are there learners with a visual impairment who need the handouts in large print?

Handouts can be used as an *aide mémoire*, or to test learning, or to provide instructions for activities. Here are some examples of different kinds of handout:

Cloze

Cloze exercises ask learners to fill in gaps. For example, you may be teaching about homonyms, words that sound the same but are spelt differently. You can ask your learners to choose which word is appropriate in a number of sentences. Here, your learning resource is being used to reinforce their learning, or test their knowledge by asking them to apply it to the examples you have created.

Cloze example

> Two, to and too
> Choose which word belongs in each sentence
> I went . . . the shops to buy a coat
> There are . . . many flies on this beach
> One, . . . , three, four
> Do you like this film . . . ?
> She told me that there were only . . . seats left.

Case studies

Here, learners are given an example of a situation which they must then discuss, or develop a strategy, plan or undertake an activity. For example, you may want your learners to think about what design they would create for a number of different gardens, or types of room. Your handout will contain the information in the case study and instructions for the activity.

Moving house

Gregory and Dulcie have just moved into their first house. It was previously occupied by an elderly couple who could not manage to do any decorating for the past 15 years. Gregory and Dulcie have got a maximum of £500 to spend and they intend to do as much of the work as possible by themselves. They have the following rooms:

- a kitchen with formica cupboards, a gas cooker which is at least 30 years old, plumbing for washing machine;
- lounge/dining room with radiators under windows, old stained carpet;
- bathroom with white suite and high-level cistern, cracked linoleum;
- bedroom with radiator under the window, floral wallpaper and carpet which is worn threadbare by the door;
- second bedroom which has bare floorboards, window and a crack in the corner.

A plan of the house is attached. In your groups, decide how you would advise Gregory and Dulcie so that they can redecorate their house in the next year. Create a list of materials and their cost for each room. Devise a timescale to undertake the work. Prepare a ten-minute presentation to show an example of one room that you have designed from your plan.

Each person in the group must keep records of the work done for the portfolio. Presentations will take place on Friday 20th March. Portfolios to be handed in on Monday 30th March.

Diagrams

Diagrams are visual representations. Sometimes they can be used to show how an apparatus for an experiment was set up, or to show parts of an animal or plant. They can either provide information, or be used for learners to label, thus reinforcing their learning from a presentation or practical. It is important that the clarity of the image is sufficient for learners to see detail. It is a good idea to enlarge diagrams which have been created by software programs or photocopied from existing material to achieve the necessary detail. As with any handout, if there is accompanying text, make sure it is legible. Always label diagrams and, if copying from existing material, write the source on the handout. Remember that if you have downloaded images from the internet, some of the colour may not photocopy well and the detail will be lost. Craig (2000) provides helpful advice about using diagrams.

Solutions and problems

Handouts are very useful if you wish to give your learners additional problems to solve, particularly for numerical work. This does not mean that you do not need to use them if you teach a non-mathematical subject. For example, if you have to calculate how much material to buy to make a set of curtains for a child's nursery, then you could give your learners a number of different specifications, thereby helping them to use the calculation process to reinforce their learning and in addition to help you find out if they have learned this or not.

Top tips

- Do make sure that the print is legible.
- Do make sure that you have remained within copyright law.
- Do make sure that you have a clear structure.
- Do make sure that your print or writing has correct grammar, punctuation and spelling.
- Do make sure you have enough copies for everyone and a spare to keep for future reference.

Top mistakes

- Badly photocopied material, for example, too dark or too light, or not centrally positioned.
- Poor handwriting.
- Spelling and typographical errors.
- Poor diagrams and pictures.
- Not enough copies for everyone.

Copyright

Remember that if you want to provide your learners with copies from a book, article or journal, then you must remain within the copyright law.

The Copyright Licensing Agency (CLA) represents the Authors' Licensing and Collecting Society and the Publishers Licensing Society. Higher education has an agreement with the CLA about what can be photocopied within the Copyright, Designs and Patents Act (1988). The law is designed to prevent people copying material which belongs to the author without that person's permission. One of the most common infringements of the Act is where people make multiple copies of large sections of a book, photocopy music or tape-record music. It is very easy to breach the law without realizing it. If you are intending to copy a series of articles and chapters for your learners throughout the course you are running on an *ad hoc* basis, then as long as you are not copying more than one chapter from a book, or one article from a journal, you should be within the confines of the Act. However, if you decided to put all your material into a pack at the start of the course, then you are actually creating a course pack which must have clearance from the CLA.

Make an appointment to talk to your librarian, or learning resource co-ordinator, so that you are clear about what copying is legally possible. It is always difficult to find ways to make materials accessible to your learners at low cost which will not prevent the creators of that material from losing out financially. Some resources are freely available on websites (see the later section on web-based learning). Here, learners can download their own material for personal use. As resources become posted on websites and, therefore, are freely accessible it becomes increasingly difficult to know when you are operating with the spirit of the law. Even if you have found something on Google or similar browser, it is always advisable to specify where you obtained the materials. The rule is, always check that material you are intending to use has been copied within the confines of the 1988 Act.

Everyday articles and games

There are so many occasions when an ordinary article can be useful as a learning resource. Helping people to improve their observation skills and memory, for example, can use the children's Kim's Game, where a series of articles is placed on a tray. People look at these for about one minute. The tray is removed or covered up and people have to write down all the articles they can remember. This game reinforces memory and, where appropriate, language and writing skills.

Language teaching can draw upon a variety of games, as can those working with basic skills. Hangman, which helps reinforce spelling; and charades, where people have to act out the name of a book, play, film or television programme, are two very popular games. Lotto is another appropriate game for some learning sessions. This is a game where people must cover a number of written words on a board with cards with the same word on them. They can only do this when the word has been called out by the tutor. This game reinforces listening and reading skills and can be used for a number of language and literacy programmes. It is *very* important to ensure that these games are played in an appropriate manner and are not seen to be insulting to the learners.

For learners who are more responsive to smell and touch rather than sight and sound, it is often helpful to provide examples from a variety of everyday sources. One of the most creative uses of resources I have seen is where a bag is filled with a number of different items which have very unusual surfaces. Learners have to describe what they can feel. This kind of activity helps to foster a wide vocabulary and really does require the learners to concentrate on feeling, rather than looking.

Another way to help people differentiate using their sense of smell is important, for example, in many of the complementary medicine programmes. Learning to smell by working with a number of oils takes time and patience. Using a number of sources other than the oils themselves – flowers, perfumes, herbs and manufactured goods – can develop people's ability to smell quite subtle essences.

When I observe sessions, I often notice that people 'perk up' when they are asked to touch or smell something. Often, an item is 'passed around' the group and the reaction on people's faces shows that they are often surprised or perplexed by what they have just smelled or felt. This can often lead to quite humorous comment, all of which helps to reinforce a particular learning point and raise the level of energy in the group.

Art galleries, museums and other visits

Why show a picture or photograph of something if you are able to see it in the original? Art galleries and museums have staff who are specially trained to work with educational institutions. They can provide guided tours, short talks on particular topics, help devise interactive facilities on their computers and advise on numerous aspects of a visit to their premises.

The layout of artefacts and resources in most museums has become far more appropriate for the facilitation of learning. It is not necessary to take a group of learners on a tour of the whole building: it is better to select a few artefacts or pictures that you can use as examples of a particular concept or topic. You can then encourage your learners to find other examples. Many people have been put off in the past by museums because they have been left to wander around a bewildering number of displays. Decide a route before your learners arrive, and allow time for them to explore for themselves. You could follow up the visit with additional handouts or photographs, or ask the learners to draw from the originals.

Other visits include those where your learners are introduced to different forms of organization; for example, if they are studying for a business studies award. They may be looking at different childcare provision if they are working towards a qualification in childcare. The resource that is available is both complex and likely to be underexploited if you do not spend time before the visit detailing exactly what you want the learners to observe, and to discuss their findings in a subsequent session. The joy of setting up visits is that learners experience 'the real world' and they can begin to make sense of the ideas and concepts that you will have been covering in previous work.

With any visit to public places, you must carry out a risk assessment beforehand to conform to the health and safety regulations. This is to ensure that participants are aware of any rules that they must follow, such as wearing protective clothing, and to inform them of potential hazards. Your institution should provide you with a proforma to help you undertake the risk assessment. You will also need to conform to insurance requirements that your institution's policy contains.

Our bodies as a learning resource

We do not have to go far to find a learning resource that is instantly available – our bodies! If you are teaching a fitness class, or running a massage course, then you will have used your own body and those of your learners throughout your sessions. People learn a lot from looking at each other, feeling what their own bodies are telling them and then learning how to look for very subtle indications of how we place ourselves in the physical world. Alexander Technique sessions encourage people to look at how they stand, sit and walk. One member of a group may be asked to stand and sit a number of times while the rest of the group tries to look carefully at what is happening to certain parts of the body. The trained tutor will very gently place hands on the person to reposition the neck, for example. Counselling programmes encourage learners to look for body language as well as hear what people are saying. They are asked to look for how people sit, what they are doing with their arms and legs and their facial expressions.

We must remember that working with our bodies is very subject to cultural differences. In some cultures, it is strictly forbidden to touch other people, whereas in others it is quite normal to stand very close to complete strangers and touch them. You may not know what the cultural norms are for all of your learners. One way to help you is to always ask permission if you are going to demonstrate how a particular stance or activity should be done on one of your learners. If you ask people to work in pairs, be conscious that some members of the group may feel intimidated, embarrassed or unable to work with members of the opposite sex. Working with people's bodies is potentially open to misinterpretation and you must be very careful that you are not infringing both personal space or cultural norms. You are not in a position to insist that people infringe their cultural norms, but you may need to make it explicit before people join your programme what they will be asked to do. If you have any doubts, then do check with your line manager. In all circumstances where you are working with people's bodies, you must remain within the law, in terms of health and safety. You must remember that an action on your part may be perceived differently by a learner and could be seen as assault or inappropriate behaviour.

Computer-assisted learning

Using the web

Fred has been told by his line manager that the course he runs is going to be supported by the facilities on the intranet. This is part of a college-wide policy to ensure that all staff and learners are able to use information communications technology (ICT). Fred can use a word processor (typing with two fingers) and his family uses a computer for e-mailing and homework at home. He does not know much about 'web 2' facilities such as social networks although his children are becoming experts. The idea of using computers with his learners who are taking an Access programme fills him with dread. What does he need to know to be ready to use web-based learning in the new session?

Chapter 2 discussed the government drive to ensure that adults have access to and can use ICT. Some teachers and trainers have been fortunate enough to have computers at work which they have been trained to use and which they have spent time individually developing their skills. Within the last decade, there has been a marked increase in the use of computers to assist learning. There are two ways in which computers are used for learning: as a learning resource (computer-assisted learning, CAL) and as the primary medium of instruction (computer-based learning, CBL).

CAL

Computer learning resources can use a number of facilities:

- CD-ROMs, memory sticks and web-based files which store information, both text-based and visual.
- Example spreadsheets, databases and word-processed documents to be edited by learners.
- Bookmarked' websites.
- Word-processing programmes for the production of assignments.
- Graphics packages that can enhance documents and presentational material.

Memory sticks (or flash drives') and CD-ROMs store large amounts of data fairly cheaply. There are a number of multimedia sources which have animation, sound and film. They may have a hypertext structure, where the user can move from one level to another.

Increasingly, material is provided by shared websites and Google docs, for example, provides an opportunity for people to share files and edit them, particularly through the use of wikis which are essentially shared files which can be edited by users who have access to that particular address.

The internet

The internet is increasingly seen as today's teaching and learning panacea. Any educational journal, commentary on teaching and learning in the educational press, and discussions at conferences all discuss how information technology and the internet are going to revolutionize the way that we enable people to learn. In particular, the internet is seen to be a prime source for self-directed learning. People can access it at any time of day and night, they can search for any number of different topics, 'meet' other users and chat asynchronously, or even synchronously. The immense data source that exists through the internet almost defies description.

The internet is basically a number of networks that relate to each other through a series of servers. The servers link to other servers so that links have been created throughout the world, hence the term internet. The infrastructure for the internet is known as the World Wide Web (WWW) and it allows a user to move around the sites linked through the local servers. Each site on the internet has its own unique address. On many sites, there are links to other sites, and these links are usually highlighted in a different colour or underlined on screen. A potential difficulty in using the web is navigating through the sheer size of the sites and links between them.

To help access the sites, search engines are used. These are facilities that find sites through all the servers. Some of the search engines are more specific, perhaps searching primarily a national network. If you are trying to find recent reports on lifelong learning in the UK, for example, you do not want to spend time reading about all policies and reports in the world. So limiting your search to the UK is important. The most widely used search engine used in the UK is Google and this has been so successful around the world that finding something on the web is now known as 'googling'.

Using the internet as a learning resource requires a careful search of both the information and the source. Anyone can create a website on the internet and publish material. How can we be sure that the material is of quality and has been adequately researched? The short answer is that we cannot guarantee the information we can find on the internet. There is little 'policing' of the material. So when you decide to find sources of information for your learners, or encourage them to find their own, it is necessary to consider where the material comes from. One way to help you is to consider the website address. If the address is a 'gov.uk' for example, then you will know that it has come from a governmental agency. The information you have found is more likely to be of quality than from someone's personal website. Of course, this does not mean that individuals are not being careful about their published material. The checks that are found within journals, for example, are simply not being used consistently on the internet.

Hints

It is quicker to search for information which is just text-based rather than downloading the graphics that accompany information on websites. Most sites give the option to do this which is also more environmentally friendly when it comes to printing the material.

Some learning resources, for example, academic materials, are published on the internet. Accessing this material usually requires a subscription. Your institution may subscribe to some academic journals. There are databases where a number of journals are available, such as Ingenta. You may find that you have access to abstracts of journal articles that can be downloaded and, in some cases, the full text.

When searching, you need to use Boolean operators. These are a mathematical and logical system that have now been applied to searching databases. They primarily operate through using two words, AND and OR. If you want to find out about assessment of childcare programmes, then simply typing in 'childcare' will give you a massive number of sites. If you type in 'childcare AND assessment', it will limit the search and you will have a more focused response. OR increases the search, so that if you wanted to know about both nursery and primary childcare, then you should type in 'nursery OR primary childcare'. There are a number of more sophisticated ways to undertake a search, for example, by searching for words that are adjacent to one of your key words. Here are the main terms:

AND childcare and assessment
OR childcare or assessment
NOT childcare not assessment
ADJ childcare adjacent to assessment in the title
ADJn childcare and assessment adjacent to n words of each other in any order
$ truncates words, for example, 'teach$' will find teacher, teaching, teaches
? replaces letters, for example, 'colo?r' will find colour and color

If you are unsure of any of these, make an appointment to see the learning resources co-ordinator in your institution, or ask a librarian in a public library. The role of libraries as a source for expertise in learning resources has increased tremendously with the developments of the internet.

E-mail

I think that one of the most useful and most frustrating developments in electronic learning resources is the e-mail. E-mail, or electronic mail, is a system where the user can write a message on screen and send it to another person electronically. Both people must have a unique address, just the same as any site on the internet. We can ask for information, send messages, attach files and contact people anywhere in the world. We can send a message more quickly than stating the same information by telephone, and of course we can send and receive messages at any time of day or night. People use e-mail so much that sometimes we are inundated with messages and, unlike paper messages, we cannot glance quickly to decide if we are going to read the message or not. We have to 'open' every message, which takes time, although there are facilities to sift out types of messages we do not wish to receive.

As a learning resource, we can keep in contact with our learners and also encourage them to communicate with each other. When learners are working, for example, on a group presentation, particularly if they are part-time learners, then they can 'brainstorm' ideas and agree on what to present by e-mailing each other outside the session. They do not have to be in the same room at the same time before they can progress their preparation.

E-mails can also be used to subscribe to mailing lists. Once learners (and you) have joined a mailing list, then you are automatically included in copies of any message that is sent. You can put out a question on the mailbase and another user may be able to provide you with an answer. For example, you may be trying to find some web-based material for a session you wish to teach and wonder if others who have the same interest as you may have found some really good sites. By sending a message to the mailbase, you may receive numerous suggestions that will save you time. Mailbases can be found by contacting a server (e.g. try 'LISTSERV@', or 'MAILBASE@') and follow instructions when you type in 'SUBSCRIBE'.

There a number of newsgroups you may wish to consider. These are like mailbases, where people join because they share a common interest and wish to share information and have a discussion. Of course, the quality of newsgroups is highly dependent on the members. Some people 'lurk', in other words they read what others are saying but do not participate themselves. Others use the newsgroup to have a jolly good moan, and this takes up a lot of reading time for others. Newsgroups are good, though, for keeping track of developments in your field.

Some of the more useful sites are listed at the end of this chapter.

CBL

Computers which are used as the primary learning medium have specific programmes and facilities which hold information, links to other websites, chatrooms and bulletin boards, and instructional material, notes and readings that comprise the content of what is to be learned. These are known as Virtual Learning Environments – VLEs. These days, most people use the VLE as part of a programme which also involves face-to-face sessions, what is known as 'blended learning'. I have seen some very exciting and innovative forms of VLE including one that was set up to support literacy practitioners undertaking a qualification to teach in Scotland, the TQAL. This VLE was used by practitioners and tutors to share resources, communicate with tutors and fellow practitioners and in fact the practitioners were required to collaborate on some of the assignments through the VLE. This was also influential in developing the practitioners' own confidence to use the VLE with their literacy and numeracy learners although the development of such knowledge and skills was in some cases quite a painful process.

There are a number of commercially available packages that can be licensed to an individual or institution. Tutors and learners can interact through discussion groups known as conferences, perhaps after reading information which has been placed on a site. The learners can interact with each other separately in their own 'chatroom'. They can read messages in a bulletin board, and receive personal e-mails from their tutors. Learners may be asked to submit assignments by attaching these as files to their e-mails. They can discuss their work on their assignments with their peers and their tutors by posting their work in a chatroom. Until recently, a downside of this methodology was the cost of logging on and working online. Recent developments in communications and the development of an offline mode have all ensured that learning online is not so expensive. Technical support is usually offered to help set up the particular structure required by the institution and particularly as an ongoing resource to support the users, staff and learners, manage the system. There are web-based programs which are less reliant upon technicians to set up the conferencing system. Blackboard and Moodle are examples. With both of these, there is a ready-made structure in which tutors create a learning programme, write materials, post notes, create learning groups and devise activities which must be uploaded for other learners to see and respond to. The facility is interactive and, of course, can be used asynchronously. The important thing to remember with a VLE is that there are numerous packages that have been designed to enable people to learn online and it is unlikely that you will be able to match the quality by working from scratch (unless, of course, you are an expert in computing!).

When developing any materials, remember to ensure that they are 'fit for purpose'. Simply posting up a set of notes on the VLE is not going to help your learners necessarily obtain the best from it. Are there particular points you wish to think about and discuss? How does this reading fit in with other content? Are there additional sites that your learners should look at to support the material that you personally have 'uploaded'? The number of resources available to a teacher wishing to work with CBL grows daily. There are websites you can consult to help you evaluate such resources, and there are projects which have been funded by government to assist in the dissemination of both resources and evaluation of these resources. ESCalate is one such project, where its key role is dissemination of information about learning resources (see the list of websites at the end of the chapter). Another helpful source you may wish to consult is the ELICT project, which concerns the evaluation of learning with information and communication technology, a service provided through the Robert Clark Centre for Technological Education at Glasgow University. This project includes evaluations of the benefits and costs of educational technology and has a series of websites and links where you can download case studies and questionnaires.

Ethical considerations

If the medium of instruction is solely by electronic means, then it is very important to establish a set of ground rules, or 'netiquette'. It is very easy for people to misunderstand what is written on e-mails and to 'flame' their responses: that is, react much more emotionally than they would in a face-to-face discussion. People need to be reminded of equal opportunities policies, particularly, in ensuring that they use inclusive language.

If you want your learners to participate in discussion, you must consider what you will do about those who are 'lurking' too much. Will you specify that they must participate – and how will you judge the quality of their contribution? You will need to ensure that they treat any contribution with respect and deal with the contribution itself in their reply, and not introduce personal agenda into the discussion.

How will you monitor the work so that learners are not tempted to plagiarize? With the increasing possibility of downloading information and pasting it into an assignment, and even access to sites where other people have published ready-made assignments, it is difficult to be sure that learners have produced their own work. One way that helps limit the opportunity for plagiarism is by ensuring that the assignments have to contextualize the question, or apply it to the learner's personal circumstances. This is definitely a problem that has not yet been resolved and continues to cause great concern in any accredited programme.

Interactive whiteboards

A recent development in the use of computer technology is the interactive whiteboard. This is a computer screen which is operated from the whiteboard rather than from the computer. There are two main providers of this hardware and software, Promethean and Smartboard. With both of these, you need to set up the individual board you are working on every time to ensure that what you have created using the software, for example, on your own laptop or computer, is adjusted to fit the screen in the room you are using. (I forgot to do this when I tried using it for the first time and couldn't understand why every time I tapped the whiteboard, my pre-prepared text and pictures just didn't show up!) Learners can engage with activities that derive from pre-prepared items stored on the VLE, for example, by clicking on an answer, or moving one object to another on screen. Other features enable learners and tutors to create ideas which can be written on the whiteboard and subsequently be saved electronically. As with other resources, the uses to which an IWB is put affects the quality of the learning experience. I have seen science demonstrations where the learners are totally engaged by the activity of having to go to the IWB and physically move text about to make pairs of words (e.g. definitions). As it is possible to write on the board, it also helps with encouraging people to complete cloze exercises which provides spontaneity and sharing within a larger group. As the IWB is essentially a large screen, it also means that you can upload clips, sound and images to reinforce the points you are trying to convey and, of course, it means that your learners, too, can share what they have been working on, for example, through showing editing of a film or photographs. There is evidence that this kind of activity is particularly motivating for younger learners. Francis and Gould (2009) provide useful tips on using the IWB including specification of some of the features such as the timer which sits in the corner of the whiteboard and can be used for group work so that learners can keep a check on their activities in the time allowed.

Resource centres

Many educational institutions have developed learning resource centres, open learning centres or flexible learning centres in recent years. These centres provide the opportunity for learners to 'drop in' to use certain materials, use computers to write reports, create diagrams, search the web for information and even to undertake learning through web-based material, audiotapes or prescribed learning packages. This approach draws upon resource-based learning (RBL). In many cases, learners spend less time with their tutor in traditional face-to-face sessions and more time drawing upon the learning centre. One further education college I have visited recently has taken a strategic decision that all courses will include a minimum of 20 per cent contact time through the learning centre. This has meant that all tutors have to decide which aspects of the curriculum should be developed as RBL. If you are asked to undertake such a change to your own teaching, then make sure that you are fully aware of the facilities of the learning centre, and how you can be helped to devise the learning materials for independent learning by your learners. There will be technicians who can advise about appropriate programmes and format, and there may even be specialist staff who can take your original handouts and notes and create a html format to enable these to be placed on the institution's intranet. With all of these developments, the fundamental question remains. What am I hoping to achieve by using this method, and what should my learners be able to do, know and think as a result?

Being inclusive

The range of learning resources that are at your disposal will help you meet the varying needs of your learners. If you have people who do not see well, then you can take steps to increase the font size of your handouts, transparencies and text online. Remember that some colours are more difficult to see, and certainly the background colour of paper or screen can enhance the visibility of text. Black text on a yellow background aids clarity. You may decide to tape-record some of the session so that your learners can listen in their own time.

If your learners have a hearing loss, then using visual materials to support any auditory material is important. If you ask your learners to watch a podcast or listen to a tape, then provide a transcript for those who may not hear too well. If you are using an interpreter, then remember to ensure that your learning resources can be viewed by the learners at a different time from watching the interpreter. The interpreter must show the learner the source of the information, and if you decide to have text, image and sound, then you will be making the interpretation demanding for both the learner and the interpreter.

There are a number of organizations which can provide both information and support for learners who have particular learning requirements. People differ in their level of physical disability or learning difficulty. It is not easy to meet everyone's individual requirements. If you have someone at your institution who is responsible for learners who have particular requirements due to their physical disability or learning difficulty, then do make sure that you find out about the resources of the institution and how these can be drawn upon for your particular learners.

Luckily, the improvements in technology for learning have resulted in far more people having access to learning. It is unreasonable to expect that you can devise resources to meet all the situations you may possibly meet, and knowing whom to ask is the first step in ensuring that you are able to provide appropriate resources for your learners. One example of support in this important matter is TechDis, supported by the Higher Education Academy (HEA), which has a raft of valuable resources and information on making learning materials accessible.

Being inclusive is not restricted to thinking about physical disability or learning difficulties. When you decide which images to include on handouts, for example, then you must ensure that you draw upon a range of visual material that reflects the diverse nature of the population. If you always show eurocentric images when you are considering a particular topic, you are possibly excluding an enormous array of diverse material. If your course is on the architecture of medieval London, then showing examples of buildings from other parts of the world may not be appropriate, although one could argue that they could be used for comparison. If all your images are of white people, then you may be sending a message to your learners that there are no people from other races in that context.

When you choose examples, then, be aware of your learners, their differing backgrounds and of the rich diversity of their experience. There is a fine line to draw between being inclusive and finding 'token' examples. Images and examples provide a powerful message to the recipient and if you are aware of this, you may be more discerning in your choice of subject-matter and accompanying learning resources.

Conclusion

This chapter has raised many questions about learning resources for you to reflect on. I hope you will now be willing to examine your own ideas about the resources you use and why you do so. I hope that you will feel confident to try out different ways of using your resources and to add new types of resources into your teaching and learning approaches. The key principles in using resources are that they are appropriate for the learning required, their language and images are inclusive, and are accessible to the learner. Remember, too, that resources do not have to be produced by 'state-of-the-art' technology to be effective. They do, however, need to be of high quality so that learners feel respected and motivated to learn. The next stage is to consider what methods of teaching can be effective to facilitate learning.

LLUK standards

This chapter will help you to work towards LLUK standards – Domain B: Learning and Teaching and Domain C: Specialist Learning and Teaching.

Further reading and information

Further reading

Armitage, A., Bryant, R., Dunnill, R., Hammersley, M., Hayes, D., Hudson, A. and Lawer, S. (1999) *Teaching and Training in Post-Compulsory Education*. Bucks: Open University Press, Chapter 5, pp. 96–128.

British Journal of Educational Research

British Journal of Educational Technology Computers and Education

Francis, M. and Gould, J. (2009) *Achieving Your PTTLS*. London: Sage.

Gray, D., Griffin, C. and Nasta, T. (2000) 'Information technology and resource-based learning', in *Training to Teach in Further and Adult Education*. Cheltenham: Stanley Thornes, Chapter 7, pp. 139–64.

Journal of Computer Assisted Learning

Petty, G. (2004) *Teaching Today: A Practical Guide* (3rd edn). Cheltenham: Nelson Thornes.

Petty, G. (2006) *Evidence Based Teaching – A Practical Approach*. Cheltenham: Nelson Thornes.

Roerden, L. P. (1997) *Net Lessons: Web-Based Projects for Your Classroom*. Sebastopol, CA: Songline Studios and O'Reilly.

Saunders, G. (2000) *Getting Started with On-Line Learning*. Gloucester: Learning Partners.

Organizations

British Dyslexia Association

MENCAP (Royal Society for Mentally Handicapped Children and Adults)

MIND (National Association for Mental Health)

NCVO (National Council for Voluntary Organizations)

RNIB (Royal National Institute for the Blind)

RNID (Royal National Institute for the Deaf)

SKILL (National Bureau for Learners with Disabilities)

Useful websites

Blackboard (http://blackboard.com). Key words: online learning, web-based instruction.

British Educational Communications and Technology Agency (BECTa) (www.becta.org.uk)

COSE Creation of Study Environments, Staffordshire University (www.staffs.ac.uk/COSE)

Educational Technology Information and Resources (http://www2.warwick.ac.uk/services/ldc/resource/)

ELICT (www.gla.ac.uk/rcc/projects/elict/html).

ESCalate.ac.uk. Key words: educational resources, educational resources database.

Further Education Resources for Learning (FERL) (www.ferl.becta.org.uk)

Inclusive Journal of Interactive Media in Education (http://jime.open.ac.uk/)

Intellectual Property Office (in relation to Copyright) (www.ipo.gov.uk)

Interactive whiteboards

    http://smarttech.com

    Promethean (www.prometheanworld.com)

National Learning Network (www.nln.ac.uk/materials)

TechDis (www.jisc.ac.uk)

WebTeach #, Professional Development Centre, New South Wales, Australia (http://webteach.net/)

www.intute.ac.uk

www.geoffpetty.com/downloads.html

www.geoffpetty.com/whatsnew.html

www.learningtechnologies.ac.uk

www.teacherstoolbox.co.uk

6 Teaching and Learning Methods

There are many ways to facilitate learning. Just as individuals learn differently, so there are also individual ways of teaching. You may have experienced teachers in the past who gave talks that were interesting and held your attention throughout, and other teachers who managed to send you to sleep. They were all using similar methods, but the way in which they presented their talk was done differently. Once again, there is a complex interaction between the tutor, the learners and the environment. This chapter will focus on the strategies and methods a tutor can use.

A strategy is a 'grand plan' or approach. It can cover a lot of techniques but has a central philosophy. Methods are techniques, procedures or ways of doing something. Learner-centred methods are part of the strategy based upon the view that all learners are individual in their abilities, learning styles and requirements. It is assumed that learners have certain experiences and knowledge that they bring with them to the learning situation and that they should be active participants in the learning context. A tutor-centred strategy is predicated on the idea that tutors have a great deal of expertise which they should impart to their learners. The learners are not expected to have the same level of knowledge and experience as their tutor. They will rely on their tutor to impart the knowledge and are, therefore, more passive in the learning situation.

In any learning situation, it is important for the tutor to create space and time so that learners can construct meaning from what is being taught, and this is especially the case with tutor-centred approaches. Even in flexible learning environments, where learners are largely autonomous, meaning needs to emerge from their engagement with online learning. In each case, the idea of avoiding Freire's banking (see Chapter 1) applies here, that is, the notion that learners are empty vessels into which ideas are poured, without their participation in the construction of what the ideas mean.

This chapter will explore a number of methods, many of which are more learner-centred in their approach. There is a focus on learner-centred methods in much of the literature on adult learning (see, for example, Armitage et al., 1999; Petty, 2003; Francis and Gould, 2009), but it is important to remember that there are times when you do know more than your learners and it is appropriate to use tutor-centred methods.

The example of Mukesh in Chapter 4 shows that he chose a small number of teaching and learning methods from those possible. Mukesh could have covered the same material and aimed for the group to achieve the same learning outcomes in numerous ways. His choice of teaching and learning methods has been informed by a series of factors including the type of group he has, the setting, the timescale and the location. Mukesh would have drawn upon a repertoire of teaching and learning methods which he has acquired through his professional practice and from his experience of being a learner, too. Here is a list of methods which are more frequently used. They can be divided into three main groups: tutor-led presentations, interactive activities and project work.

Tutor-led presentations

- Presentations
- Lectures
- Demonstrations

Interactive activities

- Brainstorm
- Questions and answers
- Group work (often called buzz groups and syndicate groups)
- Case studies
- Discussions
- Simulations
- Practicum
- Role-play
- Games and quizzes
- Individual presentations and group presentations
- Learning sets
- Chatrooms, seminar groups using ICT conferencing
- Social websites including blogs and wikis

Project work

- Individual and group projects
- Surveys and interviews
- Experiments
- Visits to museums, galleries and organizations

Very few of the methods above exist in isolation from each other. For example, in a two-hour session, learners may listen to a short presentation, discuss the main points in pairs, join together to identify three key points in groups of four, feed back in a plenary session, brainstorm the implications of these points, and then work on a case study.

'Priming' learners is a fundamental part of many teaching and learning methods. Learners need to know what is required of them when they watch a video, discuss in groups or visit a gallery. Therefore, with each of the methods listed, a consideration throughout concerns what information is required to brief the learners before they undertake the activity. This briefing requires clear instructions, providing opportunities for learners to check that they understand what is required of them and offering appropriate resources to enable them to carry out the activity.

Let us consider the advantages and disadvantages of each of the methods, and how they can be used effectively to maximize learning. With each method, there are some fundamental questions we should ask:

- What are we trying to achieve by using this method, that is, aims, objectives, learning outcomes?
- What resources do we need for this method?
- What previous learning can be reinforced by this method?
- What previous knowledge and experience are required to use this method successfully?
- Can this method help me assess what people have learned?
- What is the timescale required for this method to be successfully undertaken?
- Do I need to make any special arrangements to meet individual learning requirements, particularly in order to be inclusive?
- Could an alternative method achieve the learning goals more effectively?

Tutor-led presentations

There are a number of ways that tutors and trainers can present information to their learners. In all of the examples that follow, the tutor generally is responsible for deciding what will be presented, how and for how long.

Different forms of presentation

There are different forms of presentation, including lectures, presentations, web presentations and demonstrations. Usually, lectures occupy more time, and are seen to be more formal. It is not unusual to find that a lecture has been timetabled for one hour, and in higher education this can be for up to three hours. This does not mean, of course, that learners in higher education sit through three hours of non-stop lecturing, although it has been known! Presentations are usually shorter, and do not necessarily need to be given by the tutor. Learners are often asked to make presentations, either as individuals or in groups. It can be a summary of group work, an idea for discussion, a project plan, or a summary of learning over the previous months. The theme throughout all these teaching and learning methods is that information is portrayed by one person or group of people to another in a more 'didactic' fashion.

Web-based presentations involve websites, PowerPoint sliders or graphics, podcasts and may include interactive activities through each workstation and interactive whiteboard. As with more traditional presentations, the information is chosen by the presenter. The use of multimedia requires careful planning. Why choose certain websites, what is their informational value, and do they illustrate key learning points? The following section describes each of these presentations and discusses their strengths.

Presentations

The traditional lecture or talk can be delivered to large groups of people at one moment in time, videotaped and seen again at later stages, taped and listened to by people not present, and can be repeated on numerous occasions. It requires careful preparation, particularly, if handouts and slides are to be used.

The main disadvantage of a traditional presentation is that people do not have much chance to interact. They may be able to ask questions, either during the presentation or at the end, but it is not the same as a discussion, where there is far more input by the learners.

A further disadvantage of a lecture or talk is that people do not concentrate for long periods of time. They will, therefore, miss what is being said if they are also trying to take notes. Additional audiovisual resources and handouts which summarize the main points provide the necessary support to this teaching and learning method. Not all presentations are recorded, and once a presentation has been missed, then the individual learner has lost an opportunity to obtain information, especially if it is not available in written form. Lecturers and speakers often embellish their talk with asides, anecdotes and humour which help to reinforce the main points being made. Lecture notes do not capture these. There is often little opportunity for people to negotiate the content of presentations: they are primarily tutor-led. This is not necessarily a bad thing. When there is information to be given to a great many people in a short space of time, presentations and lectures are a highly appropriate strategy. It has become very fashionable these days to consider 'lectures bad, group work good' (Brookfield, 1998, p. 140). Lectures and presentations which are well prepared, delivered in interesting ways and paced to keep the interest of those attending, can be very effective.

When should we use presentations and how can we make them effective?

Consider the content. Is it something that can be found in books, DVDs or in websites? Why do you think it would be appropriate to use a presentation format for this? Are you trying to give your learners the background to a large, complex topic, an introduction to a new topic, a summary of different theories? These questions will help you reflect on whether the presentation method is suitable.

How should you present the information and content? Remember that people do not listen attentively for long periods. Can you break the information into smaller units? One way to ensure that people do not have to sit passively for any length of time is to create activities which reinforce learning points that you wish to make. Imagine that you are presenting information on saturated and unsaturated fatty foods. You can ask your learners to talk to their neighbour and think of two examples each of foods that have heavily saturated and unsaturated fats. It is not necessary to spend time afterwards asking each of the pairs to feed back to the whole group. By asking learners to think for themselves and then to discuss their ideas with their neighbour breaks your presentation into smaller parts and enables them to engage cognitively with the information they have just received. It also provides an opportunity for learners to raise questions if they have not fully understood the points you have just made. This 'buzz group' activity creates energy in the group, and as a result people are more likely to attend to the next part of your presentation.

Try to ensure that your ideas are presented logically. It is very distracting to listen to someone present a series of disparate points which do not seem to relate to each other or do not lead the listener to a conclusion. Remember, too, that communication is about ensuring that what you have to say reaches your listener without loss of information. This means that you must ensure that all your learners can hear you, or that they have the necessary equipment and resources to do so. The same point applies to any visual material you use. Can everyone see the computer screen or the slides?

People have many idiosyncrasies in their mannerisms, and their use of language in presentations is one way in which these are demonstrated. This is where being observed by an experienced tutor or trainer, particularly, if you have the chance to see yourself on video, can provide you with feedback about your own mannerisms. I do not think that we should try to be polished performers who never hesitate or have to use 'ahs' and 'ums' during our presentations. This could make our presentations bland and possibly stilted. However, it is very informative to watch ourselves in action and to find out how often we do use particular words or phrases. A more serious matter is how we use language. Our language should be inclusive when we use examples. Do we tend to use 'he' for senior staff, talk about husbands and wives, describe older people as having limitations on their learning abilities, and so on? Once again, observing ourselves on video provides an important opportunity to listen carefully to what we say and to view our body language.

Individual and group presentations

Any presentation which learners are asked to undertake requires clear instructions. What are they being asked to present, how long have they got to do it, and in what format? Learners require time to prepare for presentations, particularly, if they are working in groups. If they are full-time learners and there are timetabled sessions to work on the presentation, then it is more likely that they will be able to cover the requirements in time. Part-time learners, particularly, those who attend one session per week, will find it extremely difficult to meet up as a group if they are not given time within their contact time to prepare. Before asking learners to make a presentation, tutors should decide why the presentation is necessary. Is it to help the learners apply their knowledge? A case study may be used where learners are asked to identify a strategy for action and the presentation provides the opportunity to summarize this. Is the presentation to enable individuals to identify their own learning? This can be an extremely effective way of enabling learners to look back over their learning experiences and to decide for themselves what have been the most effective aspects of their learning, the surprises and the frustrations: it helps them to 'own' the learning process. Presentations can also help learners decide on future actions. If learners have to undertake a project, a presentation is a helpful way to clarify what they plan to do. I have found that my learners who are studying for a postgraduate degree find the idea of presenting their project both daunting before they do it and useful once they have done it. The feedback from their peers is an important part of this process. After each presentation, we ask questions for clarification and then identify if there is anything that can be further refined, or provide information that will be useful to the presenter. As a result, the final proposal is more carefully thought through and details have been clarified.

Presentations can incorporate other learning activities, such as case studies and demonstrations, which are described below. The process of working on group presentations can benefit enormously from the use of e-mail, video-conferencing, creating wikis and blogs and as more people gain access to free software such as Skype, they can keep in touch with each other and even see into each other's offices and homes if they have webcams on their laptops or computers! The pressure to meet together and discuss ideas and preparation for group presentations has been significantly reduced through the use of recent developments in technology. People even use their mobile phones to photograph what they are working on for instant information sharing with their peers.

Checklist for presentations

- Is the material relevant to the programme objectives and learning outcomes?
- Does it fit the learners' expectations and requirements?
- Does it build upon previous learning?
- Does it take account of learners' current abilities?
- Is the material presented in a logical order, building upon simple ideas towards more complex ideas?
- Are there concrete examples which can illustrate abstract ideas?
- Are there key points to help learners remember?
- Are there opportunities for learners to ask questions during the presentation and at the end?

- Are there questions at intervals to check learners' understanding?
- Are there audiovisual materials to illustrate learning points?
- Are there handouts to help learners remember after the presentation?
- Is the pace neither too slow nor too fast?
- Is the tone of voice varied and lively, rather than delivered in a monotonous way?
- Is there eye contact with the learners?
- Is the accommodation adequate – not too crowded, seating comfortable, everyone can see and hear?

You will find many of these items in observation schedules used in teacher training courses and in quality assurance procedures. A reflective teacher will find such a checklist helpful as it affords a rich source of information for future development. Of course, one person's idea of a lively and interesting pace will be another's idea of something which is too fast: it is impossible to meet everyone's idea of a perfect presentation. We must monitor our use of presentations, checking that they are both an appropriate teaching and learning method for the particular content and learning outcomes, and that we are using this strategy as effectively as possible. We cannot all be the equivalent of award-winning actors and actresses performing on stage, and there is no one way of presenting information that we should all aspire to. We should try to find what is most effective for our learners, and develop our own professional practice accordingly.

Demonstrations

Demonstrations are often associated with skill-based learning. When we use demonstrations, we must ask ourselves what skills are to be acquired and whether the demonstration will provide enough information for the learners to try it out for themselves. During a demonstration, the tutor or trainer has to give verbal instructions at the same time as demonstrating the skill or method. In exercise programmes, this requires a good level of fitness, otherwise learners have to work out what is being said throughout the huffs and puffs of their demonstrator during the physical exertion!

Once more, planning is important. Does the skill follow on from previous learning? Are there jargon words which need to be explained? Will the learners require the process to be broken down into small steps? Can this be done in certain activities which require cohesion? For example, if learners are trying to acquire serving skills in tennis, is it possible to break down the process of serving into short activities like throwing up a ball and letting it drop, before learning to swing the racquet?

Let us return to the cooking class. In advanced study, the term for 'cookery' is now food technology, or instead of 'cake decorating' it is sugarcraft. Let us imagine there is a group of learners who are working towards their City and Guilds Sugarcraft at NVQ Level 2. The session we are going to consider is fondue icing. The learners are all experienced at icing cakes and many own a small enterprise in birthday and wedding cakes in their local community. What should the tutor consider in the demonstration?

Learners need to know what ingredients and resources they will be using during that session. They may require written information in the form of a handout. When they come to the session, are they able to gather around the tutor to see the demonstration? Will they all be comfortable standing? Are there stools for those who are unable to do so? Is there information written on a whiteboard to which they can refer? When the demonstration begins, does the tutor set the scene, reminding learners of previous sessions and learning? Does the tutor inform learners about the criteria for this particular activity and how it relates to the relevant unit or units in the qualification? Does the tutor use questions to involve the learners while the demonstration proceeds. Questioning is an extremely useful way to check people's learning and to help them think about why certain procedures are necessary (see later section on the use of questions and answers). For example, the tutor may ask people why it is necessary to maintain certain ingredients at a particular temperature. The knowledge that underpins the skill of sugarcraft can, therefore, be introduced and reinforced.

Jargon which is introduced should be explained. It is always a good idea to try to encourage your learners to begin using such terms as soon as possible, and to apply them in their own practice.

Sometimes, learners can be asked to participate in the demonstration. You may decide that you wish to develop a certain method and, therefore, start with the process the learners have already used. Then you can step in and demonstrate the alternative, more advanced technique. You could decide that you will give instructions to a learner who performs the demonstration. Demonstrations do not have to be totally tutor-centred. Asking learners to participate can often be fun, particularly if making mistakes is taken as a necessary part of learning and not to be avoided.

Health and safety are extremely important issues for consideration in any learning activity, and they are a legal requirement. We are all responsible for ensuring that we work in safe conditions under the current Health and Safety Act. In practical demonstrations, our responsibility under the Act is paramount. If we are using electrical equipment, particularly, those which involve heat, penetration or cutting, we must take care that we use the equipment safely and that we instruct our learners how to do so too. The tutor acts as an important role model in these situations. Are the learners aware of the requirements of using the equipment? Have they been trained to take the necessary precautions before use? Do they have and wear any protective clothing?

One of my most worrying moments regarding safety occurred when observing an art class tutor. I was watching learners who were drawing a model who sat on a rotating dais. As it was winter, there was a small electric heater placed on the dais connected to the wall. At intervals, one of the learners would turn the dais around to draw the model from a different angle. The heater had to be removed from the dais while it was turned and subsequently replaced, otherwise it would have fallen over as the dais moved. However, the heater was not always removed as the dais was turned, and it certainly was never turned off at the power socket. There could have been a serious accident where the model could have been burned if the fire had fallen on her. The tutor I was observing had spent a great deal of time explaining to the learners how important it was to remove the heater before moving the dais, but the learners continued to act in a dangerous manner. As the studio was very large and the class had many learners, she was not able to monitor the situation constantly. This was clearly an example where the tutor and her learners were in breach of the Health and Safety Act.

Checklist for demonstrations

- Do I have the necessary equipment, resources, materials?
- Is the equipment in good working order?
- Are the steps in the process broken down adequately?
- Is the commentary clear?
- Are there clear instructions for the learners to follow?
- Can the learners see and hear well?
- Are there alternative arrangements for those who need additional support?
- Are the processes or skills performed according to the criteria or industry standards?
- Is the demonstration within the parameters of the Health and Safety Act and additional codes of practice?
- Have the learners got appropriate protective clothing if required?
- Are there notes, handouts or diagrams for learners to refer to during or after the demonstration? If so, do these capture the stages in the process demonstrated?

Interactive activities

The second group of teaching and learning methods is far more interactive for the learners. These methods still enable information to be communicated to learners, but they also build upon the learners' own knowledge and experience. Below are some examples of the methods and how they can be used.

Brainstorming

Brainstorming occurs when people can think together on a topic and state their ideas out loud. These ideas are recorded, usually on a flip-chart or whiteboard, so that all the group can see what has been said. Brainstorming can also apply when people think alone about an individual topic and make 'scattergrams', diagrams or lists of their ideas. It is a useful way of establishing what people already know about a certain topic, or what questions they have for the session. As their ideas are written down, there is a record which can be kept and referred to during the session or even at the end of a learning programme.

Brainstorming does have pitfalls. Learners can feel that they are doing all the work and the tutor is not 'teaching' them anything. If the ideas are simply written down and no further attempt is made to analyse what has been said, then the activity may feel pointless to many of the participants. Not all people feel able to contribute in a large group and, of course, there is the danger that some people will commandeer the contributions and overly influence what is being recorded. Brainstorming requires great skill on the part of the tutor in asking questions and teasing out from the contributions what has been said. It is important to record what the learner has stated and not what the tutor wants to say. However, sometimes it is not quite clear what has been said, or by agreement a particular term is placed next to a previous contribution because it refers to a similar aspect. Being able to draw ideas from a group of people who are not particularly forthcoming is one of the great challenges of brainstorming!

There are many ways to conduct a brainstorming session. Learners can be asked to work individually or in pairs and small groups first before making contributions. When they return to the large group to discuss their ideas, a plenary session is held. They may have been given particular tasks which relate to one aspect of a topic and only after each group has fed back can a full brainstorming session take place. Brainstorming is very useful at the start of a programme so that everyone can negotiate how the group should behave (see Chapter 7).

Interactive whiteboards are helpful for brainstorming as people can work together around the board, drawing or writing ideas which can then be saved so that everyone has a copy – the main disadvantage of using flip-chart paper or traditional whiteboards for brainstorming is that often the discussion is lost at the end of a session. Not every brainstorming record makes sense after the event but IWBs do provide a wonderful opportunity to share and further develop ideas, in much the same way as wikis and blogs.

Checklist for brainstorming

- Are my instructions clear?
- Have I got the appropriate resources to record discussion and points: flip-chart, pens, whiteboard?
- Have I allowed learners time to think before they discuss?
- Have I used *their* words, not mine?
- Have I ensured everyone can participate?
- Have I managed the group so that no individual 'hogs' the contributions?
- Will I make a record of the brainstorm and distribute it to the learners?
- How will I build on the brainstorm in subsequent teaching and learning activities?
- If I intend to use diagrams, or ask my learners to create diagrams and pictures, what will I do with these afterwards?

Questions and answers

It may seem trite to say that if you want to know what someone knows, ask a question! It is extremely useful to check what your learners have understood from your teaching, and using question and answer sessions is one way to do this. It is, therefore, also a technique of assessment (see Chapter 8). People's learning can be reinforced by asking questions immediately after a presentation, or a learning activity. This method can be applied informally, such as 'Can anyone tell me what test I use for the presence of glucose in a liquid?' or formally where a set of written questions is given under examination conditions.

The way in which a question is asked will affect the form of response. Closed questions are those which result in a simple Yes/No answer: they are useful for confirming an aspect of knowledge. Thus: 'Can I use bleach with domestic lavatory cleaners?' will tell us whether the learner knows about the rules of using bleach with other chemicals. However, the answer could have been arrived at by guesswork. If we ask the question 'What happens if we mix bleach with domestic lavatory cleaners?' we may be given an explanation of how bleach can react with the agents included in domestic cleaners to give off chlorine and why this is dangerous.

The second type of question is known as an open question: it provides an opportunity to describe and explain. The answers to the questions provide us with information about what our learners know and whether there are any inaccuracies in their knowledge that we need to address. As a teaching and learning method, therefore, it is informative to both tutor and learner. It helps with incremental learning, identifying gaps, reinforcing learning, and works at the cognitive level, requiring that learners apply their learning to new examples or explain what is the case.

Many people feel uncomfortable waiting for learners to answer their question. They do not know how to make use of silence. It is really important not to jump in as soon as you ask a question if no one responds. People may not be responding because they need time to think through the answer and if you supply it, you have taken away an opportunity for them to think independently and you also won't know what they do know (see Chapter 8). If people respond in a way that shows that they have got part of the idea but are still confused about other aspects, you will have more information about what you need to do to help clarify this.

You do need to manage the answering process. If everyone talks at once, you won't hear what is being said and neither will your learners. It is particularly important to have a rule about only one person speaking at a time if you have people who have a hearing loss or are easily distracted. Of course, people are bound to speak at the same time if they all want to answer your question, it is what you do next. Remember that it is helpful to ask people by name to answer a question as one way to manage this process (see chapter 7).

Checklist for questions and answers

- Is there a mixture of open and closed questions to enable exploration and confirmation of learning?
- Are the questions used at appropriate points in a learning programme or session?
- Are the answers discussed, particularly if further explanation is required?
- If questions are asked in a group session, has everyone a chance to 'have a go'?
- Have I ensured that quiet members have an opportunity to answer, perhaps by using small groups?
- Have I given my learners the opportunity to ask me questions?
- Have I checked with my learners that I have understood their questions and their responses correctly?
- Have I given people time to answer the question – have I respected the need for silence?

Group work

'Group work' is a term that covers a variety of activities. I have mentioned previously that 'buzz groups' and 'syndicate groups' are terms for working in pairs and smaller groups. However, it is what people have to do in their groups that is the important consideration. Many of you will have experienced working in groups if you are undertaking your teaching qualification. You may have noticed that you are given a task, perhaps to look at some case studies (see below) and discuss, or you may have been asked to find examples of a particular situation to report back to the whole group. In any group activity, there must be a directive from the tutor about what is required, by when and how the information should be recorded. I have participated in, and witnessed, many group sessions where the members are not quite sure what they have to do. I have seen group members ignore the task totally and talk about some other pressing subject – and I have even seen group members argue, or individuals leave the group and go home. Therefore, it is vital to enable the group members to undertake the activity and to see how it fits into the learning session. Group work is fully covered in Chapter 7, where I discuss the dynamics of groups and how to facilitate learning within them.

As noted before, groups do not need to be working face to face. The use of e-mail, tele-conferencing, video-conferencing and wikis and blogs are, particularly, useful to support group work that can be conducted outside of sessions but you may need to assist people in working with new software and you will need to respect their autonomy while needing to provide a structure for their activities.

Case studies

Case studies are examples of a specific situation, providing contextual information which participants must then apply to a particular problem or identification of action. The 'case' can be a series of cameos, describing people with certain characteristics. It can be a description of an organization for analysis for a human resource strategy. It can be a description of medical symptoms which require diagnosis. Case studies are particularly useful when learners have acquired the generic aspects of the topic but need to apply these to specific situations. If we think of professional practice, there are many situations which are very similar: for example, a dentist will meet many people who have cavities and will undertake routine action to fill them. However, there will be occasions where there are complications. Deciding how to act calls upon the wealth of professional knowledge that has been acquired. Case studies enable a training practitioner to meet such examples 'theoretically' and to discuss appropriate strategies without doing actual harm to a patient.

As with group work, using case studies requires careful preparation. The information provided must be relevant. It must draw upon the current knowledge of the participants. It is not helpful to give case studies to people who have not already learned the jargon or technical terms, or who cannot spot the important points because they have not been introduced to them previously.

Case studies are often used in problem-based learning (PBL) where learners must seek information for themselves in order to address the points raised by the case study. Here, although the learners require some background knowledge, the case study is being used to stimulate the acquisition of knowledge.

Case studies can be built and developed through the use of wikis, where information is gathered and shared and then the learners can undertake the necessary decision-making or analysis of the evolving nature of the case being studied.

Checklist for using case studies

- Is there sufficient information to allow the learners to discuss and act upon the case study?
- Are the instructions clear?
- Is the information relevant?
- Have I given clear guidelines for further action, information gathering and presentation based on the case study given?
- Have I allowed sufficient time?
- Have I provided the learners with information of where to locate additional sources?
- Are my handouts clear?

Discussions

Within group work, a major feature of activity is discussion. To be effective, learners need to be given a specific issue to discuss, with perhaps guidance on what to have read beforehand, or how many points to identify before feeding back to the main group, or a task sheet to complete. Learners will engage in discussion if the activity is stimulating. Where it is used simply to break up a long session, and no guidance given, learners may be tempted to wander off the subject and even rebel and not discuss the issue at all.

One of the considerations for tutors who lead discussion groups is whether to sit in on the discussion or not. I used to feel that I should be doing something while my learners were in discussion groups. I have since observed many tutors doing the same thing. Often this results in tutors wandering around each small discussion group, sitting in on the discussion and interrupting the flow. Learners then stop to explain to the tutor what they have been saying so far and this results in valuable time being taken up revisiting the issues. I have also seen some learners 'show off' when the tutor comes round, either by asking difficult and penetrating questions and almost sabotaging the group discussion, or steering the direction of the discussion away from the topic given. If you do want to join in with a group discussion, allow the learners time to settle down to the task before wandering around to ask if there is anything they wish to clarify. It is perfectly acceptable to join in a group discussion as long as there is time to do so with all the groups, and that by doing so you are facilitating the group process.

One of the more telling moments in observing a class that has been asked to divide into discussion groups is how the learners settle down. Do they look around to find out what they have to do from their peers or ask questions of the tutor, do they have experience of this kind of activity and 'know the rules', do they start the activity quickly or is there a lot of procrastination? Remember that introducing this kind of activity to people who are unused to working in small discussion groups requires good direction so that they begin to develop their skills in both talking and listening as group members.

Checklist for discussions

- Are the instructions clear?
- Have I allowed enough time for the discussion to deal with the material and issues?
- Have I decided how (if at all) feedback from the discussion will take place?
- Have I ensured that everyone can participate?
- Have I ensured my learners understand why they are asked to participate in a discussion?
- Have I established rules of respect and tolerance?
- Have I helped my learners to develop listening and speaking skills?

Simulations

Simulations provide opportunities to practise newly acquired skills and knowledge in a safe environment. A simulation is an attempt to place the learner in a situation which is as close to the actual or 'real-life' example as possible. An example is where pilots learn to fly aircraft. They are placed in a flight simulator which has all the controls and switches. The difference is that they do not actually fly but they are given the equivalent of a flight that they must control. In some simulations, the situation is deliberately manipulated by the instructor, to provide experience of controls not working, or dangerous situations that cannot be undertaken because of the risks involved. More mundane examples of simulations occur in hairdressing salons and construction sites in colleges which are as close as possible to those found in industry. Here, learners gradually acquire the skills of the trade but under control- led conditions, directed by tutors and instructors.

Simulations require careful planning. Simply placing learners in a situation and letting them get on with it will not necessarily enable them to learn effectively. They need to reflect on what they did while in the simulation, why they acted as they did, look at the products of their work and discuss if these could have been achieved differently. The role of the tutor in providing feedback from the simulation is vital. It requires careful observation of the learners to provide general learning points for future action. For example, in a workshop, if most of the learners forgot to undertake a safety check of the electrical equipment before using it, it would be appropriate to remind all the group members as well as the particular individuals.

Remember to provide opportunities for the learners to ask questions and make com- ments when they have had the experience in the simulation, even if it is simply a chance to say 'I didn't realize that it was going to be so difficult to do x and y at the same time' or 'I must remember that I should check a before I do b'.

Varieties of simulations

I recently saw an example of a simulation using the 'second life' social network, where learn- ers were undertaking an exercise in anger management. They were training to work with people who had mental health difficulties and needed to practice their skills at managing their clients' anger. Another example involved showing them what it was like to have schiz- ophrenia and here, the simulation involved hearing the voice of the person as he walked around his house. This is an invaluable use of new technology but as in all examples, it is important to ensure that learners are briefed and debriefed, particularly if the content involves dealing with emotions and difficult situations.

Not all simulations require equipment and resources. You may have already undertaken microteaching if you are on a teacher training course, which is a simulation. Here you sup- ply the learning resources and use an aspect of your teaching upon your peers, who in turn give feedback on a number of points, including whether you met your objectives, if your lan- guage and instructions were clear, the pace and effectiveness of your learning resources.

Practicum

A practicum is a term usually applied to an activity which often uses simulation or role-play to enable a learner to both experience using a technique and develop particular skills in that technique. It is often used in counselling courses, where learners must both try out their active listening and counselling skills and be observed by their peers doing so, in order to further their own skills. An example of how this can be set up is as follows.

Each individual is asked to think of an issue to 'present' to a peer who will act in the role of counsellor. The presenter and counsellor are given fifteen minutes to discuss the issue. In the meantime, two other peers observe the interaction. At the end of the fifteen minutes, the presenter and the counsellor state how they experienced the interaction. The two observers then give feedback on what they have observed. At the end of the feedback, ideas for further action and refinement of counselling skills are identified for the counsellor to work on. It is then the turn of the next presenter.

The practicum provides a safe environment for people to try out their skills and to receive feedback from their peers who have all been briefed in terms of what to observe. It also provides an opportunity for each learner to act as a presenter, a counsellor and an observer. These roles enable trainee counsellors to experience the complex nature of the counselling interaction. This form of teaching and learning would be repeated many times, using a variety of contexts and enabling individuals to experience the process with different peers.

Role-plays

The characteristics of role-play are that the people participating take on a role which then requires them to behave as though they were the person in the role. The rationale for role-play is that people have an opportunity to experience what it is like to act, particularly verbally, in the role and from this develop an understanding of how to behave in future situations. Role-play is often used in personal development programmes, such as developing assertiveness skills. By playing the part of someone different from oneself, it is possible to develop strategies and skills to deal with situations that have been causing difficulty in ways that would normally be quite alien. Role-play can also be used to enable people to develop empathy for others who are very different from themselves. It is used for developing client-centred approaches in a variety of professions. For example, by acting out the role of a confused patient, a trainee doctor would begin to identify with the patient's fear and confusion, thereby developing more empathetic approaches when dealing with future patients. They experience the situation from 'the other side' as a result of undertaking the role-play.

Language learning can draw upon a variety of simulations and role-plays to reinforce learning. Examples include having conversations about what to eat in a restaurant, ordering from a menu and asking for the bill. Role-plays can be good fun, but not everyone will want to join in. Role-plays must be carefully managed. People need to be taken 'out of role' at the end of the session, or be 'debriefed'. This is most important if the activity has been directed at sensitive issues including race and sexuality. If this is not done, there is a danger that the participants will stay in role and act out their parts in future learning sessions. If the participants have been asked to deal with controversial matter upon which they disagree, there is a possibility that feelings of anger and frustration will stay with them, rather than being dealt with as part of the role-play. It is extremely important, therefore, that using role-play is carefully thought through and that sufficient time is allowed for the debriefing stage. This is another aspect of group dynamics which is discussed in Chapter 7.

Checklist for simulations, practicums and role-plays

- Is the accommodation an accurate reflection of the 'real-life' context?
- Are the resources appropriate and in good working order?
- Are the instructions clear?
- Do the learners understand their role?
- Are there opportunities to provide feedback after the simulation has ended?
- Are learners 'debriefed' after the end of the role-play?
- Are any issues arising from undertaking a role dealt with quickly?

Games and quizzes

Learning does not have to be done under serious, formal conditions. Games provide a wonderful opportunity for learners to acquire skills and knowledge. There are many verbal games that can be used in language and literacy contexts, as noted in Chapter 4. Games can be used to simulate a situation, for example, where people are given a certain sum of money and asked to participate in an activity where they have to maximize their income. The tutor may have created a set of conditions so that those who start with more money make more, thereby illustrating some of the principles of capitalism.

Games must be managed carefully. Some people will feel insulted that they are being asked to participate in something they only played as children. Others will feel insecure and embarrassed. You must, therefore, check that your learners understand why they are being asked to participate and what they will gain from the activity.

Quizzes can be a fun way to assess your learners' knowledge part-way through a programme of learning. These can be done individually, in groups or for the whole group. They can be produced with pen and paper, on a whiteboard, read out loud by the tutor, or even produced on computers. The answers reinforce learning, or show people where they have gaps in their knowledge. Again, the point of quizzes is that they help people to learn and should not be seen as something childish, or threatening. And, of course, they need to be pitched at a level that people can participate in. I saw a quiz being used throughout a ten-week course on financial management where the tutor divided the learners into teams and they were given 'virtual' money at the start of the course and then gained or lost it as they competed in the quizzes. Given that the nature of their course was on financial systems, it also demonstrated how money is made in the industry. The downside of this idea is that sometimes, one team member becomes all important and the rest of the group cease to participate or benefit from the exercise.

Checklist for games and quizzes

- Is the learning outcome clear to the participants?
- Are the resources appropriate?
- Can each learner participate fully in the game?
- Are the instructions clear?
- Can learners opt out if they wish?
- Is the language appropriate for adults?

Learning sets

So far, most of the learning methods described contain tutor input which is most directive when using lectures, demonstrations and presentations and less directive at the brainstorming end of the scale. However, one method which draws heavily upon the learners themselves is the learning set. Here, learners work together in autonomous groups. They may be placed there initially by their tutor or they may be self-selecting. Once formed, they decide what it is they wish to discuss and to work on. They provide support for each individual member, and the members control the agenda. Members of learning sets should not have to rely on the tutor but should be facilitated in such a way that they can function effectively and autonomously. This means that all the learners in the set must take responsibility for any action that has been negotiated and must agree to participate fully in the set. Chapter 7 discusses this particular aspect of group dynamics. Learning sets are often used in vocational and competence-based work, particularly at the higher levels, where learners have to make sense of vast amounts of performance criteria. Members can help each other identify appropriate evidence from the workplace and can use brainstorming and other problem-solving techniques to assist in their portfolio development. Learning sets do not work well where the group members feel they have been forced together, or if they feel cheated of instruction from their tutor. Learning sets require very careful creation, so that everyone is clear about the process and the benefits from working in this way.

Checklist for learning sets

- Do the learners know why they are placed in learning sets?
- Are their instructions clear?
- Do they have sufficient time to establish how they will work together in the learning set?
- Will you take part at all in the process or leave it entirely to the individuals to operate their learning set?
- Are there resources and accommodation for the sets?
- Is there time for reporting back on their work?

Using ICT conferencing

An extension of learning sets is the use of conferencing. Here, learners can discuss their work and how they feel about it asynchronously using e-mail and conferencing facilities. In many distance learning courses, learners are encouraged to communicate with each other this way, partly to mitigate against the fact that they are not meeting to learn together as a group in one place. Conferencing and social networks can provide various forms of support to the learners. They can ask each other how to go about working on a particular set task, develop ideas in similar ways to brainstorming, and provide each other with helpful advice in finding resources for projects and assignments. They can also provide support in the form of empathy and encouragement, the sort of thing that can happen during coffee breaks in more traditional programmes of study. As far as the tutor is concerned, it is important to encourage learners to make use of these facilities. Although some learners may be less forthcoming and even 'lurk' – that is, read the correspondence but make no contribution – there is evidence that learners benefit from participating (Hammond, 1998).

Seminars based on ICT conference facilities are similar to traditional seminars, where learners are asked to discuss a set reading or task and to present their own interpretation of it, or general points that can be applied to other aspects of their learning. The difference with ICT conferencing is that the discussion can take place asynchronously, giving learners time to think about and read about the issues before responding. The skill for the facilitator or animateur is to monitor and manage the threads in the discussion, offer advice and points for further debate but not to take over where the discussion is leading. With all discussion activities, it is important to draw out main points, ideas for further exploration and summarize the issues covered.

Checklist for ICT conferencing

- Are the instructions clear?
- Has there been a requirement for all learners to participate?
- Do learners understand their role in the conference?
- Is there a time limit on the asynchronous conferencing?
- What are the mechanisms for summing up the conferencing?
- Have learners been given time to prepare for the conference?
- Have learners access to the necessary hardware and software to be able to participate?
- Have rules of 'netiquette' been established and agreed?

Project work

There is sometimes an artificial distinction between teaching and learning methods and methods of assessment. Project work is one example where learning can be encouraged by undertaking a project but where the product can be used for assessment. Here, learners are asked to undertake a study, a series of tasks which drawn together are presented in a format which can be assessed, either informally or formally. The idea of project work is that learners are given some criteria which they must satisfy but there is flexibility in the content or in the way in which they go about gathering their information. As a teaching and learning method, it has the advantage that learners have to take responsibility for their own learning by discovering information about the topic and compiling this in some agreed format. Often, learners choose the content of their projects and, therefore, have more likelihood of engaging actively with the process. Project work enables learners to be self-directed. However, simply asking your learners 'to do a project on x' without clear guidelines may result in a variety of offerings of varying lengths, and probably a group of learners who have experienced some anxiety about what they were supposed to do. Often the first thing your learners will ask when you discuss project work is 'How long does it have to be?' and 'When does it have to be in by?' Decide what the project is about and why this is an appropriate way for your learners to find out about the topic. Are there parameters in the content? Can the project be done using video, web-based presentation, audiotape and through artwork? How will the project be assessed? A fuller discussion on assessment is found in Chapter 8. As a learning method, what will the project achieve?

Younger learners are familiar with project work through their experiences of compulsory schooling and increasingly will have this through the use of the Diplomas and A levels which have extended projects. Some older learners may be less secure about this method and will need some guidance about how to go about deciding on what to do, to plan the timescale and resources necessary and subsequently undertake the project. With all project work, the planning part of the process is most important. Therefore, when you decide to use this method, make sure you allow plenty of time for your learners to decide what to do and to plan their projects, with consultation and tutorial time built into the learning programme. The use of planning is a fundamental approach to learning, not just with project work but with all aspects of studying. Part of any learning curriculum is learning how to learn, and project work highlights this aspect in its emphasis on self-directed learning.

Individual and group projects

Projects can be undertaken by individuals or in groups. As noted above, both require clear guidelines and sufficient planning. Individual projects require supervision by the tutor or instructor. Group projects can be more demanding to organize because of the dynamics involved in individuals working together (Chapter 7). They also require time for the individuals to meet together to plan and then undertake the activities required. In any group there will be some members who tend to lead and organize, and others who will 'coast'. If the group has to make a presentation at the end of the project, there may be competition between the individuals to be the presenter, or there may be a reluctance to do so. Where the negotiation has led to each person having a specific task to do and to present this, the timing of the presentation may be particularly fraught. I remember one group presentation of five individuals, where the first took up three-quarters of the time allowed and her colleagues had to rush their own part of the presentation.

It is not possible to plan for every contingency using group projects, and there will be occasions where learners do not get along, cannot work together, and the resulting project is less than adequate. How you as a facilitator engage with such a situation is something for you to reflect on before you decide to use project work, and then while it is ongoing, to consider strategies that will enable your learners to complete the task.

Surveys and interviews

Research methodology can be employed in project work, including the use of interviews, questionnaires and surveys. There is not space to discuss these methods in detail, but there is a variety of textbooks available covering these methods including those specifically aimed at people working in the Learning and Skills Sector (see Hillier and Jameson, 2003). Here, I simply wish to state that learners can gather a lot of useful information for their projects if they employ qualitative research methods. As with all research, it is necessary to identify exactly what the learner wants to find out, then how best to go about this and what will be done with the information once it has been acquired. Planning is central to the success of any qualitative research method. The way in which questions are asked will provide a particular type of response. If research methods are going to be used as a teaching and learning method, adequate supervision of the planning and subsequent work is required. Permission must be sought before learners set off to ask questions of the public at large, and issues of confidentiality must be thoroughly dealt with. However, these methods do enable learners to find things out for themselves, and they often become enthused by the responses they obtain and put a lot of effort into their work as a result. It provides them with learning opportunities in the processes of gathering information and making sense of it, again, learning how to learn as well as learning the content of the project.

Checklist for projects

- Are the instructions clear?
- Is there an agreed timescale?
- Are there sufficient sources of information to be able to complete the project?
- Do individual learners know their responsibilities if the project is to be undertaken as a group?
- Are there ways to monitor learners' work and progress on the project?
- Are there clear criteria for the project?

Experiments

Most people associate experiments with the study of science. Here, a particular learning point is established by asking the learners to conduct a practical activity from which they can draw conclusions. Experiments are based in a scientific hypothetico-deductive method of thought, which basically states that if x, then y. For example, if we want our learners to know one of the laws of thermodynamics, then our initial hypothesis might be, 'If we heat water to 100 degrees centigrade, it will boil.' We then set up the experiment where our learners have water, test tubes, bunsen burners and thermometers. They have to heat the water until it reaches boiling point, and identify what the temperature is.

They might be asked to do this with different amounts of water, and with different levels of heat. By finding out that no matter how long it takes to boil or how much water is used, the temperature is always 100 degrees, we are beginning to establish a scientific law. (Of course, we can then look at the pressure of air, as this law only holds true for pressure at sea level.)

Experiments provide an opportunity for learners to discover laws that have already been established in the scientific community. They also learn techniques of measuring, observation and use of laboratory equipment. As with other teaching and learning methods, it is important to draw out learning points at the end. Experiments follow a particularly standard protocol and learners must acquire knowledge of these. As mentioned previously, health and safety issues are of paramount importance in any laboratory work.

Not all experiments need to be conducted in a laboratory with lab coats and goggles. Learners from a variety of disciplines could be asked to conduct experiments. For example, people studying floristry might be asked to place a set of flowers in two types of water, one from the tap, one using a sugar solution. They might be asked to observe which solution is more effective in preserving the flowers, or which flowers respond better to each type of solution.

Experiments are very useful in establishing logical rules and in encouraging deductive reasoning. Experiments are just one of a range of research methods that can be employed.

Checklist for experiments

- Is the equipment in good working order?
- Are the instructions clear?
- Have the learners got appropriate clothes and safety equipment to wear?
- Are there opportunities for all learners to participate?
- Are there handouts and written instructions?
- Do learners know how to record the experiment?
- Do learners know and apply the protocols in their experiments?

Visits to museums, galleries and organizations

A number of disciplines involve the study of artefacts. Where learners are working on characteristics of the artists, or of stages in the development of the art, it is helpful for them to see 'real-life' examples. An interesting consequence of the use of technology, where learners can bring up on-screen examples of paintings which they can compare side by side, is that more people are now visiting the originals in art galleries! As a teaching and learning method, visits to museums and galleries have the advantage of showing learners what has been discussed in the classroom. They provide opportunities for them to wander off and look at alternative examples and to see for themselves what has been discussed in books and in presentations. However, simply sending learners off to a museum and asking them to look around will not guarantee that they learn effectively. They need to know what they are looking for, perhaps with a task sheet to complete, or an assignment for which they must gather information found in the museum. On the other hand, much informal learning is derived from wandering around museums and galleries, which can be drawn upon in future learning sessions.

Visits to organizations require some careful planning if learners are to gain the information required. Careful briefing of both learners and organizational staff must take place in advance of the visit.

Checklist for visits to museums, galleries and organizations

- Has the organization been given notice in writing and confirmation received about intended visits?
- Do the organizations meet the necessary health and safety requirements?
- Has there been prior discussion about the purpose of the visit and negotiation of people to meet, things to observe, exhibitions to view?
- Have the learners clear instructions about what to look for or investigate during the visit?
- Are there handouts and are these to be given prior to the visit?
- Do learners need to undertake background reading prior to the visit?
- Are there any physical access requirements?
- Do learners know where to go and will they do this independently?
- Are there sufficient resources to meet the costs of the visit?

Conclusion

This chapter has discussed the main teaching and learning methods that are available. There are, of course, numerous permutations of each of these. As a reflective teacher, the process is one of deciding which to use and why, trying these out and then identifying what worked well and what did not work so well. The questions every time you try a particular method are: 'Did this method enable my learners to learn?'; 'Is there anything I need to do to improve my use of this method?'; 'Were there learners who did not learn so well with this method?'; 'Can I adapt the method to ensure that such learners can benefit from the method?'

LLUK standards

This chapter will enable you to work towards the following LLUK standards – Domain B: Learning and Teaching and Domain D: Planning for Learning.

Further reading

Armitage, A., Bryant, R., Dunnill, R., Hammersley, M., Hayes, D., Hudson, A. and Lawes, S. (1999) *Teaching and Training in Post-Compulsory Education*. Buckingham: Open University Press.

Bell, J. (1999) *Doing Your Research Project: A Guide for First-Time Researchers in Education and Social Science* (3rd edn). Buckingham: Open University Press.

Cohen, L. and Manion, L. (1999) *Research Methods in Education* (5th edn). London: Routledge.

Curzon, L. B. (1990) *Teaching in Further Education*. London: Cassell.

Fawbert, F. (ed.) (2003) *Teaching in Post-Compulsory Education: Learning, Skills and Standards*. London: Continuum.

Francis, M. and Gould, J. (2009) *Achieving Your PTLLS Award*. London: Sage.

Hillier, Y. and Jameson. J. (2003) *Empowering Researchers in Further Education*. Stoke-on-Trent: Trentham.

Minton, D. (1997) *Teaching Skills in Further and Adult Education*. London: Macmillan.

Petty, G. (2004) *Teaching Today: A Practical Guide* (3rd edn). Cheltenham: Nelson Thornes.

Saunders, G. (2000) *Getting Started with On-Line Learning*. Winchcombe: Learning Partners.

Working in Groups

> **Working in groups**
>
> It is the last week of the first term of a full-time, two-year Early Years Foundation Degree. Eighteen trainees have been divided into three groups of six and have been asked to produce a project on learning through play for 3-year-old children. They must choose activities which use a variety of materials including sand and water. They must specify what the children should learn from using the materials – for example, naming colours, developing their dexterity and verbal skills. They must create two resources to reinforce the learning – for example, a storyboard which uses colour and number. The project must be submitted in two months, and the group must make a presentation of one aspect of their chosen project as part of the assessment criteria.
>
> One group works well. The individual members divide the project into tasks, having discussed the overall project and what they wish to do. Each person in the group has a set responsibility, with agreed timescale. All individuals must report back to the group at set intervals, to show what they have done and to discuss if they need to make any changes.
>
> The second group takes longer to start work. The members do not all agree on the project idea and it takes a couple of meetings before they decide what needs to be done and by whom. When they do start work, some of the group members do not achieve what they have agreed to produce in time. When it comes to the final presentation, these individuals are absent from the session.
>
> In the group meetings, there are signs of a breakdown in communication. The initial idea for the project has been changed three times. One member tried to take control of the project and set the tasks for everyone else to follow. Her peers objected and refused to participate. A second member then came forward with alternative ideas. This was accepted by half the group and rejected by the others. When the final decision for the project idea was reached, valuable preparation time had been lost. Throughout the time allowed to work on the project, there were numerous arguments between the two members who had originally proposed ideas which had been rejected. One member simply ignored all group decisions and undertook her own 'mini' project. When it was time to make a group presentation, the project was unfinished, the individuals could not agree on who was making the presentation or on what. The individuals failed their assignment.

What processes did the individual group members go through in this activity? How can we ensure that groups of people work together effectively? If we are asking learners to work in teams, can we create activities which will foster team work and develop the skills of interacting with individuals? What is the role of the tutor in facilitating the learning through group work?

When people come together in groups, their behaviour is affected by a host of factors. Groups behave like people; that is, they are all different and have varying characteristics. This diversity in turn affects the individuals within any group. So there is a complex interaction between the individuals within the group and their effect on the group behaviour, and vice versa. The study of this complex interaction is known as group dynamics and is central to understanding how to facilitate the learning of group members.

Groups are very complex. The number of possible relationships in a group can be defined mathematically by the number of people in the group multiplied by that same number minus 1 and the result divided by 2. So, even with a group of 10 people, there are 45 possible different relationships that can occur at any given time.

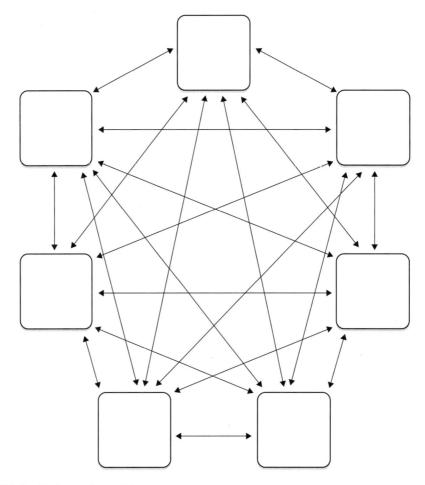

Figure 7.1 Possible interactions within a group

From such a permutation of interaction and diversity, we must consider how we can best facilitate the learning of individuals in any group setting. People who work with groups are called facilitators. The role of the facilitator is to enable members of a group to achieve certain objectives and goals while recognizing that group behaviour can take many forms.

What are the conditions for successful group work?

One of the first questions we can ask about groups is, what are the basic requirements for successful group work? Here are some of the main considerations:

- Groups need a clear purpose; where it involves learning, the aims, objectives and outcomes should be explicit.
- People need to understand the purpose of the group and be aware of whether or not they agree with this.
- People in groups need to know what is expected of them in terms of what they should contribute, and how.
- People in groups should be given the opportunity to make their expectations explicit. This helps to identify whether these are realistic.
- People need to know for how long the group will be working and meeting.
- People need physical space – when they work together in small groups, they need to be able to concentrate on their own work without hearing what is going on in the other groups. They need room to work, particularly, if they are performing an activity which involves, for example, writing on flip-chart paper.
- People need comfort – a room that is too hot or cold is uncomfortable. People need ventilation too!
- People need to know what the parameters are concerning timekeeping, whether late-comers will be tolerated, whether the group session will always start on time. If this does not happen, people will be more likely to arrive later.
- On the other hand, people are late for a variety of acceptable reasons. It is better that a facilitator does not repeat everything that has already been said each time someone arrives late!
- Timekeeping also involves finishing on time. Some people will leave early for understandable reasons. If sessions do not finish on time, there will be an increased tendency for people to drift away.
- People need to say how they wish to be addressed, particularly if they have a name which is not their formal name on a register.
- People need to feel accepted, needed and included in any group.
- People's need for safety may include being able to sit near the door, or near the facilitator, to opt out of certain activities, to think quietly.
(from Kindred, 1987)

As you can see from the list, a facilitator of a group of learners has much to consider. Not all of this is your responsibility. Heron (1989) helpfully provides a model of facilitation based upon the level of control that the facilitator uses. At the beginning of the life of a group, a facilitator may make most of the decisions about the content and the way in which the group will run. Later, this control may shift to individuals in the group and, in some cases, the decision-making will eventually rest entirely with the group itself. Where learners must meet a particular curriculum requirement, the level of autonomy will be reduced, but the way in which they decide to cover the curriculum can be negotiated and the individual members may be able to take responsibility for deciding when and how they approach the topics within the overall constraint of the curriculum.

Heron describes this variation in terms of modes of facilitation: hierarchical, co-operative and autonomous modes. He argues that these modes deal with the 'politics of learning': that is, the way in which people's experiences are managed in the learning situation. An effective facilitator will be able to move from mode to mode depending on the changing situation in the group. The three modes refer to all the activities involved in facilitation of learning: that is, planning, structuring, developing meaning, confronting, challenging, feeling and valuing.

Group members should be able to learn about the content and the tasks required, how to undertake the tasks, the process of performing the tasks and also learn how to identify processes for undertaking tasks. The learning, therefore, can be divided into two domains: 'learning about' and 'learning how to' (Heron, 1989, p. 21). The role of the facilitator is to enable each member of the group to not only learn about the matter at hand ('learning about') but also to learn about the process of doing this ('learning how to').

When groups come together to learn they go through stages within the life of the group. They begin with high anxiety and low trust – what Heron calls the 'winter' phase. They then begin to develop trust, ideas can creep through, they enter the 'spring' season. They then begin to fully function, bursting with life and activity, they are in the 'summer' phase. Finally, they begin to reach the end of the life of the group, they reflect on what they have achieved and the benefits they have reaped, the 'autumn' of their group's existence.

A different model is advocated by Tuckman (1965) who describes the phases of group life as forming, storming, norming and performing. His model allows for the way in which people 'jostle' for position within a group. Leaders emerge and then are sometimes succeeded by other contenders for the position. People begin to challenge each other's ideas. Tempers may fray. The norming phase occurs when the individuals within the group acquire a group identity and the activities of the group are performed well. There is consensus about the way in which activities are performed. This leads to the performing phase, which is similar to Heron's 'summer'.

The storming phase of a group's life is often challenging for the facilitator. People may behave in a variety of negative ways, including criticizing and directing anger at the facilitator, who 'draws the flak'. It is sometimes difficult to identify whether this is simply a result of the storming phase or whether there are justifiable criticisms which need to be acted upon. The reflective practitioner will expend much energy during this phase of a group's life.

Things that can challenge the life of a group

- Bids for leadership.
- Feeling left out.
- Subgroups which are exclusive.
- People becoming too involved with the welfare of individuals within their group.
- People who are quietly subversive by saying nothing, or making what Michael Kindred (1987) calls 'borderling remarks'.
- Hidden rules (also known as group norms).

- People's emotional barriers which are not acknowledged or confronted (for example, people who cannot cope with anger and so make the peace in any situation).
- Projection of aspects of an individual's personality onto others (e.g. calling someone else volatile when being volatile).
- Transferring emotions (being reminded of someone else and attributing that person's characteristics to a member of the group, for example, thinking someone is lovely because he is like someone's father).
- Scapegoating (blaming someone within the group for problems of the whole group, for example, 'We would have had a better mark if so and so hadn't messed up the presentation').
- Stereotyping (e.g. not paying attention to a particular member who is labelled 'the snob'.
- Scoring points off each other.
- Bringing 'baggage' from previous experiences, for example, a particular viewpoint like 'The tutors don't know what they are doing'.
- Overdependence on the facilitator.
- Not saying what is on people's minds (or waiting until everyone has left).
  (from Kindred, 1987)

How can a facilitator possibly deal with all these issues? One way to address them is to face them head-on at the very beginning of a group's life. This is done using a group contract.

Starting a group: the contract

One of the main features discussed in the literature (see Bion, 1961; Egan, 1976; Jacques and Salmon, 2007) is that of safety and how individuals within any group experience the presence or lack of it. Any facilitator of group learning must, therefore, recognize that all the individuals within the group are feeling and experiencing varying levels of safety. It is important very early on to establish a level of safety for members so that they can contribute to the work of the group and benefit from it.

How can this be done? One method is to ask individuals to create and agree a 'contract'. This is a negotiated agreement which identifies what is expected of each individual in the group, including the facilitator. It may include such items as timekeeping, respect for each individual's viewpoint and the right to express this. The idea that a contract should be agreed at the outset is an alien one to many people, particularly, if they have not studied for a long time and have expectations that the tutor is in charge. Introducing the contract, therefore, requires both sensitivity and planning.

Here are some ideas that can be included in a contract:

- Confidentiality
- Giving constructive criticism
- Not attacking, or putting down others
- Expressing feelings
- Observing timekeeping
- Honesty
- Listening to others
- Only one person to speak at a time
- Asking questions of clarity
- Right to keep silent
- Acceptance of the diversity of individuals within the group
- Sexist, racist language will not be tolerated
- Inclusive language to be used throughout.

Some of these terms will be unfamiliar to the group members and, therefore, it is important that they are explained fully. Some of the items may require discussion before acceptance. There are bound to be different interpretations of the meaning of some of the terms. The important thing is to ensure that people are treated with, and agree to treat others with, respect.

The act of negotiating a contract engages people in a dialogue with each other and with their facilitator/tutor. This is an important part of developing the life of the group, where individuals make their views known and learn about others' ideas. Facilitating this process requires skill in negotiation, patience and openness. Some of these values are those espoused by Carl Rogers (1983) who argued that we should have unconditional regard for our learners.

It is all very well establishing a set of guidelines in the form of a group contract, but how are these maintained? It is useful to write the agreed list on a flip-chart which can be kept for future reference. In some cases, it helps to put this up on the wall at the beginning of every session and remind participants of its status. This can also be written up and stored on the VLE which provides both a record of what was agreed and a reminder for when the group moves away from its contract.

Getting groups started: icebreakers

When people come together at the start of a learning programme, tutors may decide to use an 'icebreaker' to begin the first session. There are numerous ways to do this, some involving games and all using strategies to help the participants get to know something about each other. They can be placed on a continuum of safety and to a certain extent formality.

One of the least demanding icebreakers is to ask the people in the group to form pairs and then to ask each other their name and perhaps why they came along to the learning programme. People can then introduce their partner to the whole group.

A more game-like approach is to use a small object like a soft ball which is thrown by one person to another and the recipient has to provide information, for example, a name. A further extension of this activity is that the person with the ball has to state the name of the person to whom they are throwing it. Francis and Gould (2009) offer ideas for ice breakers which are useful for new groups of learners. Groups benefit from a variety of exercises which are like warming-up exercises throughout their lives. Jo Malseed (1992) has developed a series of activities that she categorizes as low, medium and high risk. The low-risk activities are very useful as icebreakers. The medium- and high-risk activities are better used once people have begun to know and trust each other as a group. An example of a medium-risk activity is where one person leaves the room and those remaining decide on an adverb. When the person returns, she or he must ask three of the group members to perform a task in the way specified by the adverb. The person must try to guess the adverb. Three guesses are allowed. The activity is repeated with a new person leaving the room.

An example of a high-risk activity is called Medusa's Raft where the group forms a tight circle, leaving one person outside of the circle. A chalk circle is drawn around the ring. The person outside has to try to get inside and the rest of the group has to try to prevent this happening, without stepping outside the chalk circle. The activity can then be repeated with someone from the inside trying to get out.

Great care must be taken with choosing warm-up exercises. Some groups are particularly experienced in using such activities (e.g. drama groups) and members will be prepared to put themselves into very unusual and demanding situations. New groups and certainly people who are very anxious about participating in games will need low-risk activities initially. The advantage of warm-up exercises is that they can prepare group members for working and mixing together. They can also raise the energy level in groups, particularly after lunch or passive periods. They can provide fun and help people enjoy their learning.

Group activities can help members reflect on how they are performing together as a group. One of the more interesting group activities I have observed and participated in is an activity called moving the piano (with thanks to Ann Wake for this). Here, the full group is divided into two groups. The first group is asked to decide how to move an imaginary piano (or an object which represents the piano) from one side of the room to another and then actually move the piano. The other group observes how the first group performs the task. The roles are then reversed. This activity is great fun but also shows how people take on the task, someone invariably becomes the leader, others may make suggestions which are not heard, and the final decision and carrying out of the task may not be executed effectively. The activity ends with the opportunity for reflection by the individuals on how people work in groups. They can then apply their insight into future group work.

Once a group has been formed, icebreakers employed and a contract agreed, the spring and summer phases, or norming (and storming) must be managed. How can we facilitate the full and effective participation of individuals within our groups? First, we can think about how the individuals will respond to each other. We rely on a number of signals that we interpret when we meet new people: the way they talk and what they talk about. We also gain a lot of information from what people do not say, in other words their non-verbal behaviour: their dress code, their actions, their mannerisms.

Non-verbal behaviour

People learn a lot about each other from their non-verbal behaviour. When individuals come together for the first time, they make a lot of judgements about their peers simply from observing behaviour and the way in which people project themselves through choice of clothes, hairstyle and accessories. This information is often misleading and can create difficulties in the future. Dress is particularly subject to cultural values. My own son, who chooses to wear his hair long with 'grungy' clothes is often avoided by older people in our local supermarket, presumably because they think he is threatening. He nearly caused a heart attack in one elderly couple when he approached them as they were standing by their trolley in the car park. He had only offered to help them load their shopping into their car! Such judgements really can colour the way individuals are responded to within any group situation. The facilitator, therefore, must take great care to ensure that all participants are not only treated with respect but that they are also given the opportunity to express themselves and demonstrate 'who they really are'.

Such individual differences can become polarized in small-group work. For example, some women may feel uncomfortable working with a man, or vice versa. An older person may not wish to work with a younger one. The reasons for this should be both challenged but also respected. This makes the role of the facilitator very demanding. How can we respect individual differences and values and then act to challenge or change them where they clearly contravene a code of inclusivity? Some facilitators achieve this by stealth, asking people to work in different groups throughout the life of the learning programme. Others do not direct the choice of individuals, provided the choice is one which is not deliberately exclusive. This aspect of group facilitation is one that you will develop your own particular strategy for dealing with. If the overarching criteria is one of respect and inclusivity, then it will guide you when you observe the way in which people choose to work together in small and large groups.

Speaking and listening

For any learning situation we must ensure that we facilitate the communication between ourselves and group members and between the learners in the group. We know that people respond to each other according to what is said and heard. Not only can words be misinterpreted by a listener, the way in which these are said, including any accent or dialect, will influence the interpretation by the listener. We are subject to very subtle cultural influences in how we receive messages from other people. A person's background is often judged on the strength of their accent. This clearly goes against the grain of inclusive practices, but it is difficult to be fully aware of how we respond to people's ways of speaking. We are influenced by cultural 'norms', and since the past century, by the projection in the media of such norms. For example, in the early days of radio, cinema news and television, only those with 'Home Counties' accents would be working in broadcasting, despite the number of well-qualified people with dialects from across the country and indeed the world.

Active listening

If groups are to work successfully, then individuals within them must develop skills of listening as well as talking. The skill of listening is one of paying attention, and ensuring that what has been said has been accurately received. This form of listening is called 'active listening'. Many of us will have experienced as children talking to an adult who murmurs 'Yes', 'Ah', 'Really' every so often but who seems preoccupied with another activity. We may have done this ourselves as adults! We are not listening actively here, but getting on with our own thoughts while trying to give the impression that we are hearing every word that has been said. Active listening, on the other hand, involves paying attention and being able to check that our interpretation is what was intended by the speaker. We, therefore, need to reflect back to our speaker what we think has been said, thereby, giving an opportunity for any immediate misunderstandings to be cleared up.

Egan (1990) has provided a helpful list of minimum requirements for active listening. These are as follows:

- face the speaker squarely
- adopt an open posture
- lean towards the speaker at times to suggest engagement
- maintain eye contact
- be relaxed.

Note that this list is one which will be acceptable in Western cultures but may not be acceptable in others (as noted in Chapter 5). Our behaviour may suggest engagement to one person but will be an invasion of personal space to another. In all our interactions, we are in danger of transgressing the personal space of another, and as facilitators we must be alert to this within our own groups.

It is self-evident that we need to develop our active listening skills – and so do our learners if we are to communicate effectively in our groups. It can be useful to bring this skill into focus with any group learning situation, so that learners can both establish and practise their skills. It can be extremely illuminating to listen to a particular small group during their discussion, looking out for examples where the members do reflect back to the speaker what has been said, or asking questions to clarify. Summarizing what has been said is another important feature of active listening. Asking people to get into discussion groups without having established the criteria for active listening may result in an erosion of the communication that takes place.

What can we do to improve the way in which our learners listen actively? One way is to practise the skill explicitly. For example, ask your learners to divide into groups of four. One person is asked to talk about a topic of their choice for five minutes. Another has to listen actively. At the end of the five minutes the listener is asked to reflect back to the speaker what has been said. The speaker can then either acknowledge that the reflection is accurate or specify what was inaccurately reflected. During this interchange the other two individuals observe the process. At the end they feed back to the speaker and listener how well the interchange captured the intended message. Everyone in the group has a turn to be speaker, listener and observer. Although this is a lengthy process, it does alert the individuals to how important active listening is and helps them develop and hone their skill in future discussions.

A second important requirement for group management is that the facilitator must be very clear in the instructions given to the group. Thus, if the individuals are being asked to discuss a reading, then what do they have to discuss and do they have to make a record of their discussion? The facilitation of the group, then, depends not only on how each individual respects those in the group, but also on the skills of listening and speaking and on clear guidelines for the activity to be undertaken.

Group dynamics

There are a number of models of how groups interact. These include psychodynamic and existential analyses (Bion, 1961; Erikson, 1978; Rogers, 1983; Yalom, 1980). Psychodynamic models focus on the idea that people will transfer their unconscious feelings to others. This transference can block effective learning. The individuals and the group as a whole may become defensive, and the role of the facilitator is to anticipate this possibility through expressing and modelling values of safety and trust. An existential approach does not explain people's behaviour from what has gone on before, while recognizing that they are in their current situation as a result of this. Rather, the existential model recognizes that individuals can be responsible for their actions and is, therefore, more forward-looking than the psychodynamic approach. Space does not allow for a full discussion of the underlying models of group dynamics. You may find Brockbank and McGill (1998) a useful resource if you wish to consider this topic in more depth.

The facilitator must be alert to the dynamics of the group and be able to identify some of the processes which are at work. For example, it may be that one person in the group ignores another or even makes dismissive statements that are not observed by anyone else in the group. The facilitator will be able to 'name' this situation, and enable the process of reflection to take place. This may result in feelings of aggression by the learners. It is not an easy thing to challenge learners, particularly on the emotional aspects of group dynamics. Facilitators will be in the firing line for many of the emotions being experienced, such as aggression or childlike demands for security. The way in which the situation is dealt with is both demanding and fraught with danger. Facilitators are *not* trained counsellors and should not attempt to be so. Groups learning together are not therapy groups. However, ignoring the emotional context of group learning is unhelpful too. Reflective tutors will continually analyse the discourse of the groups with whom they work and search for the explicit and hidden indicators of thoughts and feelings of the group members.

Emotion

Have you experienced sitting in a group and wanting to run out of the door or feeling so angry that you want to explode? Have you found yourself wondering why you came along to a group, as everyone else seems to know each other and you feel an alien? Have you ever thought that you may be exposed as an imposter any minute now and perhaps you had better keep very quiet and not draw attention to yourself? These are all examples of how people *feel* when they participate in groups. At any moment in the life of a group, people may be feeling a number of emotions: fear, anger, frustration, enjoyment, safety, warmth, insecurity, boredom. People have different ways of showing their emotions, or even of hiding their emotions. They usually demonstrate this through their body language. In Western cultures, people who are more positive towards a situation or another person may show this by sitting with their arms away from their body, facing the other person and engaging eye contact. When they are feeling negative, they may draw their arms around their chest and look down or away from other people. Great care must be taken with inferring people's emotional state from their body language. Body language has often been taken to imply one emotion when the person is actually experiencing something quite different. For example, it is often said that people who sit with their arms and legs folded are demonstrating negative feelings about some aspect of the group situation. In fact, it could be simply that they are very cold!

In groups, people are not going to experience warmth, security and positive regard for their peers just because they have all chosen to come to the same learning situation. In fact, if they are there because they are required to be, either due to an employment training programme, or as a compulsory component of a qualification, then they may begin with negative attitudes of suspicion, boredom or even anger. Other people may arrive with feelings of insecurity, anxiety and lack of confidence. When they come together, they will 'play out' their emotional feelings in a variety of ways. Some will deny these feelings and act as though they are experiencing the reverse. Many learners may act confidently, talk loudly and 'hog' the conversation to overcome their own feelings of panic and insecurity.

Others may simply be very confident and talk a lot. Therefore, it is not the case that all people who talk a lot are insecure! Heron (1989) distinguishes between two types of anxiety. The first, 'existential anxiety', is the sort that is perfectly normal, and includes such worries as 'Will I fit in?', 'Will I understand what to do?', 'Will I be able to do everything?' The second form of anxiety, 'archaic anxiety', is the type that draws upon a person's previous history of distress from the past, for example, hurt experienced in childhood, perhaps from parents who criticized educational failures. Although we all bring with us these emotional anxieties, when they are severe they become threatening and can result in dysfunctional learning.

Should the emotional state of group members be an issue which is discussed openly by the facilitator? People may not wish to have their feelings acknowledged in public, and certainly not to the whole group in the first session. They may choose to confide to another individual over an informal break. The facilitator can do quite a lot to bring the issue of emotion to the attention of the learners by modelling. This can be done by a technique called the critical incident technique (Flanagan, 1954) where an example of a case is identified and described from which general characteristics can be derived. For example, if we look at the 'Return to Study' programme discussed in Chapter 3, Sunil may decide that he wants his learners to think about their own doubts and fears and expectations in coming to college for the first time. He could describe a critical incident from his own learning, perhaps his first day at school. By describing this, particularly from an emotional viewpoint of being very lost and lonely and not knowing the rules, he may demonstrate that it is both acceptable to talk about such emotions and also spark off similar memories for his learners. There is a danger that this technique could lead to an overemphasis on negative emotions and, therefore, it is important to choose examples which exemplify positive and negative emotions. Once his learners have seen their tutor as an ordinary human being with hopes and fears, they may begin to feel more comfortable about owning up to their own feelings. Again, it is important to respect the right of group members not to disclose their feelings. Brookfield describes this well when he talks about the discomfort of sitting in a large circle and having nowhere to hide (1995, p. 9).

Brockbank and McGill discuss the way in which we should recognize the force of emotion in the learning situation of groups through the following factors:

- responsibility for emotion by 'owning' it
- storing up emotions
- assertiveness and the expression of emotions
- knowing your own emotional states
- 'parking emotions'.

Here the emphasis is on recognizing what emotions we are experiencing, acknowledging them, being able to assert to others how we are feeling in appropriate ways or waiting to deal with them appropriately at a later stage, something Brockbank and McGill call 'parking'.

Not everyone is able to recognize or label their emotions. People may repress or hide their emotions, and they may project them onto others, that is, they accuse another person of being angry, jealous or bored when in fact it is they who are experiencing the emotion. It is fair to say that working with groups of people is an 'emotional minefield', and acknowledging emotions can provoke very strong reactions in the group. The role of the facilitator, therefore, has to be one of managing the emotional turmoil but not to be responsible for other people's emotions. This is no easy task, particularly if the emotions being expressed are both forceful and negative.

Empathy

If people display such a range of emotions, how can we possibly understand or show that we understand how they are feeling? One way to do this is to have empathy for our learners. When we sympathize with people, we express our sorrow for what is happening to them. When we empathize, we do not necessarily know how they are feeling but we acknowledge that this is what they are feeling. Empathy is, therefore, quite distinct from sympathy. Carl Rogers proselytized the use of empathy when we work with other people. We remain 'unconditionally ourselves' even though we can identify with what the other person is experiencing. The role of empathy is fundamental to working with a diverse group of individuals, who may have a range of cultural backgrounds, beliefs and practices. With empathy, we are not trying to *pretend* to be the same as they are, but to try to understand from their perspective. If we are empathetic, we can begin to understand a situation from another person's perspective, and this helps us to work together. Being truly empathetic requires that we are able to communicate accurately what another person is experiencing. For example, in a group of learners, one person may be experiencing difficulty with the task. A peer would be empathetic if she could state 'You feel anxious because you can't see what we have to do with this tasksheet' rather than saying 'I think you are anxious.' The first statement expresses what the other person is feeling and the source of that feeling, the second is just making a claim that could be totally inaccurate.

A facilitator can do much to acknowledge another person's feelings. One of the annoying phrases used excessively these days is 'I hear what you say' when in fact the opposite is the case. A better way is to reflect back to the speaker what has been observed, as in the example above. Not everyone will show their emotional state explicitly. For example, if someone in the group is not participating the facilitator might make a comment like 'I can see you are not saying anything at the moment, Surinder. I wonder if you are a bit at sea over the task I have set? Are you feeling a bit lost?' This statement offers an opportunity for Surinder to either acknowledge his difficulty with the task or to inform the facilitator of what actually is the case. However, Surinder may decide to hide behind a more publicly acceptable excuse like 'I was thinking about the next assignment' or 'Sorry, I was daydreaming.' People do not have to own up to their private feelings and they certainly should not have to do so just because a facilitator asks them. On the other hand, not acknowledging feelings may get in the way of the group's activities or individual's learning.

When we acknowledge other people's feelings in the group, we must make sure we do not go on to make judgements about these, or offer interpretations or advice. Beware of statements like 'If I were you . . .' or 'Don't worry, you'll be OK.' It is important to encourage your learners to avoid making judgements too, while acknowledging the emotions and opinions of their peers. This skill will be particularly valuable for team work and can be evidenced for the key skill of 'working with others'.

Dealing with conflict

There are numerous examples of challenges arising from people's behaviour in groups that we need to manage. These include learners who talk to each other persistently, or who may distract other learners, using mobile phones and texting throughout a session, 'messing about' with inappropriate behaviour such as throwing paper or knocking someone else's belongs over. Such annoying behaviour is the kind of thing that becomes disturbing over time even though each individual incident is not in itself really serious. Yet, not dealing with it straight away makes it much harder to tackle later on. Sue Cowley (2010) provides very helpful advice on how to deal with younger people in these situations. In the example at the beginning of this chapter, one group was unable to work effectively. Two members argued, and one did not work with the rest of the group. Conflict often occurs in group work. It is something that few of us have been trained to deal with. We have all experienced it in different ways and contexts in our lives, and we may have developed strategies for coping with it ranging from fear, avoidance or by aggressive confrontation. Egan (1976) helpfully describes a way of dealing with conflict through reflective dialogue. He suggests we can develop three skills to deal with conflict: empathy, confrontation and immediacy.

The form of empathy required is a more advanced version of the previous account. Here Egan suggests we offer to the other person a tentative 'understanding of the world from another's point of view', as we are not sure that the person is aware of the feeling concerned. This is a bit like guesswork, where you might find you have to say something like 'You seem a bit cross, Paul. Perhaps you are frustrated at how long it is taking to use this particular technique?' So with dealing with conflict, it is possible for the facilitator to offer a possible description of the emotion being experienced by a person in the group and a reason for this occurring. It is by bringing the emotion out into the open that the next part of the process, confrontation, can begin.

Confrontation is where the facilitator attempts to make the learner aware of the resistance or blocks to learning. This does not mean that the facilitator should act in an aggressive way, which is another interpretation of the word 'confrontation'. It may feel like this to a learner being challenged, but the facilitator must offer the challenge in an 'enabling way'

(Brockbank and McGill, 1998, p. 202). It helps if the facilitator can offer choices when confronting a learner. For example, if a learner is avoiding written work due to fear of failure, then the facilitator may offer not just a view that this may be happening but suggestions of alternative approaches. Confronting can be positive, too. For example, 'You said you wanted to have another go at the assignment and I would like to hear how you think you will now go about revising it.'

The third component in Egan's approach to dealing with conflict is immediacy. This is 'the ability to discuss with another person what is happening between the two of you in the here and now of an interpersonal transaction' (Egan, 1976, p. 201). This is a particularly demanding skill of interpersonal relations within groups. It can be described as not only stating one person's view of the other person's feelings, but also acknowledging how it is being experienced. For example, a facilitator may say 'I sense that you are feeling very negative about this module and I can see that you are not participating in the group discussion. I feel worried about this.' Immediacy, therefore, involves a high level of self-disclosure and describes what is going on at that moment in time. A facilitator who models the three skills of empathy, confrontation and immediacy will both challenge his or her learners and also enable them to develop their own reflective skills.

One danger to avoid is what Heron (1989) calls 'pussyfooting and clobbering'. He warns us against 'pussyfooting' which is avoiding confrontation by 'skirting round the issue' and the reverse, 'clobbering', which is being too heavy-handed and literally bashing the group in a punitive way. These behaviours are symptomatic of an anxious reaction which results in the equivalent of fight or flight. We must recognize that dealing with the emotional issues within a group will also create our own emotional responses which we need to acknowledge and work with. The importance of critical reflection for this aspect of our work is paramount. How can we foster an open approach to the emotional facet of group behaviour if we do not approach our own emotional feelings in the same way?

Working with younger learners

As noted in Chapter 1, one of the new groups of learners that the Learning and Skills Sector now deals with is 14–16-year-olds. They have specific needs, particularly in group settings, that require careful attention. In particular, you may find yourself dealing with issues of discipline and control that you would not normally have experienced if you have only taught mature adult learners. Most of the suggestions contained in this chapter are pertinent for this age group, and you may find that you will need to spend time identifying the most appropriate means to facilitate a successful group dynamic. You may also find that extending your reading to literature primarily aimed at secondary school teachers will give you some insights in dealing with young people who have not yet reached an equilibrium in their behaviour (see Cowley, (2010) and Francis and Gould (2009)).

Mixed-level groups and differentiated learning

So far, we have acknowledged that people within groups form complex relationships. Many tutors are challenged by the different levels of ability that people have when they come together to learn. Dealing with mixed-level groups is something that has occupied many educational theorists and it has been the subject of much educational policy-making in compulsory education. Did you experience being placed in groups at primary school, perhaps being given a colour but realizing that the 'red' group was much better at reading than, say, the 'green' group? In much of secondary education in the UK, pupils are placed in 'sets' for English, mathematics, languages and science. In further education, a sifting process has usually occurred, where young people who are predicted good grades at 'A' level tend to study in Sixth Forms at school or in sixth-form colleges, and those with lower grades in further education. In higher education, there has been a filtering process so that learners will only be accepted for study if they have satisfied certain entry requirements, which usually means that they have a certain level of ability prior to studying. In adult education, there is virtually no division into levels of ability, although there are some courses such as languages which specify a level of study such as beginners and advanced French. In business and employment training, there are certain training programmes which must be undertaken by all employees, regardless of grade and experience. Health and safety training is a case in point. With training for unemployed people, again there is no division of trainees into ability groups per se, although the level of qualification being trained for may act as a partial filter.

Thus, in post-compulsory education, people are learning together from the basis of very varied levels of ability in a range of domains. Chapter 4 discussed one example of this, a basic skills group. What strategies can be used to ensure that all learners can successfully participate in a learning programme?

Using options

It is possible to divide the content of any learning programme into a set of core activities with optional follow-on exercises and activities for people who wish to learn more or practise more. It is important to make sure that the optional activities are perceived by the learners to be just that. They are not compulsory and it is not an indication of failure if people do not undertake them. Web-based learning applies this model, where people can click on to other sites if they wish.

At times, it is helpful to ask more experienced learners to work with those who have less experience. This is not to 'keep them busy' but it helps to reinforce their own learning by working with another person. The less experienced person may find it useful to ask questions from another learner who has just been through the process rather than to ask the tutor. In practical subjects, particularly, those which are in the 'non-vocational' curriculum, learners enjoy seeing what can be achieved by those more experienced, and the more experienced learners can both motivate their peers and also celebrate their achievements.

Working in subgroups may help mixed-level learners. This should not be necessarily a division of ability, although at times it may be appropriate to do this. Great care must be taken to ensure that people feel valued and motivated to learn. Try to ensure that your learners do not always work together in the same group. Be particularly sensitive to those learners who appear diffident, or who are finding it difficult to learn the topic under consideration. There is no single 'correct' way of using small-group work. This is where experimenting and reflecting on the outcome are essential. Did it work to put the more confident learners together and to give the other learners a chance? Was it better to spread the confident learners throughout the groups? Did pair work help bring out ideas from the more self-conscious learners? The overriding factor you are seeking is how any particular group of learners can work together effectively so that each individual can benefit.

Using resources within groups

The first resource in any group is the learners themselves! Remember that individuals can contribute a great deal to a learning situation from their own experiences. However, it is your responsibility to provide the other resources for learning in groups, even if you are asking your learners to bring certain materials with them. For example, you may be working with a group of trainees on writing a curriculum vitae (CV). You can bring a variety of application forms to the session. However, you may also decide that you want your trainees to find out about some jobs they may wish to apply for and to bring this information with them to the session. You can then ask them to look at the different ways in which organizations seek applications for jobs and begin to draw out general themes or particular points that you hope they will begin to address when they create a CV.

In all group work there is a danger that much of the discussion will be lost unless there is a way to record it. You can create crib sheets for people to be reminded of the task in hand, with spaces for them to record their discussion or aspects of the task which they are completing. You may ask them to record the main points of the discussion on flip-chart sheets and place these around the room for all learners to see. It is often helpful for someone to record these afterwards and a copy to be made for the group members. However, be careful that you do not simply create lists which, out of context, prove meaningless. I can remember being very impressed by a then new piece of technology which was a whiteboard which could produce a single A4 copy of what had been drawn on it. This could then be photocopied so that all participants would have a record. When I look back at my copies of a particular training programme, I can see a lot of diagrams and writing, but it now seems like so much 'noise'. My own notes make more sense to me. Chapter 5 discussed the necessity for handouts that are going to be meaningful in the future, and diagrams and other flip-chart and whiteboard work are often 'ideas in progress'. The same argument applies to records from IWBs and even wikis and blogs can appear meaningless after the event.

Facilitating learning in groups: accommodation and seating arrangements

If you want your learners to interact with each other, then sitting them in rows facing the front is less likely to work than if they are seated in groups around a table, or in a U shape facing you (or whoever is presenting at the time). Creating seating arrangements so that there is eye contact between individuals is vital to facilitate discussion and enable the individuals to see each other more easily.

It is not always possible to use a seating configuration for group work due to constraints in accommodation. If you have a classroom which has heavy tables which cannot be easily lifted, then moving these out of the way so that people can sit in a U shape will be difficult. You must remember that health and safety rules will prohibit you from putting either yourself or your learners in danger of back injury by moving furniture in inappropriate ways.

Can you find ways around this? Can your learners work in pairs? Can they move the chairs and sit around tables in groups of three or four? I once observed a film studies class which had to be conducted in a lecture theatre to have access to the appropriate video equipment. The tutor asked the learners to discuss in small groups, the aspects of two film clips he had just shown. The learners were able to group together through a mixture of sitting closely along the rows and turning around to talk to their peers in the row behind. It was not ideal but at least the formal tiered lecture theatre format did not prevent the tutor from using small-group work.

There may be some topics that require additional 'break-out' rooms for group work: for example, where learners need to put together a presentation which is going to be assessed by their peers, or where learners need to work on case studies that also require role-play. One of the more effective case studies using role-play is where each group has to act as a board of enquiry and they have to ask questions of three people who take it in turns to visit each of the groups. At the plenary, the groups can share how they went about the task as well as what conclusions they reached from their questioning. This process is often used when training employees for recruitment and selection procedures.

Groups online

So far, I have discussed how groups interact when they are in a traditional face-to-face situation. Are there different considerations when working with groups online? We can observe non-verbal behaviour when we are sitting in the same room as our learners, but how can we know what is happening when all we can see are the messages that are being sent in chatrooms and online seminars? There are different issues for people interacting online. There is the danger that the 'tone of voice' in a message can be misunderstood more easily and, therefore, may arouse a host of responses which may be avoided in a face-to-face situation. People can also 'flame': that is, become more emotional in their messages than they would face to face. Imagine a scenario where people are being asked to discuss a particularly controversial issue online. If they were meeting in a group, they might disagree vehemently and there may be eruptions of anger. However, the individual group members and the facilitator may decide to address the conflict directly. Online, the discussion may be asynchronous. What can the facilitator do to deal with possible conflict when it is building up over an extended period of time and may only involve some of the learners? Hammond (1998) helps us here. He recommends that people need comfort zones where they can 'warm up' before discussing contentious issues. There has to be a level of trust, in the same way as for traditional group work, but there are rules of etiquette for online work, often called 'netiquette', which should be followed. For example, people need to know what part of the thread of the discussion any contribution is referring to. They need to be able to say that they agree or disagree without drawing criticism from their peers. The issue, not the contributor, is the focus of the discussion. If people have not met each other before working online, then the level of anonymity can increase the likelihood of contributions being more direct than those from face-to-face groups. People can also decide not to join in at all, but just read other people's contributions, which is known as 'lurking'. This term has somewhat sinister connotations. I would prefer a term that could reflect that people may simply not have anything to contribute, or have not yet built up confidence to send a message online.

Working with groups online is not necessarily full of 'doom and gloom'. Taking part in an online discussion for the first time can be great fun. Finding that your messages appear on screen instantly and get mixed up with other people's messages that have been sent simultaneously can read a bit like the game 'Consequences'. VLE supported discussions can be a good way to establish a learning group because they can take place synchronously and people can gain instant feedback from their comments. Their confidence to engage can be built up quickly so that they will be more likely to become involved in future group-based activities online, including conferences which may take place asynchronously.

Conclusion

This chapter has looked in detail at the complex nature of learning in groups. It draws upon the study of group dynamics and upon the notion that people react to group situations emotionally as well as intellectually. It offers ideas for undertaking group work and builds upon the ideas of planning carefully for learning in a group situation. Working with groups can be full of surprises, and many of these result in rewarding experiences. As a reflective practitioner, we can try out ideas, adapt from previous experiences and develop our confidence when meeting new groups and new situations. We can borrow ideas from observations of our colleagues, or from our own experiences of learning in groups. We can create our approaches which reflect our individual personalities and how we adapt to the very different groups that we work with. We may never meet all the situations I have outlined in this chapter. What we can do is continually build and extend our repertoire of strategies. The important issue in considering group work is whether it provides opportunities for people to engage in learning without restricting the level at which they can learn.

Now that we have looked at how we can ensure that our practice facilitates the learning of adults, our next question to be reflected upon is how we know that our learners are actually learning.

LLUK standards

This chapter will enable readers to work towards the requirements of LLUK standards – Domain B: Learning and Teaching and Domain D: Planning for Learning.

Further reading and information

Further reading

Brockbank, A. and McGill, I. (1998) *Facilitating Reflective Learning in Higher Education*. Buckingham: SRHE/Open University Press.

Cowley, S. (2010) *Getting the Buggers to Behave*. London: Continuum.

Egan, G. (1976) *Interpersonal Living: A Skills/Contract Approach to Human Relations Training in Groups*. Monterey, CA: Brooks/Cole.

Erikson, E. H. (1978) *Adulthood*. New York: Norton.

Heron, J. (1989) *The Facilitator's Handbook*. London: Kogan Page.

Jacques, D. and Salmon, G. (2007) *Learning in Groups: A Handbook for Face-to-Face and Online Environments* (4th edn). London: Routledge.

Kindred, M. (1987) *Once upon a Group*. Southwell: Southwell Diocesan Education Committee.

Luft, J. (1984) *Group Processes: An Introduction to Group Dynamics* (3rd edn). MountView, CA: Mayfield.

McGill, I. and Brockbank, A. (2004) *The Action Learning Handbook: Powerful Techniques for Education, Professional Development and Training*. London: RoutledgeFalmer.

Malseed, J. (1992) *48 Warm-Ups for Group Work*. Lancaster: Lancaster University.

Race, P. (2000) *500 Tips on Group Learning*. London: Kogan Page.

Rogers, C. (1983) *Freedom to Learn for the 1980s*. Columbus: Merrill.

Tuckman, B. (1965) 'Development sequence in small groups', *Psychological Bulletin*, 63, pp. 384–99.

Vizard, D. (2007) *How to Manage Behaviour in Further Education*. London: Paul Chapman.

Yalom, I. (1980) *Existential Psychotherapy*. New York: Basic Books.

Useful website

http://toolboxes.flexibillearning.net.acwww.icebreakers.ws

Assessing Learning

Chapter Outline

What has been learnt?

It is the last session of the course. Patrick's group are discussing what they have learned from the ten-week course they have been attending on 'The Great Philosophers'. They have a copy of the original programme outline and the learning outcomes. This stated that at the end of the programme, the learners would be able to specify the key arguments of ten philosophers, including two from Chinese philosophy. They would be able to adopt a critical reading of the works of these philosophers. They would be able to identify how the philosophers had dealt with the two themes of knowledge and ethics. However, the group discussions strayed quite significantly from the original plan and, by negotiation, the group had decided to concentrate on the work of Kant and Spinoza. What have the learners achieved? Does it matter that they have covered different topics from the original plan? Some of the group members find it difficult to say if they have achieved some of the learning outcomes. They know more about the work of Kant and Spinoza, but are they sure that they now can apply critical approaches to their analysis? What can Patrick do to help learners identify what they have learned? Why should he do this and who needs the information?

Learning from mistakes

Gladys is upset with her project, making a children's mobile. She could not make the model work. Her pieces of cardboard went soggy when she stuck them together and they did not create the structure that was necessary to support the little bells that would provide the sound required for her mobile. She was exasperated with it and did not think she would meet the assessment criteria for the task. Gladys's tutor, Camille, sat down and asked Gladys what she realized she needed to do to make the mobile work. They went through the stages of planning, finding resources, making the mobile and evaluating how well it had been created. By the time this process had been conducted, Gladys realized that although the *mobile* had not worked, she had learned a lot about materials and how they behaved, how necessary planning and testing out ideas are to the process. She even had the kernel of a new idea for her next attempt.

In both scenarios, the learners do not necessarily realize how much they have learned from their activity. Sometimes they may have focused on the criteria for the particular assessment task and they may have missed key areas of learning, which are to do with learning how to learn. How can you ensure that your learners are able to realize what they have learned? What are the difficulties in assessing learning?

This chapter discusses assessment, why it is necessary, what can be assessed, how it can be done, difficulties with the assessment methods, and strategies to ensure that learners are assessed fairly. I will discuss qualifications and how tutors and trainers may be required to be qualified to assess. Throughout, the varying needs of the individuals who are assessed will be central to the issues raised.

Why assess?

An obvious answer to this question is that it is demanded by awarding bodies and learning organizations. Those of you who are involved with learning programmes leading to qualifications will know how much of your time is taken up with assessing your learners' work. However, how much of their learning must you assess? What can you do to ensure that your view is an accurate one? These are complex and demanding issues. So much of a learner's subsequent life-choices may depend on the assessment decisions that you make.

From our learners' point of view, assessment always defines the actual curriculum (Ramsden, 1992, p. 187).

There are other reasons for assessing our learners apart from needing to know that they can meet the criteria to gain qualifications. Assessment helps you and your learners know how much progress they are making while undertaking a programme of learning. It provides evidence for funding bodies or purchasers of learning that the quality of provision is having an affect, that is, that people are learning. Assessment can be used to diagnose whether people are ready to take a particular learning programme, or have the necessary skills and knowledge to embark on a programme. This is known as diagnostic assessment. Chapter 3 showed how important initial assessment, including diagnostic assessment, is when identifying your learners' requirements prior to joining a learning programme. Assessment can occur, therefore, at the beginning, during and at the end of a programme of learning.

In compulsory schooling, children in the UK are increasingly subjected to tests to establish if they are learning at a level appropriate for their age. There is a range of national qualifications for which they study when they reach secondary age. These qualifications are also available to adult learners. The difference between the two groups is often that schoolchildren must follow a national curriculum and are expected to take certain subjects, particularly at GCSE level, in English language, mathematics, sciences and a foreign language. Adults may need to gain a particular qualification in order to progress to further study, employment or to meet organizational requirements. It is vital, therefore, that they are assessed fairly and that they are able to meet the assessment requirements in appropriate ways if they have any specific learning or physical disability.

The power dimension

There is an important power dimension to assessment. Many assessment processes contain a series of checks and balances to ensure that learners are assessed fairly and that assessors are not compromised. In some situations, examination papers, assignments and portfolios are assessed by two people. Often, the learner's name is not known to the assessors at the time of marking. This system protects both learner and assessor, as there have been cases in the past where assessors could abuse their power and demand certain favours of their learners, or learners could attempt to influence the grades that they obtained. Authority, of course, resides with the assessors who judge the quality of the work and this is an important and necessary feature of any assessment process.

Many people acknowledge feelings of powerlessness when they know that their tutors or trainers can influence whether or not they gain jobs or places on courses as a result of the assessment outcome. We often forget, as tutors and trainers, that even though we are behaving professionally in all of our assessment practices, our learners still feel vulnerable. The more explicit our assessment procedures are, the more reassured they may be.

Formal and informal assessment

Assessment takes place all the time, even though there is a temptation to think that assessment means taking tests and examinations. Think about a group of learners whom you teach. When they ask you a question, you may be able to judge how far they have grasped a particular concept that you may be covering by the type of question asked. If they discuss an issue that you had introduced earlier, then you find that they are using ideas that they have developed from earlier sessions and are now building upon them. You did not need to set them a test in order to find out that they are learning about the topics you have introduced. This informal means of assessing provides a great source of information to you when you go about planning subsequent learning activities and sessions. For example, you may see that the way that your learners had difficulty in answering some of your questions, or the way in which they asked you a lot of questions, means that they have not yet learned the topic or concept being covered to the required level. You can then make adjustments to your teaching so that they can have the opportunity to learn what is necessary. You may find that they have learned far more about the topic than you realized by the way they drew upon concepts and ideas in a discussion or piece of writing. You may then decide to spend less time on that part of the programme and move forward to the next stage. Informal assessment is, therefore, a feedback loop which helps you constantly adjust what you teach and how you cover the content of the learning programme.

Formal assessment takes place when your learners must meet specified requirements, for example, through sitting externally set examinations and tests, or undertaking project work or assignments. The important feature of formal assessment is that it *counts*. It does not matter if the assessment takes place throughout a programme of learning or just at the end; if it is formal, then the results of the assessment activity count towards a final qualification or record of achievement.

One important factor in assessment is how useful the information gained can be. There is a tendency for learners to think of assessment as being the endpoint, as noted at the beginning of this chapter and even for teachers and tutors to do likewise. Black and Williams (1998) famously argued that school teaching was contributing to this notion and that this kind of assessment was assessment *of* learning whereas they argued it was much better to think of assessment *for* learning. In their research which became known as 'Inside the black box', the authors showed that assessment that helps give learners and their tutors knowledge of what they do know and can do and also what they have yet to learn is much more productive. With this approach in mind, the following section examines the different forms of assessment and methods.

Formative and summative assessment

Both formal and informal assessment can be used during and at the end of any learning programme. Assessment can also take place during a phase of learning, or at the close of a learning programme. Formative assessment occurs when you assess learning *throughout* a programme of learning. Summative assessment occurs at the *end* of a programme of learning, or a module of learning. Formative assessment helps you and your learners find out how much progress they have made during the course of a learning programme. Clearly, the longer the programme, the more use can be made of formative assessment. It is less used in short 'one-off' training sessions and workshops.

Why use it? For example, you may be working with a group of NVQ trainees. Each time they demonstrate a particular skill, you may be able to assess their performance and 'sign off' their record for their final portfolio of evidence. If you are working with a group of 'A' level learners, you may be helping them work towards module tests, all of which count towards their final 'A' level grade. With 'A' levels, you may also be helping your learners cover the content of the syllabus so that they will be able to answer examination questions at the end of the course.

Informal assessment may take place throughout a programme of learning which also uses formal assessment methods. In the example of modular programmes, as you cover each module you will be making judgements about your learners' readiness to take the end-of-module examination based on assignments and work produced. The most extreme use of informal assessment is where there is no requirement to meet any externally set standard or qualification, but where learners identify what they have gained from the learning activity. Learners in a parents' group which is preparing for childbirth, for example, do not have to sit an examination before they can have the baby, but they do need to have information and an understanding of what is going to happen and what to do!

Summative assessment takes place when a summary of the learning that has taken place is required. This is usually at the end of a course, although it also can be used at the end of individual modules or units that count towards a full qualification. Summative assessment may draw on the formative assessments that have been undertaken or it may be a completely new activity, such as an examination or a project. A major feature of summative assessment is that it provides an overview of the learning that has taken place and, in the case of qualifications, may help identify a particular level or grade of the award.

Table 8.1 shows the type of questions we could ask for the four possible forms of assessment activity. As you can see, formal assessment always contributes to the identification of

Table 8.1 Types of assessment

	Formative	Summative
Informal	Where are we so far? What do we want to do next?	What did we learn?
	Example: a fitness class for people with arthritis	Example: an introduction to art history class
Formal	How much of the assessment specification/learning outcomes have we achieved?	Did we achieve all the learning outcomes?
		What grade/level have we attained?
	Example: an NVQ portfolio development workshop	Example: 'A' levels

achieved outcomes as specified by the programme. Informal assessment does not necessarily do this.

Assessment is inextricably linked with learning outcomes. Chapter 3 discussed how important it is to plan the learning outcomes and to remember to think about how you will identify when and if these learning outcomes have been achieved. Formative and summative assessment can be used to help identify the achievement of these specific learning outcomes. In most learning programmes, there is a requirement for the learners to provide evidence of their learning outcomes and for their tutors or trainers to keep careful records of when and how this has occurred.

You may not be able to specify your own learning outcomes or the forms of assessment within certain learning programmes, as these may have been set by awarding bodies. For example, you may be teaching 'A' levels where your learners have to take an examination at the end of their course and they must meet the specific standards set by the examining bodies.

The necessity to construct learning outcomes carefully will become apparent when you consider the following examples.

History of Art Course

Learning outcome: Learners will be able to appreciate the influence of scientific developments in nineteenth-century painting.

What does 'appreciate' mean? How can we assess that someone has appreciated something? I could say that I really appreciate the coincidence that scientific developments took place at a time when painters began using different paints in the nineteenth century. What does this tell you about my learning? I could say that I really understand that, without the developments in the chemical industry, there would have been no change to the type of paint and the way in which it was used, thereby, altering how painters construed their ideas about art. This answer gives a little more detail, but it still does not provide much evidence of what I may have learned in the course. I could go into precise details about dates of the particular chemical applications and link these to dates when certain genres began to appear in the world of painting. I could similarly discuss applications to other art forms. Here, there is far more evidence that I have analysed the influence on scientific developments on nineteenth-century painting. How much do I have to know to be assessed as 'appreciating the influence of scientific developments'?

How will I show my 'appreciation'? Will I need to write an essay? Will I need to put together a portfolio with specific examples from paintings I have downloaded from a website? How do you know that I actually appreciate how these developments influenced painting if I have just produced a chronologically arranged set of paintings? Could I do a presentation where I have to explain why I have chosen to discuss certain works of art in relation to the chemical industry?

What if I do not tell anyone about my ideas but I really do understand about the influence of the chemical industry on art in the nineteenth century? Already we can see that assessing is not as easy as it seems! My learning outcome is not specific enough for me to devise clear assessment strategies. Let us look at another example.

Management NVQ

Learning outcome: Candidates will be able to conduct a grievance procedure.

How will I show that I can conduct a grievance procedure? Do I just list what my organization's procedure is? Can I demonstrate this? I might not know anyone with whom I have to undertake a grievance procedure (hopefully!). So how am I going to demonstrate that I can do this? If I do a simulation, will this be acceptable? Will my peers who participate in the simulation behave appropriately, or will they be perfect participants and not provide me with an opportunity to show how I can handle difficult situations? Will I know how to behave if the person involved in the grievance procedure is unco-operative? If I can show that I can conduct a grievance procedure today, how does this show that I can do it many times? How *well* do I have to conduct the grievance procedure?

As you can see from the two examples, it is very difficult to identify the most appropriate way to assess a learning outcome if the latter has not been specific in exactly what should take place and how. However, there is no assessment procedure which will capture every nuance of a person's achievement, and there is no learning outcome which is so specific that it is not open to differing assessment judgements. The aim of assessment practice, then, is to try to maximize the identification of what has been learned and to what level of specificity in the most efficient and effective way. This is a tall order.

What are the dangers of getting it wrong? There are two main errors which can result from assessment practices. The first is where learners really do know or can do something but the assessment does not show this. For example, people may become very nervous in a test or examination and although they have learned what is required and have revised carefully, they 'go to pieces' on the day of the examination and do not write their answers well. It could be said that not only have they failed the examination, but also that the examination system has failed them. The second type of error is when the assessment method signifies that people have achieved something when in fact they do not actually have the skills or knowledge. For example, with multiple test questions, it is possible to guess the correct answer either by process of elimination of the other choices or by chance. These two errors have serious consequences. The system of checks and balances that is built into assessment procedures is there to try and eliminate either of these errors. You have only to read the national press after the examination results of GCSE and 'A' levels to see how controversial the forms of assessment are. There are assertions that examinations have become easier, that people can cheat and that there is inbuilt unfairness. With the increasing use of technology, people have more opportunities to cheat, for example, by downloading assignments and pasting these into their own work.

Assessment methods

Let us consider some examples of assessment methods. The list below is not comprehensive. It covers formal and informal methods which can be used prior to, during and at the end of any learning programme. You may not be required to use all of these methods, but as your experience grows, you may find that you can add some of these ideas to your sessions, particularly, where you can devise your own formative assessment strategies.

- Tests
- Written examinations (seen and unseen)
- Assignments/essays
- Projects
- Multiple choice
- Oral examination
- Discussion
- Role-play
- Simulation
- Case study
- Presentations
- Demonstration
- Skills test
- Lab tests/demonstrations
- Investigation/research
- Portfolio of evidence.

Which methods do you currently use? Why do you do so? It may be that you have to use certain methods because the awarding body or course leader has prescribed these. One of the first considerations for choosing assessment methods is 'Does the method measure what you intend it to measure?' In other words, is it a *valid* method? For example, suppose

I want to assess your ability to swim. If I asked you to lie face down on the floor and show me your swimming strokes, I would be able to see you demonstrating that you can use different strokes, but I would not be able to see that you can *swim*. I would have to see you in the water, and would need to see you swim a certain length without going under water or without stopping to put your feet on the swimming-pool floor. So my chosen method of assessment has to be fit for the purpose.

There are two broad categories of assessment methods: those that measure performance and those that measure knowledge and understanding. Criticisms of certain forms of assessment are often made because they concentrate on one aspect to the detriment of the other. If you measure someone's performance, how do *you* know that *they* know what they are doing? If you measure their knowledge, how do *you* know what *they* know about?

Let us consider each of the methods above and identify when it is valid to use them.

Written examinations

Essay-style questions are very commonly used in examinations. Here, questions are set which require written responses. There is a time limit for writing the answers. In an unseen examination, the candidates (the word for learners who are now ready to 'present themselves for examination') will not know beforehand what the questions will be. The questions are usually written to test the candidates' knowledge of topics covered in a learning programme. In a 'seen' exam, or 'open book' exam, candidates are told in advance what the questions will be. They can then prepare their answers and, when they take the exam, they are really just writing down from memory what they have already prepared. In another format, candidates can take certain texts into the examination room. They are given questions which require the application of their knowledge. For example, they may be allowed to take dictionaries into a language exam but they will still need to create a letter, write a creative account or a dialogue which will require use of grammar, syntax and fluency. Mathematical and scientific examinations will have a number of problems which require set methods to find the answers or demonstrate a proof.

Examples

Written essay exam question
What evidence is there that paganism was widely practised during the time of St Bede? (1,000 words)

Mathematical exam question
Find the mean, median and mode for the following values:
2, 5, 4, 3, 6, 2, 2, 5, 4, 6, 6, 8, 1, 3, 2, 2, 4, 5.

Science exam question

What are the characteristics of mammals? From the list below, identify which animals are mammals:

Stoat
Otter
Dolphin
Chameleon
Whale
Orang-utang
Goat

Many of you reading this chapter will have experienced at least one version of these examinations. There are people who do well in examination conditions: they are able to learn a large number of facts and reproduce these in an examination. They may also apply these to novel situations. You may have personal experience of a range of emotional responses to tests and examinations including nervousness, feelings of pressure, failure and inadequacy, but some of you may have enjoyed having the chance to show what you have learned in test conditions. So, as a way of testing if people can remember facts and methods and apply them within time constraints, examinations work well. As noted earlier, the danger is that people who are nervous may make mistakes on the day, even though they really do remember and can apply their knowledge. In some situations, such as medicine, people need to show that they can perform in stressful conditions, that they can 'hold their nerve', and the examination process is one way of testing this ability.

In formal examinations it is customary for there to be a moderation process where candidates' identities are kept from the assessors. In many cases, examination scripts are double marked, so that examiner bias is dealt with. In national examinations such as 'A' levels, examiners are given training to ensure that they are aware of the criteria for the award, how to mark certain attributes in the scripts, and they undertake moderation exercises where they are given sample scripts to mark. With all these checks and balances, there is still disagreement between individual examiners on essay-style questions. There is less disagreement on problem-based examinations, particularly for mathematics and science, although at higher levels there will be differences of opinion on the methods chosen by the candidates to solve problems.

Setting examination questions

You may be asked to set examination questions, perhaps 'mock' examinations. If you are asked to write examination questions, try to ensure that your question is going to help your candidates write answers! Will they recognize what you are asking them to do? Have you got a clear idea about the necessary criteria or points that should be included in their answers? Some schemes find it helpful to produce 'model answers' although this may restrict both learners in their use of creative alternatives, and assessors from acknowledging and rewarding these alternatives.

Example 1

Poverty is a worldwide phenomenon. Discuss.

Example 2

Poverty is a worldwide phenomenon. Using one definition of poverty, compare and contrast two examples of poverty, one drawn from the South, one from Europe. From your two examples, suggest whether you can find evidence that poverty is a relative or absolute concept.

In these two examples, the first is very open and it is not clear what the candidate needs to discuss. Now, it is possible that such a free-ranging question is deliberate to help candidates draw upon a large source of underpinning knowledge. However, the second question gives more information about the type of response required. Candidates will still need to understand what the question requires, that is, a critical comparative analysis.

If your learners do have to take examinations, you will probably spend time helping them to learn how to pass an examination. There are numerous strategies that learners can employ to revise for examinations and to answer questions in the most effective manner. This 'exam technique' is something that they will not necessarily have acquired by their previous experiences. Part of the curriculum, then, is about practising the skills of performing in examinations. This is particularly pertinent in using an appropriate writing style or academic register, which in addition to spelling and grammar is often an implicit criterion for achieving the necessary pass mark.

Multiple choice questions

Multiple choice (or, cynically, multiple guess!) questions are often used in examination conditions, but not exclusively. Candidates must identify the correct answer from a number of possible answers provided for each question. In some multiple choice assessments, there is also an opportunity for making short written answers to some of the questions. These questions will specify how many marks each question is 'worth'. This indicates to the candidate how much response is required, and whether there are parts to the answer.

Example

Copper sulphate is:

  soluble
  insoluble

When copper carbonate is added to hydrochloric acid, the resulting salt is obtained:

copper chloride
copper chlorate
sulphuric acid
carbon chloride

Multiple choice questions are very useful for checking that people have acquired information and that they can differentiate between appropriate and inappropriate answers to set questions and problems. They are easy to mark, because the correct answer is supplied. There are optical scanners that can be used to read the marked answers, making it a fairly efficient way to process large numbers of candidates' results. They are frequently used in science subjects, possibly because they test facts which do not necessarily require discussion.

However, because the correct answer is supplied in every case, it is possible for candidates to gain enough correct responses by luck rather than by choice. If candidates cannot quite remember an answer but then see it written down, then their memory will be 'jogged'. Now, is this such a problem? How many of us can remember exactly what we learned at school? Yet, if we were to see answers written down, we may recognize the correct one. How many of us have to look up spellings, meanings of words, information for our own teaching that we have not quite remembered well enough? None of this means that we do not know our subject very well. So why not have a system of examination that helps our learners to find the correct answer?

Pointers when setting multiple choice questions

You may not set multiple choice questions for examinations, but you may decide to use them for formative assessment. As with other examination-style questions, it is important to ensure that your question can produce only one answer and only one interpretation. As you will also be supplying a range of possible answers for each item, try not to make all the other answers obviously incorrect, but use the answers supplied to differentiate between what will have been learned well and what has only been partially learned.

Example 1

The capital of France is:

Paris
London
Dublin
Edinburgh

Example 2

The capital of The Netherlands is:

    Amsterdam
    Rotterdam
    The Hague
    Maastricht

Assignments

Assignments can range from writing an essay to undertaking a series of discrete tasks that create an overall piece of work that will meet NVQ or other competence-based criteria. Assignments are essentially tasks that are set. You may ask your learners to read an article and discuss it critically. You may set a task that involves research, for example, finding the best rate of interest for differing amounts of savings, or the best way to save a fixed amount of money for different purposes.

Assignments can be undertaken by individuals, or in small groups. In many vocational programmes, learners are often required to demonstrate that they can work in teams. Assignments are a good source of both learning and assessment activity in this case. For example, in the Travel and Tourism Diploma, an assignment may require that the group investigate a day trip for disabled people. They must find and book transport which has capacity for two wheelchairs and access for eight ambulant disabled passengers. They must decide on an itinerary which includes a visit to one museum, a stop for lunch and two short breaks. They must establish where disabled lavatories are located in garages and restaurants *en route*. Finally, they must cost the trip. The assignment will include a short presentation to their peers which uses a PowerPoint presentation, and copies of the information that would be given to the participants on the trip.

This is a major piece of work. It has been broken down into discrete tasks and it would be possible for certain members in the group to undertake aspects of the assignment. How does this assess learning? First, there are principles about treating disabled people with respect (as, indeed, all people) and, therefore, ensuring that the itinerary is both appropriate and accessible. Learners will need to know all about local agencies which provide information on disabled access and transportation requirements, and they will need to research which museums have access for wheelchairs. The completed assignment will reflect this knowledge. If there are gaps in the assignment, is it because the learners have *forgotten* about certain facilities for disabled people or because they do no *know* about the particular requirements. The written summary and the presentation would provide an opportunity for the learners to comment on the way in which they went about choosing the itinerary and the particular facilities, which will reflect their knowledge of disabled people's requirements when undertaking a one-day trip. Thus, an assignment which includes a written require-ment and a presentation will be more effective as an assessment strategy by providing numerous opportunities for establishing what has been learned.

Pointers in creating assignments

It is really important to ensure that your learners know how much work the assignment requires. Usually, one of the first questions you are asked when setting an assignment is 'How many words?' or 'How long does it have to be?' Identifying exactly what the tasks will be, and how these will be assessed, is vital. If you had asked your learners to 'present a plan to take a group of disabled people out for the day' it would be much harder for them to go about the assignment, rather than the earlier version where they were given specific subtasks. It is also important to specify how well the task has to be done. Reminding learners what and how much to include will help them to produce assignments that are neither too sketchy nor too detailed.

Presentations and demonstrations

Presentations can be undertaken by individuals or small groups. As with assignments, these can be used to identify what people have learned, both formally and informally, and can be undertaken during and at the end of a learning programme. Presentations can even be used before a programme of learning, in much the same way as auditions.

The most common form of presentation today is a short talk supported by PowerPoint. There is a variety of alternatives, including group role-play or short cameo performances.

When asking your learners to make a presentation, what should you bear in mind? First, what do they have to do, how long should the presentation last, and are you interested in the content, process of creating the presentation, or both? If the latter, you must state on the criteria that you will be assessing how well the learners demonstrated the process. Process is often more indicative of people's learning than the final product. If you are on a programme of teacher training, you may be asked to keep a log with reflections on your teaching and on the feedback from the observations by your course tutor or line manager. When you make presentations to your peers, the ideas that you originally had and the way in which you decided to choose a particular topic all tell a story of what you are thinking about. Those thoughts include aspects of your learning while on the course.

Example

Your learners are using multimedia programs to write a short story for children. They must produce a story that has at least four linked pages with audio and video input. You want to see that they not only know how to create links and how to upload audio and video inputs into the story, you also want to see how they went through an iterative process to create the story using the multimedia facilities. If you ask them to just write a story, that is what they will do. Of course, they will go through the process of creating the links, trying them out, redesigning their pages, and so forth. But if they are not asked to keep evidence of the early stages of their design, then they cannot possibly be assessed on this. So the instructions for the presentation with the criteria must be clearly stated at the outset.

Questions and answers

Asking questions is a fundamental way to find out if your learners really do know something. This method is often used throughout a learning programme in more informal ways (see Chapter 6), and provides constant feedback to you and your learners about how much they remember, know or understand something. Questioning can also be undertaken in a formal way at the end of a programme. For example, in NVQ awards, candidates are asked questions after they have submitted their portfolios. The questions are intended to search for underpinning knowledge and to 'plug' any gaps that may exist.

Questions can be asked in a variety of ways. They can be written down, with gaps provided for answers. These are often in the form of handouts that learners can keep for later revision or referral. Questions can be asked orally, either in person or on audiotape. Audiotapes are very useful for blind and visually impaired people, as they can replay them in the same way that sighted people can refer to their written material many times. Questions can be asked on video and, for deaf people, can be in sign language.

If I want to know if my learner can tell the difference between two ways of creating a product, for example, making pastry, then I could ask a variety of questions:

1. What are the main types of pastry for making fruit pies?
2. What is the difference between shortcrust pastry and puff pastry?
3. When would you use shortcrust pastry and when would you use puff pastry?
4. Which is lighter, shortcrust or puff pastry?

I will have very different answers to these questions. The first and last questions will probably only have one or two words, and my learner may guess the answers anyway. Questions 2 and 3 will require much more information.

There are two kinds of questions that can be asked: open and closed questions. Closed questions are those which will result in short answers, which are useful for confirming but do not provide much information. They often are 'Yes/No' type responses. For example, 'Can you use margarine instead of lard to make puff pastry?' will be answered with either a Yes or No (although, of course, some people may say it depends!).

Open questions are those which intentionally offer the respondent an opportunity to give detailed responses. They tend to use terms such as Why, How, In what way? So, we could ask 'In what ways can margarine be used instead of lard?' or 'Why is it important to use margarine instead of lard?' These questions are asking different things, but both will result in a response that is unlikely to be arrived at by chance, and require a much deeper level of analysis.

Role-play and simulations

As discussed in Chapter 7, role-plays and simulations are used when it is inappropriate to use 'real-life' examples and situations. These teaching methods can be used for assessment purposes. If we return to the earlier example of a grievance procedure in a management NVQ, this can be undertaken first to learn what is required and how to go about it. It can then be done at a later stage, but this time the candidate will be assessed on how well he or she demonstrates the process. In training schemes, simulation plays a significant part in both the learning and assessment process. In construction qualifications, for example, trainees will learn how to build a wall using a variety of materials and then they will be asked to demonstrate their newly acquired skill and knowledge by being asked to construct a particular type of wall, or to choose what is the most appropriate wall to build for a set purpose and then proceed to build it.

It is very important to ensure that the simulation is an accurate representation of 'reality', particularly, if the assessment of the activity is used as evidence that the person is competent in the workplace. It is quite easy to undertake, for example, an 'in-tray' exercise where an office is simulated, but if there are no phones ringing, no urgent deadlines to be met and no previous problems still waiting to be resolved, then the circumstances do not fully replicate the way someone will behave in reality. Assessment centres which test potential employees for a variety of management skills do not necessarily provide an accurate prediction of performance. Assessment centres are designed to test candidates in a variety of ways. Usually these comprise psychometric personality tests, 'in-tray' exercises, group activities, discussion and other simulations. The raft of tests used is intended to provide a more accurate picture of candidates' abilities. Assessment centres are particularly used for recruitment and selection of candidates for management posts, but they are also used for assessing management skills in management development programmes.

Case studies

Case studies, described in Chapter 6, provide an opportunity for learners to discuss and analyse in detail a scenario in which they can apply principles and practices from their recent learning. Case studies can also provide an opportunity to test how people apply their knowledge. As with role-plays and simulations, it helps if the case study is relevant and accurate. The more detail provided in the case study, the more able the learners are to work with the material and demonstrate their own skills and knowledge.

Case studies can be given to groups or individuals to work on. They can be used in examination and test conditions, or be given in a more 'open book' situation. They can be used during and at the end of a learning programme. They are particularly useful when drawing together a number of strands. For example, in a training management programme, candidates may be asked to look at a case study of one organization. They will be asked to analyse its corporate strategy and develop a training plan based on the training needs derived from information within the case study. This assessment process will, therefore, require that the candidates apply their knowledge of identifying training needs, creating training plans, creating training resources and building in the need for careful monitoring and evaluation.

The case study is a more holistic approach than a more mechanistic way of testing candidates' knowledge by asking them to produce separate assignments on making a training needs analysis, creating an evaluation procedure, and so forth.

If assessing a case study, remember it is important to specify exactly what you want your learners to do. If you want them to relate their findings to a theoretical model, then you must say so. For example, if you want a training plan based on the idea of the 'learning organization', but you also want the learners to critically analyse the effectiveness of the model of the learning organization, then the example given above would not do. You cannot mark people down for not providing something or not undergoing a certain process if you have not asked for it in the first place.

Clinical/laboratory tests

Professional training often requires that trainees demonstrate their competence in the workplace. This involves working in clinical settings, laboratory settings or in 'the field'. It is vital, therefore, that practitioners are seen 'in practice'. Laboratory work and clinical work are not simulated, they are 'for real'. Therefore, assessment is 'in the workplace' or, at least, in conditions which are the same. Here, the assessment process must be carefully constructed because the candidates are working with 'real' patients or clients, or using materials that are dangerous. Assessment practice, therefore, must be non-intrusive so that the candidate is able to undertake the process with the client without interruption. The assessor, however, must be able to monitor any possible dangerous development and to intervene if necessary.

It is important to ensure that the assessment process in these conditions takes place at appropriate times. Candidates who are prepared to demonstrate a particular interaction with a client, for example, are totally reliant on the client being there. If the client cancels the appointment, the assessment of their performance cannot take place. On the other hand, a situation may emerge that makes it possible for a different range of activities to be assessed. For example, a client may present a problem and behave in a way that requires a different approach than was originally expected to be assessed. This 'happenstance' is something that most competence-based assessors will be dealing with when they are assessing clinical practice. Rather than regret that the original planned activity did not take place, the assessor can accredit a different set of criteria.

With laboratory work, the equipment must be in working order, the materials and resources available and the exact procedure that is being tested clearly set out. Again, laboratory work may be undertaken by individuals or groups. With all such activities, being able to see what is going on with a group of learners and assessing their performance is a demanding task. Any assessment by observation of performance is always going to be subject to constraints in what the observer sees. If you are concentrating on one group because they have reached a critical stage in the process, you may miss this occurring at the same time in another group. You may be expecting to look at one thing and not notice other behaviour or activities occurring.

Tape recording or videoing performance is a helpful way to ensure that if you have missed something, you can see it again. It means that if you are unsure, you can have another look. Make sure you have a way to record your observation. This does not have to be through video or tape recorder. You may have a checklist that you can use while observing, and tick off each item as you observe it taking place. You can then use your checklist for giving feedback to your learners after the observation, identifying what was done well and what you did not observe, so that future work can aim to 'plug the gaps'.

Portfolios

Portfolios are compilations of evidence of learning and practice drawn from a variety of sources. The word originally applied to a leather case used for carrying papers. Now, portfolios are often in the form of A4 folders and ring binders, with paper in plastic wallets, carefully referenced against a set of criteria. The competence-based assessment movement has been a key factor in the use of portfolios for assessment of learning.

If I want to know that you can teach, I will need to see you in action, but I will also want to see that you have planned for your activities, that you have prepared resources, that you have carefully thought about ways and means to create an appropriate learning situation, that you will be able to monitor the learning that takes place and assess it, and that you will evaluate this process and make any necessary changes. Watching you teach will not necessarily supply all this information. However, if I ask you to produce a series of learning plans, see a report of someone's observation of your teaching and a record of your feedback discussion, see a sample of resources that you have adapted and created, an assessment procedure that you have used with your learners, an evaluation of this and an indication of what you plan to do next time, then I will have more confidence in saying that I think that you can teach. This evidence can be put into a portfolio.

Portfolios, then, are the product of learning. They are also surprisingly idiosyncratic and I find them such a source of surprise and interest when I am assessing them. Portfolios are used across a range of qualifications from assessment awards, originally known as the 'D units 32 and 33' to a full management NVQ Level 5. There is a tendency for candidates to worry about having enough evidence, and when NVQs were first introduced at the higher levels in professional qualifications, this angst led to rather large portfolios (see Hillier, 1999).

So, if you require a portfolio as a way to assess your learners, be very clear about what should be in it and how much evidence for each topic/unit is required. Luckily, the awarding bodies have made great effort to specify evidence requirements so that candidates do not put the equivalent of the entire contents of their filing cabinets into the portfolio.

E-ASSESSMENT

Increasingly there are opportunities to assess using technology. For example, the awarding bodies enable learners to be tested anywhere at any time through their online assessment facilities. The tests are often multiple choice or 'drag and drop' in nature and are used for diagnostic testing as well as summative testing. The Skills for Life tests, for example, are available online. One advantage of online testing is that images, video clips and sounds can provide 'real-life' situations that go beyond the traditional paper-based questions. The disadvantages are that the learners do need a required level of ICT skill.

Informal assessment in large groups

Most of the methods I have discussed so far are used in more formal situations. There are numerous activities that can be undertaken with learners when they are in large groups which help to reinforce learning and also test their knowledge so far. Here is a short list of examples.

Concept maps

Here, learners can draw diagrams to help them display what they know about a certain topic.

Venn diagrams

Here, relationships between certain topics, categories or concepts can be shown.

3-minute essay

Here, learners can write down a brief description of what has just been covered, or about what they remember from a previous session, or about a certain topic.

Letter to a friend

This is a good way to find out if your learners have achieved a particular learning objective. They write to a friend describing how to do something, or what they have just learned about a particular topic. It has an informal approach but is quite searching of their learning.

Cloze exercise

Here, learners are given a paragraph or text with certain words missing. They must complete the missing gaps. This form of exercise is often used with language and literacy work, but it is also a good way to find if people have acquired definitions of concepts and jargon.

Example

Apples and pears are . . . fruits I love to eat.

There are . . . many people in this lift.

I am going . . . see the doctor today.

(two, to, too)

Norm-based and criterion-based assessment

One of the most demanding aspects of assessing learning is defining how well your learners can do something, or know about something. In sport, we often find out how well someone can play tennis, for example, by the number of wins they have in a tournament: they have a position, or 'seed'. Their position is defined against the performance of other tennis players. Competitions are very useful in making distinctions between people's performance, at least about their performance on that occasion. In the same way, we are sometimes asked to make judgements about the performance of our learners, and we have to decide in what order we must rank them. So our assessment activity must be able to distinguish how well our learners have performed the task set.

In the past, national qualifications such as GCE and 'A' levels measured candidates by ranking them in order of how well they performed in the examinations. Imagine a group of 100 candidates. They have scores on a test ranging from 95 to 30 marks out of 100. If we rank order them – in other words, put their scores in order from the highest to the lowest – we may decide that the top 20 per cent of the group will score an A, the next B, the next C, and so on. In this case, the scores of the first 20 per cent range from 80 to 95. Now, suppose a second group of 100 people take the same test and their scores are put in rank order. Their scores range from 20 to 80. With this group, the top 20 per cent scores range from 65 to 80. So we now have a situation that on the same test, one group of people scored an A when they had lower marks than the other group. This is exactly what happens when we decide to grade people according to what is known as a *norm referenced* process. We make judgements about the level of award based on the group of people we are dealing with. It is expected that the distribution of their scores is 'normal': in other words, there are more people performing in the middle categories and their distribution would look like a bell-shaped curve if we plotted their scores on a distribution graph.

A different way to measure performance is to state a set of criteria that all candidates must meet in order to pass. Here, provided everyone meets the criteria, they can all pass. For example, suppose we set an assessment activity where we asked our candidates to create a database, a spreadsheet and write a letter to a customer drawing upon information found in the spreadsheet and database. Here, we will not place our candidates in order of whether they completed the task or not, and then say that the top 20 per cent have an A. We will simply indicate that those candidates that do everything required pass and are deemed competent, and those who have not done everything will not be competent yet. If we have 100 people doing this task, we may find that a higher percentage passes. They can only pass, or not. There are no grades given. This form of assessment is known as *criterion referenced*. The advantage of this method is that people pass when they meet the criteria, and they do not have to be ranked against how well the other candidates have performed on the day. We make no assumptions about how their performance is distributed. We have to make our criteria specific in order to judge whether or not our candidates will pass.

Some people are motivated by the idea that there are few high grades awarded and they work very hard to try to ensure that their scores are in the top percentile. Others are demotivated by the idea that no matter how hard they try, their score is dependent on how everyone else performs. Both systems have problems with fairness. With norm-referenced systems, it is possible for people to fail simply because others have a higher score, whereas with the criterion-referenced system, they would have been deemed to have passed. On the other hand, criterion-referenced systems can be very unwieldy, and although they give the appearance of being explicit, still contain opportunities for different assessment decisions by the assessors. Observation of performance, in particular, is notoriously difficult to achieve agreement on. Again, an example from the competitive sport of figure skating demonstrates this. If you have seen the scores that the judges give, there is always a spread of marks, even though they have all watched exactly the same performance.

Can people be graded on criterion-referenced assessment methods? Yes, they can, provided the criteria state clearly what must be covered to achieve a particular grade or level. In higher education, John Biggs (1999) developed his SOLO taxonomy (Structure of the Observed Learning Outcome) which defines five grade levels. He suggests that particular verbs can help us identify the grade our learners should be awarded, as they help differentiate between the breadth and depth of their knowledge and skill. These are as follows:

Grade A The best understanding that could be reasonably expected: includes verbs such as hypothesize and analyse.

Grade B Highly satisfactory understanding: might contain verbs such as explain, solve, compare.

Grade C Quite satisfactory learning, with understanding at a declarative level: verbs such as elaborate, classify.

Grade D Understanding at a level that would warrant a pass: low-level verbs, also inadequate but salvageable higher-level attempts.

Grade E Fail.

Each of these levels would require assessment tasks that evaluate how well the target verbs are deployed. Biggs argues that the highest-level verb manifested becomes the final grade. Now it is possible that this taxonomy can apply to other areas of learning. Essentially this is an attempt to help the learner and the assessor identify what has been achieved from the original learning objectives and how well this has been covered. The flexibility in this model ensures that some people will provide more evidence of learning at higher levels than the original learning outcomes specified. I have seen this occur in numerous adult education classes where the participants displayed deep levels of analysis which went beyond the requirements for the course.

The levels of learning can be defined in the following way:

Extended abstract: This is where the learner can theorize, generalize and reflect.

Relational: This is where the learner can make comparisons, explain causes, relate ideas.

Multistructural: This is where a learner can describe, or list points, do simple algorithms.

Unistructural: This is where the learner can identify items, undertake simple procedures.

Pre-structural: This is where the learner 'misses the point' or does not show any evidence of having learning anything about the topic.

How can an assessment activity capture these levels? Let's consider an 'A' level biology class. The learners have been working on a topic of human anatomy, about the muscular–skeletal system. Now we could ask them to tell us what bones and muscles are found in the foot. This would provide us with information that our learners are working at the multistructural level, where their knowledge is declarative. We could, instead, ask them to explain how the muscle and bone systems interact when kicking a ball. Here, we would be testing their relational and declarative knowledge. They would have to apply their ability to name the various muscles and bones and relate these two systems. However, if we set them a problem such as how to design a shoe that would help a person who has suffered an injury to the foot to walk, then we would be not only testing their relational knowledge, but also their ability to make hypotheses and test these through designing a product.

An assessment activity, therefore, can be used to test different levels of knowledge and understanding.

We can apply different methods of assessment for the different forms of knowledge and skill that we wish to test. Table 8.2 is an example of how the methods can be used for different forms of learning.

Table 8.2 Assessment methods which demonstrate learning outcomes

Learning outcome	Level of understanding	Assessment task
Basic facts, definition of terms, e.g., state the cost of materials needed to make a brick wall	Recall and recognition, some relational and multistructural	Multiple choice, cloze, short answer questions
Distinguish between different concepts, relate facts, e.g., differentiate between fair and unfair dismissal	Relational and multistructural	Assignment, presentation, comprehension test, case study
Demonstration of skill, e.g., search a database by fields	Procedural knowledge	Presentation, simulation exercise, audio/videotaping
Converse fluently in foreign language, e.g., conduct a one-to-one conversation about the weather	Relational, functional knowledge	Role-play, audio/videotaping
Develop an argument and defend own views, e.g., specify how humour is used to portray stereotypes in 'Jeeves'	Evaluation, relational and extended abstract	Discussion, long essay, seminar presentation
Reflect on own learning, e.g., monitor own progress	Extended abstract, relational	Log/diary

Equity

How are we sure that when we use assessment methods they are going to assess our learners fairly? For example, suppose we want to find out if our learners can demonstrate their ability to take part in a discussion which will assess their communication skills for the Key Skill Level 3. We set up a group discussion on what we think may be a controversial subject to encourage everyone to participate. We choose the topic of underage drinking. All the participants are aged between 16 and 18 years and are taking a vocational qualification. This seems like an appropriate assessment method. However, we find that some of the group members do not participate in the discussion. When we think about who did participate, we find that it is mainly the young men who do, and the young women who do not. We may decide that this is because the young women do not have any experience of underage drinking. When we analyse this further, we realize that the ethnic mix of people in the group is such that there are a number of women who are Muslim but none of the men are. So, have we been fair in our assessment method? We have set a topic that may not be experienced at all by one subgroup, and this is compounded by differences in the way that both sexes may approach the task. How can we ensure that if we do want to set a discussion, it will enable people to participate so that they can be assessed on their skills of communication? We may consider dividing the group into small subgroups, where people who have similar experiences can share their ideas. We may think about doing this but mixing the subgroups so that people with different experiences can share their views without feeling intimidated. We are not trying to treat people differently, or assess them differently: we are making sure that the conditions under which we set an assessment activity do not exclude some groups.

Fairness

Fairness is, therefore, an important consideration, in terms of whether people will have the right background knowledge to approach the task, or the necessary skills. For example, if we want to know that our learners can set up a spreadsheet, we do not need to ask them necessarily to write about how to do this: we need to see them going about the process of creating a spreadsheet. If some of our learners are working in their second or third language, then the assessment method which helps them demonstrate their skill and knowledge without relying upon their use of language will be more appropriate. If, on the other hand, they must be able to describe the process as they are going to train others to work on spreadsheets, we need to assess their language skills as well. We do not need to necessarily do this as part of the assessment of their ability to set up a spreadsheet.

Often learners are judged on 'hidden' criteria, particularly, skills in reading, writing and numeracy, because the assessment activity relies on their use of these important skills. In the past, people learning to drive needed only demonstrate their skill through a test of their driving ability. They now must take a test to show their knowledge of the Highway Code, and this relies on their ability to read. One can argue that this is necessary, as people need to be able to read road signs and notices when they are driving. However, if we simply want to know if people can drive a car using gears and then park it, we do not need to assess their ability to read.

Authenticity

How do we know that the work we are assessing is authentic; that is, actually produced by the person concerned? If we ask people to take part in tests and examinations where there is an invigilator, then we can be fairly certain that the work they produce is their own. If we ask people to write an assignment in their own time, they may have copied it from someone else's work, or even asked someone to write it on their behalf. The former is known as plagiarism, and is a serious offence within higher education and examined work. Yet, with the use of the internet, there are many instances of learners downloading model answers or examination essays and pasting these into their own work. It is becoming increasingly difficult to identify whether learners have cheated, particularly where there are literally hundreds of scripts to assess. This is where it is advisable to use alternative assessment methods to supplement those which are more subject to cheating. Some learners do not realize how easy it is to tell if they have done the work themselves or not when reading the assignment. Sudden changes in prose and style, particularly where a more formal academic style appears, are often an indication that the writer has not produced everything single-handed.

Increasingly, this is a problem as websites offering essays are used by learners who try to plagiarize. At the same time, many universities, for example, use software such as 'turnitin' to check this as well as developing clear guidelines for their students on what plagiarism means and how to avoid it.

Currency

How do we know that the work produced is current? In assessment processes which incorporate learners' previous knowledge and qualifications, APL and APEL, it is necessary to consider whether their previous knowledge is current. People returning to work after a break may be asked to complete a short task, for example, type a letter using a word processor, to show that their speed and accuracy are at a level necessary to begin working again. If I learned how to resuscitate people in a first-aid course ten years ago, am I still able to do so? There have been changes to many of the first-aid practices as a result of developing knowledge and practices. My knowledge may be out of date and even dangerous. In many qualification systems there are strict guidelines concerning the currency of previous qualifications. If in doubt, the use of other assessment methods, including question and answer and demonstrations, helps to ascertain if people are up to date.

Peer and self-assessment

So far, I have talked about assessment where you, the tutor, are responsible for assessing your learners. Why should you take sole responsibility for this? It can be very revealing for learners to begin to assess their own performance. When asked to look at their own assignment and to check that it meets the criteria before submitting it, many learners find that they can make improvements. They discover for themselves what needs to be done.

However, there is evidence that learners are much harder on themselves than their assessors. They may not have the confidence to acknowledge when they have produced a piece of work which is well done. They may feel insecure about assessing themselves because they do not wish to give themselves false hope. Of course, many people have experienced an education system that wields power through the tutors and teachers as assessors. The learners simply are not aware that assessment can be done differently. Certainly there are cultural issues to consider when introducing the idea of peer and self-assessment. In many South East Asian communities, the tutor is seen to be both knowledgeable and powerful, and it is deemed inappropriate for the learners to make judgements about their own abilities and performance.

Another form of assessment that moves the power relationship into a more learner-centred domain is that of peer assessment. Here learners assess and give feedback to their peers. Peer assessment has often been conducted informally in the past in many art-based programmes, where everyone gathers round each learner's work in progress and undertakes a critique. This style of informal assessment and feedback is often directed by the tutor, but many learners continue to provide this assessment to each other throughout learning programmes, particularly in coffee breaks! In many vocational programmes and training and development programmes, learners undertake peer assessment in a more formal, structured way. They may be required to watch a presentation of their peers and then to provide feedback on the basis of a series of performance criteria. It is possible for the peers to decide their own criteria. I have used this technique with a group of learners who are experienced teachers and trainers of adults studying for a Masters degree. They were examining issues of assessment, and by devising their criteria for a group presentation later in the term, were confronted in a very real way by the necessity of making criteria explicit and of the difficulties in assessing peers. They could draw upon this experience to reflect on how they assess their own learners.

If you are going to encourage your learners to assess their own performance and that of others, what must you consider? First, many learners feel very uncomfortable stating explicitly their assessment of their peers. They will tend to use general terms and not wish to give feedback, particularly, if they think that they, too, may have not done so well.

Giving feedback

In all of the assessment methods noted above, I have referred to feedback. Implicit, then, in my description of the methods is that after the assessment has been conducted, the learners are informed about how well they did. Many of you will have experienced feedback on written work which is full of red marks, scored-out sentences, and a grade or mark which has made you wince. Many of you will also have experienced an assignment which has been marked, and a comment like 'Well done' written at the end. In neither of these examples, would you have been able to improve your written work as a result of receiving the comments. If feedback is to be of any use, it must be constructive, clear about any action to be taken, and encouraging.

If you are only going to assess written work, or if you are running a distance learning programme, where you will not be meeting your learners face to face, then it is extremely important that your written responses are going to be understood by your learners. Laurie Taylor (1999) provided a witty description of how to assess examination scripts without actually reading them. Among his suggestions included placing question marks randomly in the margin, and a series of appropriate comments, such as 'Meaning?', 'Be specific', none of which would state exactly what the problem is and how to resolve it.

Lea and Stierer (1999) have shown how important the creation of meaningful feedback of written skills is. One example of research in their book, conducted by Ivanic, Clark and Rimmershaw, investigated how six different tutors provided feedback on an assignment. The tutor who was most helpful gave explicit comments but also had a personal style. There were statements like 'This is a very satisfactory essay', 'I wanted to know more about how you intend to operationalize your ideas', 'I'm not sure what you mean by full learning', and 'Now what reservations do you have about this viewpoint?' (Ivanic et al., 1999, p. 53). The learner would not only be able to see what needed further work, but also was congratulated on the aspects that had been done well.

Giving feedback verbally has its own challenges. It is easy to give feedback to learners who have done well, met the criteria and can move on to the next activity. It is far more demanding to consider how you will feed back to learners who have not achieved the task, particularly, if they have encountered difficulty in the past on other assessed activities. How will you deal with your learner who bursts into tears, or becomes angry, or simply does not hear to what you say?

Remember that when you talk to your learner about her assessed work, you are dealing with the work itself. Concentrate on what has been done, and how. Even before you have your say, ask your learner to comment on how she thinks she has done, what she found easy, and whether there was anything she found difficult. This often results in an acknowledgement by your learner that there were areas that needed more work, or more support from you. People often feel glad to have the chance to say what they think, rather than to wait to hear it from their tutors, particularly, if their perception is that they have not done well.

Once you know what your learner thinks, then give your feedback. Start by commenting on the parts that have been undertaken successfully. Give precise examples, such as 'When you measured the calcium carbonate, I thought that you demonstrated your knowledge of the equipment very well.' Once you have identified a couple of points where you want to congratulate your learner on the task covered, then move on to the areas that may need more work, or were not done properly, and what needs to be undertaken to ensure that the learner is successful next time. Again, make sure you give precise examples. Statements that are too general should be avoided, such as 'I thought you went to pieces in the second part.' Rather, give an example that begins with 'When you had to roll the Swiss roll mixture, I noticed that you did not do this quickly enough. The mixture had lost heat and your roll cracked and did not end up as a smooth cylinder.' This statement indicates what happened, why it did, and then allows the possibility to discuss what to do to make sure that next time a perfect Swiss roll is achieved.

After you have discussed the areas that went well and those that did not, you should then decide on what your learner needs to do as a result of the assessed activity. It may be that there are further opportunities to practise a skill and your learner will need to do this. It may be that your learner will require additional learning support, perhaps, from a learning centre. You may decide that your learner requires an individual tutorial or, perhaps, needs to undertake some additional reading. Whatever you suggest, make sure that it is clear to the learner what is required, and by when. Finally, make sure that your learner has had a chance to ask questions, and that you end on a positive note. Sending your learners out of the door with a quick 'Make sure you get it right next time' is not likely to motivate them.

Good practice in giving feedback

- Focus on the issue, not the person.
- Be specific, give examples.
- Mark examples on the work and relate these to an overall summary.
- Be constructive, offer ideas to improve.
- Summarize any action required.
- Check that your learner knows what to do next.

Things to avoid in giving feedback

- Do not make sweeping statements.
- Avoid negative comments without any helpful suggestions.
- Avoid giving so much feedback that the learner is overwhelmed and does not know where to start.
- Avoid using red pen and scoring through large sections of the work.
- Avoid finishing on a negative comment.

Record keeping

How can you keep track of all the assessment activities that your learners undertake? Why is this necessary? One important reason is that learners need to know what progress they are making, and so do you. If you have a record of what they have done, you can look back over their work and identify what they have achieved, and what gaps exist. You are accountable to your learners and to the organization that employs you, or uses your services. You must show that your learners are making progress, and the record of their assessed activities will be one way in which you can demonstrate this. There are formal requirements in many qualification systems that records are kept of all the assessed work that learners undertake. These may be heavily prescribed by the awarding bodies. For example, many NVQ and other competence-based awards require tracking of each unit achieved, particularly, if candidates have already gained some previously from another centre. There are computer-based record-keeping systems devised specifically for such awards (see Figure 8.1).

Trainers in Management			
Central asessment centre			
NVQ UNIT ASSESSMENT			

Candidate Name:	
Qualification/Level:	
Unit/Element No:	
Unit Title:	

Unit requirements:		Assessors' Comments:	
Narrative			
Reflective Summary/conclusion/ Recommendations			
Knowledge & Understanding statement			
Evidence matrix/cross-referencing			
Evidence Criteria:	☞ X		
Validity			
Sufficiency			
Authenticity			
Currency			
Evidence Range			

Assessment Decision:	C/NYC	Assessor:	Date:
IV Decision:	C/NYC	IV:	Date:

Figure 8.1 NVQ assessments: example of unit assessment

However, not everyone will need to keep a track of units achieved. If you are working with learners in a more informal setting, but are required to keep a record for quality assurance purposes, then you may need to devise your own system. In many evening classes, tutors may be given a proforma to record their learners' progress. In the past, this was not a formal requirement and tutors kept a variety of records, some existing only in their heads! Keeping records may seem overly bureaucratic, particularly in more informal settings, but learners do need to know how well they are progressing, and if you have a record, you are able to motivate learners by showing them how much they have achieved (see Figure 8.2).

Remember that records must be stored in a secure place and that your learners' records are confidential. The Data Protection Act (implemented March 2000) requires that learners know what information about them is being kept and also requires that this information is not passed on to others without consent. Records, therefore, should be kept with the agreement of the learners. Openness and clarity are two guiding principles when keeping records. The Freedom of Information Act (FOA) entitles people to gain information that is kept on a variety of matters including their own records and this helps to ensure that records are held appropriately. It is certainly inappropriate to keep records which are mere value judgements such as 'Poor learner' when in fact the slow progress and perhaps diagnostic test results are all the evidence you need.

Trainers in Management
Central asessment centre

ASSESSMENT PLAN
MANAGEMENT NVQ: LEVEL 5 MANDATORY UNITS

Candidate Name: .... Date ....

Mandatory Units	Adviser/Assessor	Date
A3. Manage activities to meet customer requirements		
A5. Manage change in organisational activities		
B4. Determine the effectiveness use of resources		
C3. Enhance your own performance		
C6. Enhance productive working relationships		
D6. Use information to take critical decisions		

Figure 8.2 Mandatory unit summary records

Assessment as an evaluation tool

So far, I have concentrated on assessment as a tool for helping tutors and learners know about the progress made in attaining learning outcomes. Assessment outcomes are also invaluable in helping us, as tutors, evaluate our own performance. If we find that all our learners fail a particular test, then it may be because we have not made ourselves clear, or that we have not covered the material in enough detail for the learners to apply. We must be careful not to 'blame the learner'. This is where being reflective about our practice can help here. We can ask ourselves a number of questions when we consider how we assess. We can learn from our experiences and refine our practice as a result.

Qualifications for assessors

To ensure that there is coherence in assessment procedures, when NVQs were first introduced in the mid-1980s, the awarding bodies agreed that they would all demand that assessors and verifiers who checked the assessments were qualified to undertake these roles. There were specific units from the then Training and Development Standards, now known as the Occupational Standards and soon to be revised again, which detail exactly how assessment procedures should be carried out. They were known as the 'D units' and have become the basis of much staff development in post-compulsory education. It is fair to say that attitudes towards gaining the D units were more usually negative. Many staff in colleges and institutions felt that their professionalism was undermined by having to gain the D units. The educational literature, in particular, was scathing of the whole NVQ movement (see, for example, Hyland, 1994, 1998; Ecclestone, 1997). However, with the increasing move towards accountability and use of quality assurance procedures, more teaching staff are being asked to gain these units. The current occupational standards for learning and development have been revised by LLUK following consultation in 2010.

Lifelong Learning UK has produced a guide to new qualifications developed for the Qualifications and Credit Framework (QCF) which cover assessment and the quality assurance of assessment (LLUK, 2010).

New qualifications for assessors:

Level 3 Award in Understanding the Principles and Practices of Assessment
Level 3 Award in Assessing Competence in the Work Environment
Level 3 Award in Assessing Vocationally Related Achievement
Level 3 Certificate in Assessing Vocational Achievement

New qualifications for internal quality assurance staff (sometimes known as 'internal verifiers'):

Level 4 Award in Understanding the Internal Quality Assurance of Assessment Processes and Practice
Level 4 Award in the Internal Quality Assurance of Assessment Processes and Practice
Level 4 Certificate in Leading the Internal Quality Assurance of Assessment Processes and Practice

New qualifications for external quality assurance staff (sometimes known as 'external verifiers'):

Level 4 Award in Understanding the External Quality Assurance of Assessment Processes and Practice
Level 4 Award in the External Quality Assurance of Assessment Processes and Practice
Level 4 Certificate in Leading the External Quality Assurance of Assessment Processes and Practice

Although the demand for possession of the qualifications by awarding bodies creates resentment by many staff, others have found going through the process of demonstrating that they are competent in assessing their learners invaluable (see Ecclestone, 1997). They have to think about what they do in their normal practice and provide evidence that this meets the national standards. In other words, they do have to reflect on what they are doing, and why. If taken seriously, working towards the assessment awards can have many benefits, including becoming more organized and more consistent in assessment activities.

Conclusion

Now that you have read this chapter, take a moment to consider what you do currently. Why are you assessing your learners? How can you improve your assessment strategies? Think about the last learning programme you were responsible for. List all the assessment methods you used. By the side of these, indicate which learning outcomes these methods assessed. Now think of alternative methods that could have been used. Think about the pros and cons of these. Could they be more efficient in terms of the time you took to assess or the time taken out of the learning programme? Could the learners have assessed any of their learning by themselves? Could they have worked with their peers? Was the process inclusive? What was the outcome of the assessment activities you used? Did you discover anything about how well your learners acquired knowledge, skills, and applied these? Would you do things differently next time, and why?

LLUK standards

After reading this chapter, you should be able to work towards LLUK standards – Domain E: Assessment for Learning.

Further reading and information

Further reading

Armitage, A., Bryant, R., Dunnill, R., Hammersley, M., Hayes, D., Hudson, A. and Lawes, S. (1999) *Teaching and Training in Post-Compulsory Education*. Buckingham: Open University Press.

Biggs, J. (1999) *Teaching for Quality Learning in Higher Education*. Buckingham: SRHE/Open University Press.

Black, P. and William D. (1998) 'Assessment and classroom learning', *Assessment in Education*, 5, 1, pp. 7–74.

Cowan, J. (1999) *On Becoming an Innovative University Teacher*. Buckingham: Open University Press.

Ecclestone, K. (2005) *Understanding Assessment and Qualifications in Post-Compulsory Education and Training* (92nd edn). Leicester: NIACE.

Francis, M. and Gould, J. (2009) *Achieving Your PTLLS Award*. London: Sage.

Gibbs, G., Habeshaw, S. and Habeshaw, T. (1986) *53 Interesting Ways to Assess Your Learners*. Bristol: Technical and Educational Services.

Huddleston, P. and Unwin, L. (1997) *Teaching and Learning in Further Education: Diversity and Change*. London: Routledge.

Lifelong Learning UK (2010) *Assessing and Assuring the Quality of Assessment Guidance for Awarding Organisations March 2010* (www.lluk.org.uk) accessed August 2010.

Nyatanga, L., Forman, D. and Fox, J. (1998) *Good Practice in the Accreditation of Prior Learning*. London: Cassell.

Tummons, J. (2007) *Assessing Learning in the Lifelong Learning Sector*. Exeter: Learning Matters.

Wolf, A. (1995) *Competence-Based Assessment*. Buckingham: Open University Press.

Organizations

The QCDA provides information across the range of qualifications, and its website is particularly useful.

Learning and Skills Improvement Service (LSIS) (www.lsis.org.uk)

Awarding body information: City and Guilds, EDEXCEL and OCR all produce NVQ/SVQ handbooks, External Verifier handbooks, Quality Assurance handbooks.

Useful websites

City and Guilds of London Institute (www.cityandguilds.com)

EdExcel (www.edexcel.org.uk)

http://geoffpetty.com/activelearning.html

Lifelong Learning UK (www.lluk.org.uk)

Qualifications Curriculum Development Agency (qcda.gov.uk)

Standards Verification UK (www.standardsverificationuk.org)

Part 3
Evaluating and Developing Professional Practice

Evaluation

Chapter Outline

Sunil has run his Return to Study course, the healthy-eating programme has come to an end, Patrick's class has finished and a new one is due to start in the following term. How well did the courses run? What have the tutors learned from the way their programmes were conducted? Would they need to make any changes? Can they repeat the successes? Do they have to tell anyone else about the good points and the areas that need improving? Were the learners satisfied with the outcome of their endeavours?

These are questions that are asked when we evaluate a programme. The word 'evaluate' contains the word 'value'. Evaluating involves making judgements. When we evaluate, we ask questions such as 'How well?', 'What worked?', 'What didn't work?', 'What needs changing?' Answering these questions requires information from a variety of sources. We should not only ask ourselves what was worthwhile: we also need to know what our learners thought and, where appropriate, what their employers or sponsors thought. We need to decide what we want to evaluate, too. Learning, although undertaken by individuals, takes place in a social environment and there are many influences on the teaching and learning situation. When we evaluate, we should consider as many factors as we can.

Why evaluate?

If we reflect on our teaching and on the learning that has taken place, we will want to know if there is anything we have done that has worked well for our learners, so that we can continue doing this for future learners. If there is something that has gone wrong, we will want to know about this so that we can try to prevent it happening again. Sometimes we will think that our programme ran quite well, and, yet, our learners may be going away with a different view that our sessions were boring, or that we allowed the talkative people to interrupt the discussions all the time, or that our notes were not detailed enough. If we do not ask our learners what their views are, we will not know if we have been meeting their expectations.

The learning situation does not involve just the learners and their tutors. All the chapters so far have dealt with aspects of the complex teaching and learning interaction. Our learners need information before they join a programme, and they require good advice to enable them to make decisions. They need information about the outcomes of any programme of learning they undertake. They need resources to help them learn successfully. They need feedback on their learning and they need to know if they have successfully met any criteria for qualifications and awards. Each of these important areas must be evaluated to ensure that they can meet the demands of future learners.

There are requirements placed upon learning organizations and institutions to evaluate their activities. Most further education, adult education and training organizations are funded partly by government. As noted in Chapter 2, the funding agencies require that their funded institutions provide evidence that they have met the objectives for funding. This will include the identification of how many learners have been recruited, retained on the learning programmes and then achieved a qualification. Funding for community education programmes may have similar requirements for 'outputs' of learning. Training that takes place within organizations may be evaluated for its impact on achieving business objectives. The agencies and bodies which require such information are 'stakeholders' in the learning that results from teaching and training activities.

So we need to evaluate to satisfy ourselves that we are enabling people to learn. We want to identify ways to improve this. We also need to evaluate because our activities are funded and supported by a variety of bodies – public, private and voluntary – all requiring evidence that their objectives are being met.

The number of stakeholders may seem daunting. If we want to know how well a course has run, then we will need to ask those involved in the programme – the learners, the tutors/ trainers, those who provided learning facilities, technicians, library staff, and those who

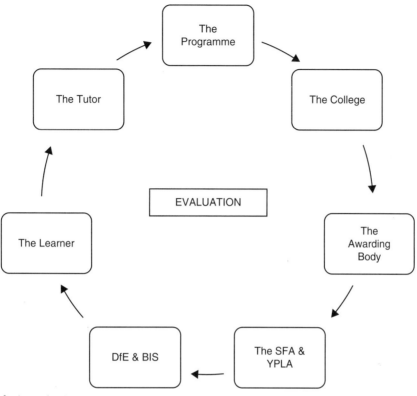

Figure 9.1 The evaluation process

are responsible for the smooth running of programmes, administrators, programme co-ordinators. In fact, evaluating how well something has run can include a number of things. Figure 9.1 shows how far-reaching evaluating can be.

Professionalism

We should want to evaluate our learning programmes to satisfy the requirements of all the stakeholders identified above, and to satisfy ourselves. Being professional (which is something the following chapter discusses) includes striving for excellence. How can we know that we have done a good job if we do not evaluate our programmes of learning, from as many perspectives as possible? Evaluation can, therefore, be seen as an intrinsic part of our professional practice, and not the ubiquitous determinant of whether or not our programmes will be funded in the future.

We also need to ensure that we can strive for the best possible conditions for our learners to succeed. If we do not evaluate our programmes, we may be doing our learners a great disservice. For example, we may need to improve the level of learning resources available so that the learners can gain the maximum level of award possible. We cannot know that our funding is inadequate to undertake our job if we do not have any 'hard evidence' to support our claims. Evaluation is, therefore, a tool that can help us ask for the necessary level of resources to ensure that our learners can achieve their maximum potential.

When to evaluate

Like assessment, evaluation does not need to take place once at the end of a programme. In longer courses, there is often a 'mid-term' evaluation where the tutor and learners examine a number of factors – including progress so far, the pace of the teaching or training – and they will identify action that needs to take place so that the programme can run more effectively. It is important to record any changes made to a programme as a result of this interim evaluation and to monitor how effective these are. The end-of-programme evaluation must then take account of the changes made. For example, if a group of learners could not gain access to a learning resource centre because it was timetabled for another group of learners, it may be possible to change their own timetable so that they were free to use the centre at a different time, or to negotiate access for the learners by arrangement with the co-ordinator of the other programme. If the resulting change meant that learners' work was greatly improved, it is important to recognize this feature so that future programmes would take account of the timetabling arrangements.

Institutions implement quality assurance procedures which include a cyclical evaluation of programmes. There may be a five-year review of particular programmes, and here information is drawn from the five 'cohorts' of learners to identify how well the programme has run during this time and to judge whether it should continue or be replaced by a different programme. Therefore, evaluation can take place during a programme, at the end of a programme and at the end of a review period.

Awarding bodies also require that reviews take place before they approve a programme to run for a second period. The review is not exactly the same as evaluation, but the procedures are often similar. Awarding bodies require assurance on a number of central issues such as the support for staff development, the infrastructure for learning, including library, technical and computer facilities, equal opportunities and health and safety policies. Evaluation can, therefore, be seen to be a process of making judgements that can be done at an individual level, all the way through to institutional and even regional and national level. The cumulative effect of evaluation to satisfy all the 'external' stakeholders is that we sometimes find ourselves asking so many questions of our learners and colleagues that we seem to be evaluating more than facilitating their learning.

If you have just run a one-day workshop, you may feel rather overwhelmed by the prospect of evaluating this if you have to ask everyone shown in Figure 9.1. In fact, your role may be only part of the picture. You do not personally have to talk to all of the stakeholders. Some of the information gathering will be done by people with a quality assurance brief.

Your role may be limited to collecting evaluation feedback from your learners. So let's look at ways in which this can be done.

Evaluation methods

If you want to know what your learners thought about your teaching and the programme they have just completed, then why not ask them? But what do you say? Confronting a group of people during the last five minutes of the last session with a question such as 'Did you enjoy the course?' is not likely to provide you with much information. It is a 'leading question' in that people will feel that they should have enjoyed the course, and they may not be prepared to tell you face to face that they did not. On the other hand, there may be some people who feel very strongly about their experience and launch into a tirade of criticism that leaves you feeling like giving up your job altogether! Neither is much use to you at this late stage in the programme.

So, first of all, let us establish what you want to know, and why. Are you interested in particular aspects of the programme you have just run? If you have taught this course for the first time, you will not have any previous experience to build upon. You may deliver a programme on a regular basis, but perhaps you have just introduced a new way of assessing your learners, or some new method of group work, or new learning resource packs for independent study. If so, then you will want to judge if your new ideas have worked in practice. So you will want to include questions about your *learners'* viewpoint. Remember that you, too, have an important role to play in evaluation. Your own perspective is a key part of the evaluation process. You may have noticed that your learners did not perform so well with your old way of introducing a particular complex issue and that your new idea seems to have done the trick. Your learners will not know that you have done this differently, so they may not have any comment to make on this issue. No comment may mean that people are satisfied, but it is dangerous for you to make this assumption. This is where asking for comments does not work. An alternative way is to ask people to rate how well they think you have performed on certain criteria.

Evaluation of learning

Example of an evaluation sheet with open-ended questions

Assertiveness skills workshop

What were your objectives for attending the workshop?

I wanted to know how to stand up to my boss at work.

Were these achieved?

I don't know yet.

What was most helpful about the workshop?

> *Practising how to say no.*
> What was least helpful about the workshop?
> *I didn't need to know why it is important to be assertive. I just wish I could be!*
> Please comment on the accommodation.
> *Very nice.*
> Are there any areas that you would like further development on?
> *I would like a follow-up once I have tried changing how I am at work.*
> Thank you for your comments.

Example with rating scale

Ten-week Car Maintenance for Beginners

Please rate the following using the scale: 5 = excellent, 4 very good, 3 = satisfactory, 2 = fair, 1 = poor

	5	4	3	2	1	Comments
Information about the course	☒	☐	D	D	☐	Very useful
Content of course	☐	☒	D	☐	☐	Interesting
Pace of sessions	☒	☐	D	☐	☐	Spot on
Handouts	☒	☐	☐	☐	☐	Liked them
Equipment and resources	☐	D	☐	☒	☐	OK
Accommodation	☐	D	D	☐	☐	Really cold

Thank you for your comments

What do you do with the information from learner evaluations?

I am guilty, and I know a lot of my colleagues are too, of rushing into the office after we have just finished a workshop or programme to look through the evaluation sheets, not so that we can calmly and carefully identify our successes and failures, but to check that it went well enough and that there were no really awful comments. Brookfield talks about this as the 'perfect ten', in other words getting full marks (1995, p. 17).

I don't think we should ignore our own need for positive feedback, and I am also aware that with any set of evaluations we will find a variety of viewpoints, some of which are completely contradictory. This makes it difficult to work out if we were successful or, more importantly, if we need to make any changes to what we do next time. One way to think about this is that those learners who were stating positive things may reinforce our teaching and learning strategies, but those for whom it did not work remind us that we have a variety of individual styles and preferences to work with. We, therefore, need to identify ways to ensure that future learners with those styles and preferences are able to learn successfully. If we completely change our practice to meet the points made by one set of people, we may then adversely affect the learning of a different group. Such situations can cause cynics to claim that evaluation is, therefore, unnecessary or at least unhelpful because you can't please all the people all the time. It is at times like this that we must remember that we are trying to maximize the learning that can be undertaken by each individual. We are, therefore, setting ourselves a difficult challenge. If we are reflective teachers, we will continually aspire to meeting this challenge.

Let us return to the two examples above. In the first, we have a number of comments made by our learners and quite a few returned with just ticks. Some of the responses are very detailed, and the comments run over on to the other side of the page. It is normal to have different levels of detail. Does this influence our collation of the replies?

It is tempting to think that those learners who provide full responses must have strong feelings that should be taken into account, whereas those who have just given one-word answers like 'Fine', 'Good' or even 'Lousy' don't much care as they have not taken the time to write in sentences. This is a mistake. People these days are suffering from 'happy sheet' overload. They are constantly asked to fill out customer satisfaction questionnaires (CSQs). If they are unhappy about something, then they will let us know. So it may be that a nil response or a one-word response is an indication that they are satisfied.

One way to analyse the written responses in your evaluation questionnaires is to use a blank proforma on which you record the responses from all your learners for each question asked. You can then identify if there are any trends. For example, if most of the learners were satisfied with the information given to them but over half of them thought the content was too difficult, then you may decide that you need to change the precourse information to ensure that they were aware of the level of the programme.

Assertiveness workshop – overall summary (twelve participants)

What were your objectives for attending the workshop?

To stand up to the boss (three responses).

To be able to say no (seven responses).

To learn how to say things without backing down (two responses).

Were these achieved?

Nine yes, three not sure.

What was most helpful about the workshop?

Practising (ten responses).

Time to try things out (two people).

What was least helpful about the workshop?

Being told how important assertiveness was (five responses).

Nothing unhelpful (five responses).

Accommodation

Very nice (nine responses).

OK (three responses).

Further development

More practice (five responses).

Follow-up workshop (three responses).

Saying no to assertive people (two responses).

Not sure (two responses).

Introduction to Car Maintenance Workshop
(twenty participants)

	5	4	3	2	1	Mean score
Information about the course	10	6	4	0	0	4.3
Content of course	8	8	4	0	0	4.6
Pace of sessions	12	6	2	0	0	4.5
Handouts	5	10	3	2	0	3.9
Equipment and resources	1	3	8	6	2	2.75
Accommodation	0	1	4	10	5	2.05
Total	36	34	25	18	7	

With the second example, we can create an average score for each of the items. We may decide that any score lower than the mid-point (i.e. 3) indicates that something is not going well. However, I have seen feedback sheets where the learners have divided into two opposing camps about certain points. The overall score suggests people were satisfied. It helps to see the spread of responses as well as an average score so that you can identify if most people were satisfied or if there were differences of opinion.

You may not be required to analyse your learners' evaluations. In some institutions, the quality assurance process that is conducted centrally will do this. You will be given information about the result of the learners' evaluations for whom you are responsible. The centrally devised and conducted evaluation process may not include questions that *you* want to ask your learners. If this is the case, then you may need to consider additional means to gain feedback. So let's look at other ways to evaluate with your learners.

Negotiated feedback in sessions

In programmes that are conducted over a series of sessions, it is helpful to find out how things are going throughout the programme, so that you can make changes along the way. In many programmes a learner is chosen by the group as the 'course representative'. This person is responsible for gathering the views of the group and representing them on course committees where staff and the representative discuss issues of course management.

An alternative evaluation process appoints one person in the group who gives feedback at the end of the session about certain aspects: pace, content, group interaction, and so forth. The view is not to be taken as representing the whole group, but a personal view. This gives each learner an opportunity to express a personal perspective.

If your learners have expressed their personal learning goals at the beginning of the programme, then they can be asked to think about these and judge how well they have been met when evaluating the programme. I have sometimes asked people to write on a 'yellow sticky' their main learning goal at the beginning of the first session. These are then posted on flip-charts which I save and at the end of the last session I bring them out for everyone to see. It is a helpful way to identify what has been achieved. It leaves scope for recording another set of 'yellow stickies' which state the unintended consequences and outcomes of the programme.

Giving feedback does not have to be done in writing. One of the most liberating methods I have experienced is where I asked my learners to think back over their programme as a learning journey and to draw this on flip-chart sheets. We then exhibited these around the room. The learners could *see* how their peers had experienced the programme. Some things are more easily expressed in pictures than in words, and it is a particularly useful strategy if your learners are less confident in their writing or language skills.

Electronic feedback

For programmes which are delivered on the web, then feedback can be gained from conferences, or given as electronic questionnaires. The advantage of electronic questionnaires is that they are easy to collate. Electronic feedback can also be obtained by e-mail from groups of learners. This method does not only work for distance or e-learning programmes. As increasing numbers of people have e-mail addresses, it is becoming more appropriate to ask for evaluations by e-mail rather than through sending questionnaires by post. It is, of course, also cheaper! However, due to evaluation overload, may people do not respond to electronic forms of evaluation and the response rate can be poor. This invariably leads to skewing of the data, as often those who are particularly aggrieved will respond and those who are essentially happy with the programme will not. This can be overcome by offering prizes such as entry to a draw for vouchers or book tokens but the lack of engagement is a problem.

Anonymity

Not everyone wishes to express their views in public. In some institutions protocol requires that tutors do not gather in the evaluation forms of their own learners, so that they will not be able to identify particular learners who may have been giving unfavourable feedback. I would expect that a truly professional tutor would not treat any learner differently on the basis of their feedback about a programme – but clearly some managers do not leave this to chance.

It is, however, the case that some people feel uncomfortable expressing their views, particularly, if these are negative, unless they can return the feedback forms anonymously. If they are asked to express their opinions verbally, they may choose to remain silent. If they are given forms requiring written feedback, they may feel more willing to state their views. Remember that the whole point about obtaining feedback from your learners is so that you can appreciate their experiences of the programme. This knowledge can help you maintain and develop the quality of learning. It is not meant to be a 'name and shame' exercise, or one that only asks for feedback about the things that did not go so well.

There is a trend for people to complain if they are dissatisfied with their programme. This is often because people now act as 'consumers' of learning, rather than being passive recipients of the teaching that was done 'to them'. People have paid for their programmes and expect quality in the delivery. They are less likely to put up with badly prepared classes, poor handouts and a tutor's superficial knowledge of the content. Indeed, where learners have signed learning agreements, and where the programme defines learning outcomes and teaching and learning methods, then people have a right to expect that they will achieve what has been defined. Evaluation, therefore, is a key part of the process of identifying whether the elements in the programme have been delivered and met.

As learners can be seen to be consumers of learning programmes, there will be aspects of their experience, and yours, which they comment on that are outside your own control. For example, if you have been working with a group of trainees in a room which is extremely hot in summer and cold in winter, or which has out-of-date equipment, then you cannot possibly deal with this by yourself: this is information that must go to the appropriate manager of central services in your organization. However, if you do not inform anyone of the difficulties you and your learners have been encountering, nothing will change and next time you will no doubt be receiving exactly the same feedback from a different group of disgruntled learners! This situation, therefore, is not one that can wait for an end-of-programme evaluation.

Informal evaluation

One of the most potent sources of information for evaluating a programme can be derived from the conversations that learners have during their breaks! Not every tutor will spend their coffee breaks with their learners, but when this does happen, learners will often comment on aspects of their experience of the programme, perhaps about the friendliness of the 'front-line staff' or how they are having difficulty finding certain resources in the library. This informal feedback is extremely useful for tutors who can either take action by informing the appropriate colleague or manager about gaps and difficulties in services or pass on the positive comments. Remember that staff in organizations hear about complaints far more frequently than compliments. It is so rewarding to hear that a particular colleague has been helpful to a group of learners, or that the newly refurbished cafeteria has made a difference to the learners' leisure time. If you do receive positive feedback, then do make sure you pass it on to the appropriate people in your institution.

Closing the circle

What do you do when you have undertaken an evaluation of your programme with your learners? There is no point in keeping a series of evaluation sheets if you do not do anything about the feedback given, or take any action. This part of the evaluation process is the most important and yet the most neglected in many institutions, and indeed in organizations generally. What can you do to prevent this happening?

Quality assurance procedures should involve identification of action plans as a result of evaluation. The procedures should monitor the action that subsequently takes place. It is like a feedback loop. One way to think of evaluation and monitoring is to think of how room temperature is maintained. The actual temperature of a room is monitored by a thermometer. It simply records how hot or cold the room is. If no action is taken, the room will stay cold or hot. If we want a room to remain at a particular temperature, say, 20 degrees centigrade, then we want to ensure that if the temperature falls below this, the heating will be turned on until the room reaches the required temperature. If it becomes hotter than our desired temperature, the heating will be turned off. The device for ensuring that the temperature remains constant is a thermostat. Now with evaluation, if we want to ensure that our learners are achieving certain skills, knowledge and understanding, we may think that the results of their assessment activities will give us this information. Once again, all we know is how well they did. If we want to improve what they do, then we will have to take certain action until their scores or grades go up. Now it is not as simple as keeping the temperature constant, and we certainly do not want to stop our learners obtaining even higher grades or scores! What we do not know for certain is what action will absolutely improve our learners' scores, or their achievement rate. We work in a complex situation with numerous factors. The work on achievement and retention in further education, for example, identifies an array of factors that are involved (Martinez, 2000). However, our evaluation will help provide us with information about how certain of our actions are affecting the final outcome of learners' achievement. Much small-scale institutional research has begun to uncover the impact of cross-institution initiatives on retention. For example, if all learners are contacted once they have not attended for a period of three weeks, then some of these learners may be encouraged to return. They may have felt that once they did not show up they were not welcome back, or they may have been encountering financial difficulty and the institution would be able to provide advice on how to resolve part of this. So a new procedure may influence the outcomes across an institution. Your part in this may, therefore, not simply affect your own group of learners but have an impact on the college's overall rate of achievement and retention.

Evaluation of the programme

The two examples above deal specifically with the learners' viewpoint. If we return to Figure 9.1, we can see that one of the stakeholders is the institution in which the learning programme is located. What form of evaluation is possible at this level?

The information that we are monitoring, that is the *performance indicators*, can tell us a great deal about the programme in its wider context. The sources of information we need can include the following:

- Course design
- Course management
- Recruitment, retention and achievement rates
- Staff development and qualifications
- Observation of staff
- Resources
- Library
- Record keeping
- Learner feedback
- Employer feedback
- First job destinations of learners where appropriate.

The evaluation of these aspects can be used to identify if a programme should continue to run, if it needs more resources, if it fits the mission and aims of the organization or institution, and whether action is needed to ensure that it reaches quality indicators set by the institution.

The next stakeholders are the awarding bodies and the funders. Here, evaluation will focus on the institutional procedures. External verification relies on the information gathered internally, either across the college by an internal verifier co-ordinator, or a quality assurance manager. Much of this information is derived from the list above. City and Guilds, for example, applies the following criteria when a centre is being approved to run its programmes.

- Recording systems which enable evaluation of candidates' achievements in relation to the centre's equal opportunities policy.
- Procedures to communicate with senior managers about the implementation of the qualifications.

- Resources in relation to an individual scheme's requirements will be identified and provided.
- Staff have sufficient time to undertake their designated roles and responsibilities.
- A staff development programme is provided.
- The centre has an appeals procedure for candidates.
- The centre has an explicit policy on equal opportunities.
- The centre has an effective system for quality assurance of assessment.

Targets and performance indicators

How do we know that value has been added to a learning programme? We can obtain feedback from a variety of sources including our learners, our tutors and colleagues, and from our external verifiers and examiners. We also need to know if we are making improvements over time and to measure the effect of any initiatives and developments we have introduced. This requires us to identify whether we have met targets that have been set. For example, in many colleges there are numerous targets set for learner recruitment and retention. There are national benchmarks for these set by the funding body. These benchmarks are used to measure an individual college's performance on each scale/item. It is possible to observe trends over time so that in a certain programme of study, say, Business BTEC, the learners in one college may have achieved passes at a lower rate than the national average. By introducing a series of measures in the programme, including the setting of course work and an enhanced personal tutor system, the following two years may show steady increases in the pass rate measured against the benchmark. It is, therefore, possible to use targets and benchmarks to inform the evaluation of certain aspects of the learning programme or to identify college-wide trends.

Once we have set targets, we need to know if they are being met. The way we do this is to look at our performance indicators. If we wanted to increase the use of the learning resource centre, we may decide that we shall count the number of times people enter the centre. This is one indication of the use of the centre. However, it does not tell us if we are recruiting new learners to the centre, or if the same people are making more use of it. So we need an indicator that can tell us about who is using the learning centre, and how often. Our performance indicator may, therefore, require a logging-in system that the learners must undertake every time they come into the centre. Now we will have more information about the use of the learning centre and we can use this performance indicator to help us judge whether or not our target of increasing the use of the learning centre has been met.

Many people are suspicious of setting targets. They are aware of the lack of impact that these have made in many commercial organizations. The public is unforgiving that targets are not met. For example, on the railways, a target of 95 per cent trains arriving on time will not impress those travelling on the 5 per cent that do not! The sanction applied for poor performance (usually a fine) does not necessarily improve the travelling conditions for the passengers. Setting performance indicators which cannot be met, or which do not ultimately affect the experience of the 'end user', in our case the learners, is, therefore, likely to cause cynicism and frustration.

Setting targets for human behaviour is far more fraught with complications. Our learners are people with widely differing circumstances. Simply assuming that an increase in numbers will provide us with homogeneous groups of learners is mistaken. We may decide that our target for an early years course is for an increase in recruitment by 10 per cent, and a retention rate of 90 per cent. However, if we recruit our additional 10 per cent from groups which have lower GCSE qualifications, we may find that we have to do a lot more to enable them to meet the criteria of the programme. If we have not changed our programme in any way, we may not fully support our new group of learners, and the achievement rate may be adversely affected. It does not make sense to set targets that are not coherent, and it certainly does not do to set targets that cannot be achieved if the infrastructure of the central services is not there to accommodate any increase in recruitment of new and different groups of learners.

On the other hand, it is helpful to identify if there are any changes in the outcomes of learning over time. We cannot take action to stem a drop in achievement or retention if we do not know there is a drop in the first place. We need this information across the whole learning organization, but we also can take action at the level of teaching on one programme. We may discover that a new strategy we have introduced actually has not worked, and being able to refer to past performance can help us decide if we should continue with our strategy or make changes.

Self-evaluation

So far, everything we have covered is about evaluation of what has gone on externally. How about our own practice? Arguably, reflective teaching takes self-evaluation as a given. Yet evaluation is not exactly the same as reflection. Evaluation is about making judgements, not challenging assumptions. Evaluation is necessary to inform reflection. It provides information and judgements about this information that can then lead to the searching and questioning that critical reflection demands.

What can we do to evaluate our practice?

Self-evaluation asks 'What is my role in all of this?' Did I provide a stimulating learning environment? Did I treat my learners with respect? Did I create clear guidance and work within clearly defined boundaries? Can I improve the way that I use my teaching and learning strategies and methods? Have my assessment activities worked? Did my learners stay on the programme and what can I do to encourage and facilitate their learning? Did the learners enjoy my programme? Did I enjoy teaching on this programme? How did I work with my colleagues? Did I take action when it was required and what happened as a result? Were there learners who needed more support and did I give this effectively? What content do I want to change next time? What resources do I need to create for next time? What worked well and what will I do again? Have I anything to tell my colleagues that they may like to experiment with? Is there any development I have identified that I need to undertake before my next programme? What support do I need from my colleagues?

One way to evaluate our practice is through using a professional log or diary. We can keep weekly records of the planning and delivery of our learning programmes. We can make notes about how we thought the sessions went, what changes we wish to make and points for action for the following sessions, or for the next programme. When we evaluate how the programme went, we can look back through our log and look for areas that we are happy with and will continue to use and we can look for aspects that we wish to change.

Professional log

Another way to use our professional log is to use a critical incident technique (mentioned in Chapter 1). Here, we can record incidents that are examples of situations or themes we wish to explore. For example, if I have a group of learners and one of these learners does not seem to be making satisfactory progress, I may begin to explore what I am doing in the sessions. I may decide to think back to one incident where I could see my learner was not achieving, and examine that situation to identify what I was doing at the time, what she was doing at the time and what the content of the session was, what methods I was using, and so on. I may begin to find that there are trends. I may discover that my learner just cannot undertake tasks if she is given oral instructions only. As I tend to become more softly spoken over a period of a few minutes, I may then further discover that she has a slight hearing difficulty. By keeping a log, I begin to gather information that leads me to reflect on both my performance and the impact it is having on my learners.

Critical incident technique is very powerful for enabling us to consider challenges that confront us. If we have a group of learners who seem particularly disaffected, can we find any examples of activities that did engage them? Can we work out why they were effective and can we use this knowledge when we plan future sessions, especially if we are going to meet new learners with similar circumstances?

We are not going to be able to identify for ourselves all the aspects of our teaching that we can feel pleased with and those aspects that need to be developed: this is where the quality assurance procedures of the organization can help. We may be observed teaching or training, particularly, if we are working towards a qualification in teaching or training. The feedback we receive from the observation can help us evaluate our own performance. If we are observed on a series of occasions, we can establish if we are making progress in our teaching and learning practices. Whenever we have the opportunity to discuss our practice with our colleagues, we can draw upon their experiences to help inform our own. Self-evaluation, therefore, is not a solitary activity but one which draws upon the views of our learners, our peers and colleagues.

Taking action

Once we have derived our information from the variety of sources, established if there are any trends and, measured our performance against any benchmarks, what do we do now? One of the dangers is that we have a mass of information that we then do not use to inform our future practice. The wealth of data that has been collected in the name of inspection procedures would probably provide jobs for life for some statisticians and analysts! With each of our stakeholders, evaluation can lead to further action. If we know that our learners do not have an acceptable retention or achievement rate, not doing anything is hardly likely to improve matters. We must decide what action to take on the basis of the information that our evaluation processes have provided.

You may not be able to effect changes necessary across the sector, your programme area or your institution. You can, however, make changes at 'local level' – that is, with your own learners next time. Closing the circle, then, is not just about monitoring how all the stakeholders are performing: it involves making choices. Sometimes this may involve drawing information to the attention of managers. You may be aware of initiatives in your field which will impact on the provision in the institution. Your learners may be experiencing changing situations when they are in the workplace that may affect the way in which you run your learning programmes. As a professional, you will continually strive for the best possible conditions for your practice and for your learners.

If you do make changes, though, it is necessary to monitor the effect of those changes and then to evaluate these. So evaluation becomes a key component of a cycle: identify learners' needs, abilities and desires, create and deliver learning programmes, assess learning, evaluate the programmes and make decisions based on the information and your reflections ready for your next programme. These steps may not necessarily take place in a neat chronological fashion. The role of critical reflection is to help heighten our awareness of the need to continually ask questions about what we do. This constant questioning becomes central to our professional lives.

Conclusion

Self-evaluation is an important part of making judgements about our professional practice. Being a professional can mean many things but essentially it involves a commitment to achieving high standards in our practice. To do this we need to know what the standards are and how we can develop our practice to work towards them. In the next chapter, the focus turns to ourselves and how we develop our professional practice.

LLUK standards

This chapter will help you work towards LLUK standards – Domain A: Professional Values and Practice, Domain D: Planning for Learning and Domain E: Assessment for Learning.

Further reading and information

Further reading

Armitage, A., Bryant, R., Dunnill, R., Hammersley, M., Hayes, D., Hudson, A. and Lawes, S. (1999) *Teaching and Training in Post-Compulsory Education*. Buckingham: Open University Press.

City and Guilds (2000) *Ensuring Quality Policy and Practice for Externally Verified Assessment* (9th edn, October). London: City and Guilds.

Edwards, J. (1992) *Evaluation in Further and Adult Education: A Practical Handbook for Teachers and Organizers*. WEA.

Useful websites

Learning and Skills Improvement Service (LSIS) (www.lsis.org.uk)

www.ofsted.gov.uk

Improving Professional Practice

Looking back

It is the end of the year. You have managed to teach your programmes successfully. Your learners have achieved their qualifications, your trainees have obtained vocational qualifications and some of them have been successful in gaining employment. Others have gone on to apply for further education and training. Your evening class learners have been very satisfied with their progress and wish to enrol for other programmes next year. You look back over the year and from the evaluations of your learners, peers and your own records, you realize that there are some areas of your professional practice that you wish to develop. You are unsure how best to use technology effectively in your teaching. You are really not quite sure about the changes to credit-based programmes and how you should be assessing your learners' work. You know there are new developments in your curriculum area and you wish to know more about them. How will you go about developing and improving your practice?

Being observed

The inspectors are visiting your institution. There is a great deal of preparation by the institution to provide evidence that the programmes of learning are of the appropriate quality. Part of this preparation involves an observation of your teaching by your line manager in readiness for the inspection. You are given a pro-forma which outlines the areas she will be concentrating on. You discuss the appropriate time for her to visit your group. After the session she arranges to provide you with feedback. When you sit down together she asks you how you thought the session went. You describe what you are happy with and the parts of the session where you know things could have gone better. She agrees and then begins to identify aspects of your teaching that could be developed. She has noticed that you answer the questions you have just asked your learners if they hesitate even for a second. They do not get the chance to answer before you step in. Your writing on the whiteboard is difficult to read from the back of the room. There were a few typographical errors in your PowerPoint and handouts. The younger learners have not engaged with the topic and have been disruptive in your session.

As a result of your observation, your line manager suggests that you may wish to join in the staff development programme offered in the institution. It will provide you with an opportunity to meet other tutors and to share aspects of your practice that are both successful and those which continue to challenge. In particular, there is a new series of seminars on dealing with 14–19-year-olds that may be particularly helpful for some of your programmes next year.

These are two examples where individuals can begin to look for ways to improve their professional practice. The first originates from a personal decision that there are aspects of the practice which can be developed. The second results from a line manager's recommendation. There are many reasons why you may be asked to take part in formal professional development not simply because someone thinks that you are not teaching appropriately. Professional development is part of the new requirements to practice as well as your personal search to achieve high standards in teaching and learning, to maximize the learning that will take place in your classes.

Institutional support for professional development

We do not always know what we need to do to develop our professional practice. Sometimes there are specific requirements made by our institution. For example, we may be required to attend a health and safety workshop. We may be offered a programme of staff development that is voluntary. How do we make judgements about what to attend? Why should we attend? If you have a full-time or fractional appointment in your institution, you will be asked to take part in an appraisal of your professional practice. Appraisals are meant to identify how you have met the targets set from the last appraisal, to review your performance, to check that your job description is accurate, and to identify any changes that have taken place. You will be asked to consider the strengths and weaknesses of your performance and will set new targets for the coming period. If you have undertaken any development activities during the last period, you will be asked to consider how much effect these have had on your performance.

If you are an hourly paid tutor, you may not be given an appraisal but you may be asked to meet with your programme co-ordinator or line manager to discuss your teaching. You may be observed on a certain cycle, almost certainly the first time you work for an institution and then possibly once every two to three years afterwards. Institutions have different quality assurance procedures and demands in this regard. With any form of appraisal, the important thing is to think of how it can work for you. What development do you think would help you do your job better? If you are asked to take on a completely new group of learners without any support regarding their teaching and learning requirements, then you are going to find it a difficult and challenging job. You must also take responsibility for finding out about your learners and part of your professional practice concerns keeping up to date with pedagogical issues, including how to work with varying groups of learners.

What can you expect from your institution?

Legislation in Europe has enabled those who work part-time to enjoy the same rights as full-time workers (European Directive 97/81/EC). Many of you reading this will be working part-time for training or educational institutions. Back in 2000 the then FEFC reported that part-time staff should be offered a range of professional development activities:

- All staff who are newly appointed to an educational institution should have an induction.
- They should have access to relevant qualifications and professional updating.
- They should be given adequate information about the college and its courses.
- They should be informed about current curriculum initiatives, which include key skills, basic skills and Curriculum 2000 (see Chapter 2).
- They should have mentors or other staff with a specific role in providing advice and support.

Ten years later, this entitlement has not changed but been strengthened by legislation. For information, visit the University and Colleges Union (UCU) website where a summary of entitlement for hourly paid and fractional staff can be downloaded.

If you have not been given any information about new curriculum developments, make sure that you go and talk to your curriculum co-ordinator or line manager. Sometimes, these colleagues are so overwhelmed with their own work that they have not managed to ensure that all staff, particularly those who only work a small number of hours per week, are kept informed. Is there a college intranet (internal network) where you can log in and obtain news and information? You have responsibility for keeping yourself informed as well as relying upon others to pass that information to you.

In all colleges and adult education institutions there is a governing body with staff representation. Make sure that you know who your staff governor is. Keep up to date with developments at a college-wide level by reading minutes of formal meetings in the college as well as your own programme area team meetings. In this way you can make sure that your views are represented. Staff in institutions who are fractional and hourly paid provide a large amount of the teaching but by virtue of their contracts and other responsibilities elsewhere have less opportunity to be involved in decision-making. This in no way reflects their lack of commitment. Recent research has identified that part-time hourly paid staff continue to feel isolated and estranged from their institutions, even though they also value support from their line managers and have immense commitment to their learners (Hillier and Jameson, 2004, 2006). Full-time staff, too, must ensure that their views are heard, as it is often too easy to become bogged down with all the day-to-day activities. Otherwise decisions will be made by others that may be subsequently difficult to implement.

Being responsible for keeping up to date and playing an active part in decision-making processes in an organization are part of the role of a professional teacher or trainer. What does it mean to be a professional?

Being professional

Developing professional practice suggests that we know what it is to be a professional. When you ask a neighbour whether the local plumber did a good job, you may be told that it was 'very professional'. When you visit the dentist, you may conclude that her skill in filling your tooth and the way in which she talked to you was 'very professional'. What exactly does it mean to be a professional?

In many occupations, being professional involves meeting strict criteria, including having entry qualifications before being able to practise. The medical and legal professions are prime examples where, following a number of years of initial training, further training is undertaken while practising until people become fully qualified and certified to practise. In other occupations, being professional includes taking examinations to become members of a professional body, and again this membership licenses people to practise. Jocelyn Robson researched professionalism for further and higher education staff and provides a careful summary of characteristics of professionalism including having autonomy, agency and practicing according to codes of conduct (Robson, 2005).

Once qualified and practising, people maintain their professional practice through further training and development, often called continuing education (CE) or continuing professional development (CPD). Professional practice is, therefore, seen to be practice that has met threshold standards, is continually developed and takes account of new research and development in the field.

Some professions have specific codes of practice that members must adhere to. The medical profession, in particular, is governed by a council, Acts of Parliament and ethical committees. The teaching profession for compulsory education is governed by the General Teaching Council and Acts of Parliament. Before 1999 there was no equivalent body for those who work in post-compulsory education. In 1999 the national training organization for further education, FENTO, was created to fill this gap. There were two other training organizations which had standards relating to teaching and training adults, Employment Training Organization, ENTO and PAULO, which was the training organization for adult education. Under the Learning and Skills Council, FENTO's remit, in particular, was far reaching. FENTO devised and proselytized a series of standards for teaching and management. All teachers new to further education were required to have a teaching qualification and must cover the FENTO standards. The standards were seen as a compulsory way to ensure that staff in further education were trained and qualified to teach. The three NTOs were subsequently drawn together to form the sector skills council Lifelong Learning UK (LLUK), as a result of government legislation which attempted to rationalize the training organizations. The LLUK is an employer-led organization with one aim 'to ensure that the lifelong learning workforce is the best it can be' (LLUK, 2010). It is responsible for community learning and development, further education, higher education, libraries, archives and information services, work-based learning and career guidance. The Higher Education Academy (HEA) replacing the Institute for Learning and Teaching (ILT) was set up to support teaching in the higher education sector. It produced a separate framework reflecting the distinctive needs and demands of teaching in higher education while providing flexibility to develop specific institutional needs. As more higher education teaching is undertaken by those in further education, any teaching standards require careful consideration, to ensure that both higher and further education sectors are covered.

The Standards Unit supported the quality of teaching and learning in the sector, as noted in Chapter 2. This activity has now been subsumed with LSIS. Useful material to support subject-specific teaching was created, building upon good practice in the sector. A reflective teacher now has a set of standards against which to measure her or his performance and to identify what can be done to meet these.

In 2004 the DfES announced its analysis of the consultation on initial teacher training for FE, and argued that the teaching qualification should provide a license to practise in further education. The Institute for Learning (IfL) would be responsible for managing the register. The proposals, outlined in *Equipping Our Teachers for the Future* (DfES, 2004a) include a two-tier level of qualifications, with a 'passport to teach' for new teachers in the sector, and a full teaching award, which entitled them to be qualified to teach in the learning and skills sector (QTLS). This was an important departure from the previous regime, where schoolteachers gained qualified teacher status (QTS) following their training, but further education teachers did not. Such a licence may help work towards addressing the anomalies in the system, where 14–19-year-olds are taught by teachers without QTS in further education. The second important feature of the proposals addresses CPD, where professionals are required to continue to enhance their knowledge and understanding of teaching and learning, and a professional development record is used to capture this important activity. As a result of these changes, it is even more important that you continue your own professional development and keep a careful record of your activities, and importantly what you have gained from them.

The standards

Standards underpin teaching qualifications. There are three levels: PTLLS, CETLS and DETLS. LLUK standards for teachers in further education are divided into three elements: professional values, professional knowledge and understanding, and professional practice. The following are six key areas in teaching known as domains.

Domain A: Professional Values and Practice
Domain B: Learning and Teaching
Domain C: Specialist Learning and Teaching
Domain D: Planning for Learning
Domain E: Assessment for Learning
Domain F: Access and Progression

Each of the domains contains a series of statements about what teachers should be able to demonstrate at certain stages in their programme of development. The combination of the three elements provides a comprehensive and potentially demanding set of standards. In addition to the generic standards, there are standards for literacy, numeracy and ESOL. The standards are used for teaching qualifications at Levels 3, 4 and 5 in the QCF. Here, practitioners are expected to have a specialist knowledge of literacy, maths or language. A Level 4 qualification is the equivalent of the first year of an undergraduate degree programme. It is possible to gain a teaching qualification with a basic skill specialism through a number of higher education institutions or further education providers.

Interpreting standards

Sometimes it is hard to work out exactly what the standards require. This is where attending staff development programmes and, particularly, those which lead to qualifications are so useful. You meet other tutors and trainers from a wide range of backgrounds and contexts and by sharing your own practice you can learn from your colleagues. In many programmes, you will be asked to identify your strengths and weaknesses as a practitioner, possibly at the beginning of the programme and certainly at the end, where you think about what you have learned and how you intend to apply your skills, knowledge and understanding. There is an expectation, in all of the accredited programmes for developing teaching and learning, that you will continue to develop professionally. No one expects that you will sit back comfortably having completed a qualification in teaching and learning and expect to repeat your practice annually until you retire!

Not everyone agrees on what good practice in teaching and learning is. You may find that colleagues in your own subject specialism disagree about how certain concepts and topics should be covered. Using technology to support learning may be an area where there are 'champions' who use it all the time and others who state that they are fighting a rearguard action against computers at the expense of the face-to-face learning in which they believe strongly. This kind of debate is healthy because it forces us all, as professionals, to examine our practice and to identify where new ideas can be implemented and evaluated. It is the lack of discussion and argument that can stultify our practice.

In addition to the standards for professional practice, we must also abide by government legislation governing safe practice. This includes the Every Child Matters legislation (ECM) which has five tenets that children and young people will

- be healthy
- stay safe
- enjoy and achieve
- make a positive contribution
- achieve economic well-being.

We are also required to work within health and safety standards primarily through the Health and Safety at Work Act (1974) and the Management of Health and Safety at Work Act (1999). We must ensure that we are aware of the Disability Discrimination Act (1995) and the Special Education Needs and Disability Act (2001) (SENDA). Finally, we are bound by equality legislation including the Sex Discrimination Act (1975), the Race Relations Act (1976), the Human Rights Act (1998) and the Equality Act (2006).

Analysing our practice

Once we have a set of standards we can begin to measure how well we match these. One way of developing our professional practice is to review what we do at certain intervals. We evaluate our teaching and training constantly, wondering how individual sessions went, how to enable certain learners to make progress, deciding whether to change a particular workshop or develop new materials which can be used on the web. This reflection-in-action (Schön, 1983) has been described in Chapter 1. We need to move beyond such reflection to ensure that we stand back from the everyday experiences and place our experience in a bigger context. Have we found there are changes we should be making at a deeper level? For example, if we have noticed that our learners have learned particularly well from some of our activities and not from others, should we change our overall approach to certain topics? Have we decided that technology can be used to support some of the learning that can be done autonomously by our learners? It is not easy to analyse our practice by ourselves, but at least the standards provide a framework against which we can begin to think about what we currently do and whether we could change some of our practice. I do not think we should assume that we must constantly change everything. The role of reflection in teaching and training is to both affirm what works well in addition to helping us to see what could be changed.

The LLUK standards are not the only means by which we can judge our professional practice. If you talk to your colleagues, you will probably find that you have quite different opinions about good practice. You would almost certainly find it challenging to work out what LLUK standards mean and how you could demonstrate you are meeting them. I think that sharing practice is one of the most fundamental rewarding, challenging and useful things that teachers and trainers can do. It is not necessary to sit down with a checklist and ask whether items can be ticked off. What is more important is to observe how other people practise, watch how other learners go about their work, read about ideas and debates in learning and teaching. If you are fortunate enough to attend conferences, you will notice that you learn more from the informal discussion at the breaks than you will necessarily do from the speakers. If your institution provides a staff conference, then do try to attend as you are likely to benefit enormously from talking to your peers, either from your own programme area or from a completely different part of the provision.

Staying informed

How can you become involved in the debates about teaching and learning? How can you find out about the current issues? You may belong to a professional body in your own subject. There are, in addition, bodies that are specifically involved in the education and training of adults. The National Institute for Adult and Continuing Education (NIACE), in particular, is an extremely useful source of information and acts as a lobby to government and policy-makers. Their monthly journal, *Adults Learning*, is written by practitioners in the field of adult education and training. There are sections on activities and conferences taking place, book reviews, website reviews and then a series of articles, sometimes about a particular feature, written by practitioners. Reading this journal will keep you informed about the major developments and debates in the field. There is a similar body for trainers. The Chartered Institute of Personnel and Development (CIPD) is a more formal body as it is a chartered institute and trainers and developers must undertake a variety of accredited programmes to become members. Its journal is *People Management*. The LSN provides an enormous amount of support in the sector. It disseminates information about large- and small-scale projects that it has managed, produce publications and, importantly, responses to government consultations about new policy initiatives. These are particularly helpful for staying informed about current debates (see www.lsn.org.uk).

The Learning and Skills Research Network (LSRN) has regional groups of members interested in research in the sector who meet locally. There is an annual conference held by each active region and a number of practitioners have contributed to a publication of their research having won an award for their papers in a series of annual conferences held nationally between 1997–2003 (Hillier and Thompson, 2004).

All of these bodies, and a variety of others, provide information through their websites. You can usually find lists of their publications there. Reading about teaching and learning can be done through searching library catalogues, websites, visiting your local library and obtaining recommended lists from your staff development managers and curriculum managers. There are a variety of sources you can consult. There are policy documents about widening participation in learning, lifelong learning, paying for learning. Many of these can be obtained from the DfE and BIS websites.

There are books, like this one, on general issues in teaching and learning. A search on a library OPAC system (Open Public Access Catalogue) for a subject or author will provide another source of information about aspects of teaching and learning. Those of you who want to know more on assessment, for example, can follow this up through searching for 'assessment' and 'adult' on your local library catalogue.

Then there are subject-specific books and articles. Certain subjects have bodies that have their own journals. With adult basic skills, for example, the Research and Practice in Adult Literacy (RaPAL) group has a publication which, again, is written by practitioners. The *Basic Skills Bulletin*, with its counterpart *Numeracy Briefing* and *14 – 19 Bulletin*, offer important overviews of developments in the basic skills field. The National Research and Development Centre for Adult Literacy, Numeracy and ESOL (NRDC) regularly publishes research reports.

The teaching union for further and higher education, UCU has its own journal, the *Journal for Further and Higher Education*. This is a refereed journal, which means that articles that are submitted are read by members of the editorial board before being accepted for publication. This process helps assure the quality of the papers. Another journal worth consulting is *Studies in Adult Education*, again published by NIACE where the articles cover issues in more depth.

Research in the sector provides an important source of information and ideas and journals often are a good source of research findings. There are journals which cover themes in education across the compulsory and non-compulsory divide, like the *British Journal of Educational Research* which is produced by the British Educational Research Association (BERA). Some journals have a specific focus, like technology in learning, such as in the *British Journal of Educational Technology*, or deal solely with certain aspects, such as *Studies in Educational Evaluation*. The education evidence portal (EEP) is a useful website that enables you to search for recent research across the education sector. It is useful to look at how research in secondary schools, for example, could inform work in colleges and vice versa. The Economic and Social Science Research Council (ESRC) funded a Teaching and Learning Research Programme (TLRP) which in its third phase focused on post-compulsory education and training.

You can also read shorter articles which are about current issues in Tuesday's *The Guardian*, Thursday's *Independent* and in *The Times Education Supplement* and *The Times*

Higher Education Supplement. If you belong to the Universities and Colleges Union (UCU), you will receive a newsletter which covers issues in teaching and learning and contains book reviews. The Association of Colleges (AoC) has its own publication as does LSIS and LSN.

Finally, you may find that your own institution has a newsletter that will provide information about local and regional developments. You may have curriculum meetings that you attend where information about new qualifications, new practices and procedures will be discussed. Awarding bodies attempt to disseminate information through newsletters, formal communications with centres and through their websites. For example, City and Guilds produces its *Broadsheet* which carries information about new awards, new appointments and celebrates success of its candidates. As mentioned previously, EdExcel has a *Policy Watch* and this is obtainable from the Pearson Research Institute . One of the more helpful guides produced twice yearly is often titled *Who Does What? A Guide to the Main Education Agencies and Bodies and What They Do*, prepared by Steve Besley. This summary contains a chart showing the 'New Post 14 Order', which everyone should have on their office walls to help demystify the structure of the Learning and Skills Sector!

Professional practice which provides personal development

Acting as verifiers for your own institution or for an awarding body can provide a good source of personal development. If you are fortunate enough to be asked to work as an external verifier or assessor for an accredited programme, you will meet colleagues from other centres. By undertaking the role of external verifier, you will have to assure yourself that their procedures for recruiting, teaching and assessing their learners are appropriate. You will, therefore, observe the practice of your peers. You will discuss issues about the learning situation, how to implement new curriculum developments, aspects of assessment, issues of equal opportunities and access, and generally how the field is developing. These discussions are an extremely potent source of personal development for you. I learned so much from acting as external verifier to the range of teaching and training awards for City and Guilds. It informed my own practice and enabled me to share and disseminate practice that I observed among staff in the centres I visited. If you have gained experience in your field, and can take on the role, I would certainly recommend your applying to act as external verifier for an awarding body. The bodies must provide professional development for their staff and you, therefore, have access to further opportunities outside your own institution's provision.

You do not have to go outside your own organization to find opportunities to develop your own professional practice. If you have been invited to participate in college-wide committees, for example, a teaching and learning committee, quality committee or equal opportunities committee, you will discuss how aspects of the college's policies are implemented and monitored. This can inform both your own practice and help you disseminate ideas widely among your peers.

Membership of steering committees and course boards can also enable you to learn from your peers. Most committees require membership from across discipline areas, or external membership, and this requirement specifically aims to foster cross-fertilization of ideas. Disseminating these ideas is particularly important if professional practice is to benefit.

Acquiring new skills and knowledge

Keeping informed by reading about new developments and keeping abreast of current debate will help you be up to date in your knowledge *about* teaching and learning for adults. However, another aspect of continually developing your professional practice is the *improvement* of your current level of skill and knowledge. An obvious example of this is where you are asked to undertake a new course which you have not taught before. Not only will you need to familiarize yourself with the requirements of the programme, but you may also need to learn about the subject-matter more deeply. You may be asked to use new techniques. In many institutions, there is a move to making use of the learning resources centre. You may be asked to supply content for programmes that are being turned into web-based learning programmes. You may be asked to provide instruction through distance and web-based learning, and this may be something that you have not done before. Professional development involves learning new techniques and knowledge so that you can enable your learners to acquire skills and knowledge in different ways. If you do find yourself in a situation where you are unsure about what is required, what do you do? First, make sure you know who your programme co-ordinator and line manager are. Make sure that you take time to find out what is on offer centrally in the institution regarding professional development in teaching and learning. Do not restrict yourself to looking at accredited programmes. Your institution may have a policy of supporting its staff to learn by subsidizing learning on its mainstream programmes. This is where you could decide to investigate how to develop your own web-based learning, or to learn a new language. Remember, just as we think it important that our learners are exposed to a variety of ways to learn, so you, too, can do this and find out what it is like to be a *learner*. Not only can you honestly tell your learners that you know what it is like to juggle home, work and family commitments when studying, you can also see for yourself how other tutors and trainers work. Many good ideas for your own teaching and learning come from being in classes that have nothing to do with your own subject area. Providing you acknowledge where you have obtained your ideas, then there is no reason why you should not try out someone else's good idea in your own situation. You may find that your own portfolio is a great source of ideas to your tutors on your teaching qualification programme. You can usually tell who the teacher trainers are in any group of learners, as they are always making notes about the activities they have just experienced!

I recently took up playing the piano again and embarked on a series of lessons culminating very recently in taking an exam. I experienced the profound nervousness of having to demonstrate my practical skill of playing in front of an examiner, something I hadn't done since I was a teenager. It was an extremely humbling experience and reminded me only too clearly about what it is like to face a challenge, with a deadline and a one 'performance on the day' experience. It also provided me with an opportunity to reflect on my piano teacher's approach to teaching. I appreciated the way in which she instilled confidence in my ability to move to a much higher standard than I had ever thought was possible. This experience has already influenced how I work with my students and, of course, has given me a chance to say (with feeling!) that I really do know what it is like to undertake a course of study that is demanding and not guaranteed to end in success.

Serendipity

Much of your thinking and reflection may take place completely outside your everyday practice. Some people have their ideas in the middle of the night, on the bus, running around a park or in the bath. Allowing time for the creative aspect of your thought processes to come to the fore is very important for reflective teaching. Just a chance word with a friend could give you an insight into your practice, or an idea to take away and try out with your learners.

Next steps

Professional practice carries a variety of meanings. Implicit in the term is a notion of good practice. You may have read and heard about this in your own institution, or from material described above. It is difficult to know what good practice really is and whether you are, in fact, achieving it in your own work. Throughout this book there have been suggestions about what to reflect upon in the many aspects of the complex activity of teaching and learning. What can you do to ensure that you continue to develop your practice? You do not need to take a qualification in teaching and learning to continually develop your professional practice. However, if you think this is what you want to do, what is available? Many of you reading this book will already be undertaking a teaching or training qualification. If you are very new to teaching adults, you may be taking the PTLLS award. In this case, there are a number of further awards that are available. As you gain experience, you will have the opportunity to draw upon this if you decide to work towards a higher-level qualification in teaching and training. Each of the awarding bodies offers qualifications which are available in a wide range of centres, and DETLS and Postgraduate Certificates in Education (PGCEs) are also offered by higher education institutions.

All these awards work with the idea that there are general concepts of teaching and training that can be covered regardless of your subject specialism. Meeting other teachers and trainers on such programmes is a rewarding experience, where you can gain much from the cross-fertilization of ideas and from observing different practices. However, there are also programmes and qualifications which are subject-specific. There are times when it is particularly helpful to discuss teaching and learning issues about your own subject.

There are a number of subject-specific awards that you may wish to consider. These relate to certain subject areas including:

- Literacy, Numeracy, ESOL and IT Skills (Functional Skills)
- Complementary Health, including Reflexology, Aromatherapy
- Dance, Movement
- Distance/Open/Flexible Learning
- Exercise to Movement, Health and Fitness Training (YMCA)
- Marketing
- Resource-based learning
- Sign language teacher training
- Teaching English as a Foreign Language (TEFL)
- Teaching English for Speakers of Other Languages (ESOL)
- Technology
- Learning and Development.

Some awarding bodies offer units which create 'mini-awards'. One of the most frequently obtained is the assessor award qualification for people who assess NVQs. At Level 3 in the QCF there are awards such as Assessing Competence in the Work Environment and the Certificate in Assessing Vocational Achievement (OCR qualifications) and at Level 4 it is possible to gain awards in Internal and External Quality Assurance of Assessment Processes. Some of the awards are covered as part of a larger qualification. The Computer Literacy and Information Technology (CLAIT) is offered at Levels 1 to 3. A similar qualification, the ECDL (European Computer Driving License) is recognized internationally. Increasingly, you will be asked to demonstrate that you have a necessary level of key skill, for example, in literacy and numeracy, and the awarding bodies and higher education institutions require this as part of their awards.

Higher degrees

You may also consider working towards higher-level qualifications that provide you with a deeper theoretical basis for your professional practice. Most universities offer opportunities to study part-time for Postgraduate Diplomas and Masters degrees. Many of these specialize in education or lifelong learning. Some are particularly geared towards those working in post-compulsory education. There are programmes that suit trainers rather than teachers. Some of the programmes can be studied by distance learning. The variety of postgraduate programmes is quite bewildering. If you do want to pursue a qualification at this level, you will need to obtain information from a variety of universities. Most have this information on their websites as well as through prospectuses.

Masters-level work usually requires a significant piece of work, either a research project or a thesis. If you are not sure that you can devote the time to this, then you can often study to Diploma or Certificate level. The content may be similar: you just don't have to commit yourself to either undertaking an independent piece of work or to take so many modules of the full award. Certificates, Diplomas and short courses are very helpful for keeping you up to date with ideas and the theoretical underpinning. Most of these programmes carry credit which can be used towards a full award at a later stage. Many people decide to take one short course to see if they can manage the commitment of time and effort and then carry on to gain a full qualification. Others derive great benefit from the short course and do not feel any further study is possible or necessary. The important point is to decide why you want to study for an award or short course and to find out what is required in terms of level of study, time commitment and the appropriateness of the content and methods. You may find that your staff development manager can advise you about suitable courses, and even provide information about whether there is any possibility of funding for these.

With any of the courses described above, do remember to talk to a line manager, staff development manager or curriculum manager. They may know of other colleagues who have studied these programmes and can help you decide if they are suitable for you. It may be that your organization is particularly keen to sponsor you to undertake certain awards. Even if there is no funding from your organization, you may find out about how to obtain funding or career development loans. Remember that there are many experienced colleagues in any institution who have undertaken a variety of programmes of professional development. Their experiences can help you consider more options than perhaps you would find for yourself.

Professional values

Your professional practice is just one part of your life. It is influenced by who you are, your lifestyle, your circumstances, where you work and with whom. Just as we cannot talk about any one aspect of the teaching and learning situation without relating it to the larger picture, so we cannot talk about developing our own professional practice without thinking about how that fits in with the rest of our lives.

In the UK today there is a trend towards working long hours. We read about and experience high levels of stress at work. Our learners come to our sessions weary from their own busy lives. We are asked to meet more and more deadlines which become increasingly urgent. We have demands placed on us to reach a host of quality indicators. We have to become perfect tutors, counsellors, guidance workers, and somehow find time to deal with all the domestic demands of cooking, cleaning and shopping.

Reflection on our teaching, therefore, must also provide an opportunity to question whether what we do is adding something positive to our lives. For many, the satisfaction of watching our learners progress is enough to counteract their busy, stressful working conditions. We must take care, though, that what we believe in is enabled to flourish. If we place our learners at the centre of our professional activity, then we will find that we must challenge, from time to time, some of the policies that are implemented. We must speak out for the values that we believe in: treating people with respect, encouraging people, building confidence, celebrating success. And we must acknowledge the value in what we do and celebrate it publicly. I hope that your professional journey allows you time to reflect on the fundamental joys of adult learning and your role in it.

LLUK standards

This chapter will help you work towards LLUK standards – Domain A: Professional Values and Practice.

Further reading and information

Further reading

Brookfield, S. D. (1995) *Becoming a Critically Reflective Teacher.* San Francisco: Jossey-Bass.

Fawbert, F. (2003) *Teaching in Post-Compulsory Education: Learning, Skills and Standards.* London: Continuum.

Francis, M. and Gould, J. (2009) *Achieving Your PTLLS Award.* London: Sage.

Further Education National Training Organisation (2000) *Standards for Teaching and Supporting Learning in Further Education in England and Wales.* London: FENTO.

Hyland, T. and Merrill, B. (2003) *The Changing Faces of Further Education.* London: Routledge.

Lea, J., Hayes, D., Dunnill, R. and Armitage, A. (2003) *Working in Post-Compulsory Education.* Buckingham: Open University Press.

Journals and newspapers

Adults Learning

Basic Skills Bulletin

Basic Skills Professional Development

FE Now

The Guardian (Tuesday)

The Independent (Thursday)

Numeracy Briefing

The Times Education Supplement (Friday)

Times Higher Education Supplement (Friday)

Organizations and websites

Many of the websites can change as organizations change their names, or restructured or cease to exist. It is, therefore, a good idea to use a keyword search if the address you first use is no longer available. Keywords of education, learning, training and skills may help locate many of the websites below. Most of these websites contain links to each other, and to additional websites that may be of interest.

Academic portals

British Academy (www.britac.ac.uk/portal/)

British Educational Research Association (www.bera.ac.uk/). Conference papers – mostly as abstracts.

BUBL link selected internet resources covering all academic subject area (http://bubl. ac.uk/link/index.html)

Campbell Collaboration. Its objectives are to prepare, maintain and disseminate systematic reviews of studies of interventions (www.campbellcollaboration.org/).

Educational Evidence Portal (eep) (www.eep.ac.uk/DNN2/). This is a very useful website with links to a number of other agencies and research centres. It helps users find educational evidence from a range of reputable UK sources using a single search.

RSA (Royal Society for the encouragement of Arts, Manufacture and Commerce) (www.thersa.org.uk)

Education

Association of Colleges (AoC) (www.aoc.co.uk/)

Centre for the Study of Civil Society (formerly Centre for Voluntary Organisation) (www.lse.ac.uk/collections/ccs). Research on the voluntary sector

City and Guilds (www.cityandguilds.com)

City and Guilds newsletter, the Broadsheet (www.cityandguilds.com/Broadsheet.html)

Further education news (www.fenews.co.uk/) – this website contains video clips and has a news archive

Harvard reference system: detailed guide from Edge Hill College (www.edgehill.ac.uk/tld/student/7steps/harvard. htm)

Higher Education Funding Council for England (HEFCE) (www.hefce.ac.uk/)

Higher Education in Further Education Colleges (www.sheffield.ac.uk/heinfestratprog/materials.html) – this website provides information and materials to support the strategic development of higher education provided by further education colleges

Institute for Learning (IfL) (www.ifl.ac.uk)

Qualifications and Curriculum Authority (QCA) (www.qca.org.uk/)

Quality Assurance Agency for Higher Education (QAA) (www.qaa.ac.uk/)

Universities and Colleges Admissions Service (UCAS) home page (www.ucas.ac.uk/)

UCAS statistics and publications on student numbers and widening participation (www.ucas.ac.uk/figures/archive/ publist/index.html)

Universities and Colleges Union (UCU) (www.ucu.org.uk/)

Universities UK (www.universitiesuk.ac.uk/)

University of Leeds. Education-line is a freely accessible database of the full text of conference papers, working papers and electronic literature which supports educational research, policy and practice (http://brs.leeds. ac.uk/~beiwww/el.htm)

European Union

ALICE database (information on non-formal adult education in Europe) (www.esnal.net/alice.html)

CORDIS (EU Community Research and Development Information Service) (http://cordis.europa.eu/)

EU–CEDEFOP (European Centre for the Development of Vocational Training) (www.cedefop.europa.eu/EN/Index.aspx)

EU documents (ISBNs) and official Commission Documents (http://ec.europa.eu/unitedkingdom/index_en.htm)

Organisation for Economic Co-operation and Development (OECD) (www.oecd.org/home/)

UKRO European News (news on EU-funded opportunities for research and higher education) (www.ukro.ac.uk/)

Libraries

British Library catalogue (http://blpc.bl.uk/)

COPAC (http://copac.ac.uk/copac/). Access to the merged online catalogues of 24 of the largest university research libraries in the UK and Ireland, *plus* the British Library and the National Library of Scotland.

Institute of Education (library catalogue) (www.ioe.ac.uk/library/librarycatalogues.html)

London School of Economics library catalogue (www.lse.ac.uk/library/)

Newspapers and journals

Guardian Education (www.guardian.co.uk/education)

Independent Education page (www.independent.co.uk/news/education)

Times Education Supplement (http://info.tes.co.uk)

Times Higher Education Supplement (all subscribers have access to all archived articles through this site) (www.thes.co.uk/). Use your subscription number to obtain your own user name and password.

Publishers

Cambridge University Press (www.cambridge.org)

NIACE publications (www.niace.org.uk/Publications/Default.htm)

Open University Press (http://mcgraw-hill.co.uk/openup/)

Oxford University Press (www.oup.co.uk/)

The Policy Press (www.policypress.co.uk)

Routledge (www.routledge.com/)

Sage (www.sagepub.co.uk/)

SARA (www.tandf.co.uk/sara/). This is the portal to request content alerts for Carfax, CRC Press, Frank Cass, Parthenon, Psychology Press, Routledge, Spon Press or Taylor & Francis journals.

TSO (formerly The Stationery Office) (www.tso.co.uk/bookshop/)

Research

British Educational Research Association (BERA) (www.bera.ac.uk)

Centre for the Analysis of Social Exclusion (CASE) (http://sticerd.lse.ac.uk/case)

City and Guilds Centre for Skills Development (www.skillsdevelopment.org.uk/) commissions research and publishes a series of reports

Current Education Research in the UK (CERUK) (www.ceruk.ac.uk/)

Economic and Social Research Council (ESRC) (www.esrc.ac.uk). The UK's leading research funding and training agency addressing economic and social concerns

Joseph Rowntree Foundation (www.jrf.org.uk). Substantial summaries of research Reports

Learning and Skills Improvement Service (LSIS) (www.lsis.org.uk/Pages/default.aspx)

Learning and Skills Network (LSN) (www.lsnlearning.org.uk)

Learning and Skills Research Network (LSRN) (www.lsrn.org.uk/)

National Audit Office (independent scrutiny of effectiveness of government spending and policies) (www.nao.org.uk)

National Foundation for Education al Research (NFER) (www.nfer.ac.uk)

National Institute for Adult and Continuing Education (NIACE) (www.niace.org.uk)

National Research Centre for Adult Literacy, Numeracy and Language (NRDC) (www.nrdc.org.uk/)

Organisation for Economic Co-operation and Development (OECD) (www.oecd.org)

Policy Studies Institute (www.psi.org.uk/). Research papers on various topics that can be downloaded free

Research and Practice in Adult Literacy (RaPAL) (www.literacy.lancs.ac.uk/rapal/)

Scottish Council for Research in Education (SCRE) (www.scre.ac.uk/)

Social Research Update (University of Surrey Department of Sociology) (www.surrey.ac.uk). Each issue is a succinct article on some issue of research methods (e.g. Focus groups, finding information on the web). Free access

Teaching and Learning Research Programme (TLRP) (www.tlrp.org/index.html)

UK government

Communities and Local Government (all reports can be downloaded) (www.communities.gov.uk/publications)

Department for Education(DfE) (www.dfe.gov.uk). Latest government documents, press releases

Equality and diversity (www.equalityhumanrights.com)

Ofsted (www.ofsted.gov.uk/)

Social Survey Division of the Office for National Statistics carries out high-quality survey research for government departments and other public bodies on a range of social issues (www.statistics.gov.uk/ssd/default.asp)

Skills Funding Agency (www.skillsfundingagency.bis.gov.uk)

UK Census 2001 (www.statistics.gov.uk/census2001/)

Youth Funding Agency (www.ypla.gov.uk)

Further abroad

American Educational Research Association (AERA) (www.aera.net)

Australian Vocational Education and Training Research Association (AVETRA) (www.avetra.org.au)

Commission of European Communities (http://europa.eu/index_en.htm)

Department of Education (USA) (www.ed.gov/)

Educational Resources Information Center (ERIC) (http://accesseric.org)

Ministry of Education (New Zealand) (www.minedu.govt.nz/NZEducation.aspx)

National Center for the Study of Adult Learning and Literacy (NCSALL) (http://gseweb.harvard.edu)

New Zealand Council for Educational Research (www.nzcer.org.nz)

Technical and Further Education (TAFE) (www.tafe.vic.gov.au)

UNESCO (www.unesco.org/education)

Epilogue

When I was writing the changes to this third edition in summer 2010, I was frustrated by the quickening pace of change in the Learning and Skills System, knowing that there was a good chance that some of the agencies and activities would be closing or being overtaken by different organizations. Yet I couldn't predict exactly how they would be changed. Throughout the book, I have encouraged you, the reader, to keep in touch with what is happening in the sector, whether or not you work in the English system or further afield. The changes being introduced in England are not unique and many other countries are attempting to alter the structure and provision of further and adult education as they grapple with the deep and long-standing challenges of managing opportunities for learning with limited and often dwindling resources.

What I can now see is a sector which is undergoing significant cuts in England. The further education provision is subject to a 25 per cent reduction in funding over the next few years. Individuals who are over 23 will now have to pay for their first qualification at Level 2 and above. As Ian Nash noted

> There is something very mean spirited about a politician or bureaucrat who would shave two years off the state-funded entitlements for a 25 year old struggling to achieve qualifications equivalent to GCSE. In the grand scale of things this is at best penny pinching; at its worse it is vindictive. (Nash, 2011, p. 3)

For adult and community learning, the picture is worse. Although in the current year 2011, the budget was safeguarded to the tune of £210 million, this is a drop in the ocean compared with the overall budget for further education. BIS is currently examining how informal adult and community learning should be supported in future and queried particularly how lifelong learning provision saves the economy funds through enabling people to stay healthy and active. It is interesting to note how informal learning has become part of the discourse after the 2009 Learning Revolution White Paper turned its attention to learning that goes on beyond the boundaries of formal adult and further education. This discourse is now including terms such as 'reform and reinvigoration' as well as describing learning as being a continuum. Adult basic skills is also currently the subject of review by BIS. In fact, much of the provision in lifelong learning is being queried and tested against a backdrop of spending cuts and exhortation for people to keep investing in their own futures.

A major report by Alison Wolf (2011) has questioned the value of GCSEs and vocational qualifications which do not appear to bring any economic gain to individual young people (and to some extent adults). Her report recommended that young people should not be forced into specializing so early in their choice of subjects, allow certain vocational qualifications to be offered in schools from September 2011 and move all qualifications away from the qualification framework which she argues is suitable only for adults. She recommends that apprenticeships for 16–18-year-olds should be increased with genuine work placements. However, her major recommendation was that all young people should attain English and Maths GCSE and if they have not done so by the time they reach 16 (currently the leaving age), they must pursue these as part of any subsequent programme of study.

Of particular interest to many people reading this book is that she suggested that further education staff who are qualified in the Learning and Skills Sector should be able to teach in schools, thus finally providing parity between the qualifications from this sector and compulsory schooling. This recommendation was immediately accepted by the government.

There are other changes occurring in England affecting further and adult education. The Education Maintenance Allowance (EMA) has been disbanded and will be replaced by a more careful means-tested fund. This decision was highly contested by staff and learners in the sector. At the same time, the initiative to encourage more young people from disadvantaged backgrounds to enter higher education, Aimhigher, closes in summer 2011.

Possibly one of the most controversial decisions affects people who want to study at higher education. From September 2012, the fees charged will be increased by at least double or in some cases nearly triple to a maximum of £9000. At the time of writing, many universities are deciding to set the maximum fee, even though they are aware that they will have to demonstrate how they will recruit and retain students who would be previously from widening participation backgrounds.

All in all, the picture is one of confusion and mixed messages. The onus on individuals is increasingly to fund their learning with reduced support from the state. Yet, there is some cause for celebration. Apprenticeships are being increased; there is a pupil premium to support children from disadvantaged backgrounds and there is a serious attempt to streamline and reduce the bureaucracy which dominates the educational sector.

It is impossible to capture the many changes in these last paragraphs. It is clear that this is a time of great change and challenge. The commitment and resilience that reside in those who work in the sector will help buffer the worst excesses of policy decisions currently being made. By the time you read this, more decisions will have been made which will change the landscape of lifelong learning in this country and abroad. I hope that you will continue to keep abreast of these changes and examine how you, as a professional, can ensure that your learners continue to have the opportunities they need and deserve.

Yvonne Hillier
April 2011

Glossary

AACS	Adult Advice and Careers Service
ABSSU	Adult Basic Skills Strategy Unit
ACVE	Advanced Certificate in Vocational Education
AE	Adult Education
'A' level	Advanced Level
ALB	Arms Length Body
ALF	Average Level of Funding
AoC	Association of Colleges
APEL	Accreditation of Prior Experiential Learning
APL	Accreditation of Prior Learning
AS	Advanced Supplementary Level
BERA	British Educational Research Association
BIS	Department for Business, Innovation and Skills
BSA	Basic Skills Agency
CAL	Computer-Aided Learning
CALL	Campaigning Alliance for Lifelong Learning
CBI	Confederation of British Industry
CBL	Computer-Based Learning
CE	Continuing Education
CETLS	Certificate in Teaching in the Learning and Skills Sector
CETTs	Centres for Excellence in Teacher Training
CGLI	City and Guilds of London Institute
CIPD	Chartered Institute of Personnel and Development
CLA	Copyright Licensing Authority
CLAIT	Computer Literacy and Information Technology
CoVE	Centre of Vocational Excellence
CPD	Continuing Professional Development
CPVE	Certificate in Pre-vocational Education
CSE	Certificate in Secondary Education
DCSF	Department for Children, Schools and Families
DDA	Disability Discrimination Act
DES	Department of Education and Science
DETLS	Diploma in Teaching in the Learning and Skills Sector
DfE	Department for Education

DfEE	Department for Education and Employment
DfES	Department for Education and Skills
DIUS	Department for Innovation, Universities and Skills
DoE	Department of Employment
E2E	Entry to Employment
ECDL	European Computer Driving License
ECM	Every Child Matters
EEP	Education Evidence Portal
EMA	Education Maintenance Allowance
ENTO	Employment National Training Organisation
ESOL	English for Speakers of Other Languages
ESRC	Economic and Social Science Research Council
ET	Employment Training
ETP	Employment Training Programme
EU	European Union
FD	Foundation Degree
FE	Further Education
FEDA	Further Education Development Agency
FEFC	Further Education Funding Council
FENTO	Further Education National Training Organisation
FEU	Further Education Unit
FL	Foundation Learning
GC	Guidance Council
GCE	General Certificate of Education
GCSE	General Certificate of Secondary Education
GNVQ	General National Vocational Qualification
HE	Higher Education
HEA	Higher Education Academy
HEFCE	Higher Education Funding Council for England
HNC	Higher National Certificate
HND	Higher National Diploma
IAG	Information, Advice and Guidance
IALS	International Adult Literacy Survey
ICT	Information and Communications Technology
IF	Increased Flexibility partnerships
IfL	Institute for Learning
IFLL	Inquiry into the Future of Lifelong Learning
ILP	Individual Learning Programme
ILT	Institute for Learning and Teaching

IQ	Intelligence Quotient
IT	Information Technology
IWB	Interactive Whiteboard
KS	Key Skills
LA	Local Authority
LDD	Learning Difficulty or Disability
LLL	Lifelong Learning
LLUK	Lifelong Learning UK
LSC	Learning and Skills Council
LSDA	Learning and Skills Development Agency
LSIS	Learning and Skills Improvement Service
LSN	Learning and Skills Network
LSRC	Learning and Skills Research Centre
LSRN	Learning and Skills Research Network
LSS	Learning and Skills System
MA	Modern Apprenticeship
MBPI	Myers Briggs Personality Inventory
MIAP	Managing Information across Partners
MSC	Manpower Services Commission
NACCEG	National Council for Careers and Education Guidance
NAGCELL	National Advisory Group for Continuing Education and Lifelong Learning
NALS	National Adult Participation in Learning Survey
NATFHE	National Association of Teachers in Further and Higher Education
NCVQ	National Council for Vocational Qualifications
NEET	Not in Education, Employment or Training
NERF	National Education Research Forum
NETTs	National Education and Training Targets
NIACE	National Institute for Adult and Continuing Education
NOCN	National Open College Network
NQF	National Qualifications Framework
NRDC	National Research and Development Centre for Adult Literacy, Numeracy and ESOL
NROA	National Record of Achievement
NTO	National Training Organisation
NVQ	National Vocational Qualification
OCR	Oxford Cambridge and RSA Examinations
OECD	Organisation for Economic Co-operation and Development
Ofsted	Office for Standards in Education
OHP	Overhead Projector
OHT	Overhead Transparency

ONS	Office for National Statistics
OPAC	Open Public Access Catalogue
OU	Open University
P4P	Partnerships for Progression
PAULO	Adult Education National Training Organisation
PBL	Problem-Based Learning
PTLLS	Preparing to Teach in the Lifelong Learning Sector
PGCE	Postgraduate Certificate in Education
PLTS	Personal Learning and Thinking Skills
PLR	Personal Learning Record
QCA	Qualifications and Curriculum Authority
QCDA	Qualifications and Curriculum Development Agency
QCF	Qualifications and Credit Framework
QIA	Quality Improvement Agency
QTLS	Qualified to Teach in the Learning and Skills Sector
QTS	Qualified Teacher Status
RaPAL	Research and Practice in Adult Literacy
RBL	Resource-Based Learning
RDA	Regional Development Agency
RoC	Rules of Combination
RPA	Raising Participation Age
RSA	Royal Society of Arts
RtA	Routes to Achievement
SCAA	Schools Curriculum and Assessment Authority
SENDA	Special Educational Needs and Disability Act
SFA	Skills Funding Agency
SK4L	Skills for Life
SSC	Sector Skills Council
TA	Training Agency
TEED	Training, Education and Employment Commission
TEFL	Teaching English as a Foreign Language
TOPS	Training Opportunities Scheme
TRLP	Teaching and Learning Research Programme
TUC	Trades' Union Congress
UCU	Universities and Colleges Union
UDACE	Unit for the Development of Adult Continuing Education
UfI	University for Industry
UK	United Kingdom
UKCES	UK Commission for Employment and Skills
ULN	Unique Learner Number

WBL	Work-Based Learning
WEA	Workers Education Association
YMCA	Young Men's Christian Association
YOPS	Youth Opportunities Scheme
YPLA	Young People's Learning Agency
YT	Youth Training
YTS	Youth Training Scheme

Bibliography

Adorno, T. et al. (1976) *The Positivist Dispute in German Sociology.* London: Heinemann.

Ainley, P. (1993) *Class and Skill.* London: Cassell.

Argyris, C. (1982) *Reasoning, Learning and Action.* San Francisco: Jossey-Bass.

Argyris, C. and Schön, D. (1974) *Theory in Practice: Increasing Professional Effectiveness.* San Francisco: Jossey-Bass.

Armitage, A., Bryant, R., Dunnill, R., Hammersley, M., Hayes, D., Hudson, A. and Lawes, S. (1999) *Teaching and Training in Post-Compulsory Education.* Buckingham: Open University Press.

Ausubel, D. P., Novak, J. D. and Hanesian H. (1978) *Educational Psychology: A Cognitive View* (2nd edn). New York: Holt, Rhinehart and Winston.

Avis, J. (2009) 'Further Education in England: the New Localism, Systems Theory and Governance', *Journal of Education Policy*, 24, 5, pp. 633–48.

Avis, J. (2010) 'Education, Governance and the "New" Professionalism: radical possibilities?' *Power and Education*, 2, 2, pp. 197–208.

Bateson, G. (1958) *Naven.* Stanford, CA: Stanford University Press.

Beinart, S. and Smith, P. (1998) *The National Adult Learning Survey 1997.* London: DfEE.

Besley, S. (2004) *Policy Watch January–June 2004.* London: Edexcel.

Besley, S. (2009a) 'A postscript to the GCSE results 2009', *Policy Watch*, 1 September 2009. London: Edexcel.

Besley, S. (2009b) 'Who does what in the 14–19 system', *Policy Watch*, April 2009. London: Edexcel.

Besley, S. (2010a) 'Keeping track of what happened in education in February 2010', *Policy Watch*, 26 February 2010. London: Edexcel.

Besley, S. (2010b) 'Meeting the needs of young people during the recession and beyond', *14–19 Learning and Skills Bulletin*, Issue 11 Spring 2010. Cambridge: Circa.

Besley, S. (2010c) *Policy Watch Priorities and Investment for 16–19 Provision for 2010/11.* London: Edexcel.

Biggs, J. (1999) *Teaching for Quality Learning in Higher Education.* Buckingham: SRHE/Open University Press.

Bion, W. (1961) *Experiences in Groups.* London: Tavistock.

Bloom, B. (1956) *Taxonomy of Educational Objectives.* London: Longman.

Brennan, L. and Gosling, D. (eds) (2004) *Making Foundation Degrees.* Work Brentwood: SEEC.

Briggs, Myers I. (1993) *Introduction to Type.* Oxford: Oxford Psychology Press.

Brockbank, A. and McGill, I. (1998) *Facilitating Reflective Learning in Higher Education.* Buckingham: SRHE/Open University Press.

Brookfield, S. D. (1988) *Training Educators of Adults: The Theory and Practice of Graduate Adult Education in the United States.* London: Croom Helm.

Brookfield, S. D. (1990) *The Skillful Teacher.* San Francisco: Jossey-Bass.

Brookfield, S. D. (1993) 'Breaking the code: engaging practitioners in critical analysis of adult education literature', *Studies in the Education of Adults*, 25, 1, pp. 64–91.

Brookfield, S. D. (1995) *Becoming a Critically Reflective Teacher.* San Francisco: Jossey-Bass.

Brookfield, S. D. (1998) 'Against Naive Romanticism: from celebration to the critical analysis of experience', *Studies in Continuing Education*, 20, 2, pp. 127–42.

Bruner, J. (1966) *The Process of Education.* Cambridge: Harvard University Press.

Burgess, T. (2000) 'The logic of learning and its implication for higher education', *Higher Education Review*, 32, 2, pp. 53–65.

Carr, W. (1986) 'Theories of theory and practice', *Journal of Philosophy of Education*, 20, 2, pp. 177–86.

Carr, W. and Kemmis, S. (1986) *Becoming Critical.* Lewes: Falmer.

Castling, A. (1996) *Competence-Based Teaching and Training.* Basingstoke: Macmillan/City and Guilds.

Chalmers, A. F. (1982) *What is This Thing Called Science?* Milton Keynes: Open University Press.

Chown, A. and Last J. (1993) 'Can the NCVQ model be used for teacher training?', *Journal of Further and Higher Education*, 17, 2, pp. 15–26.

City and Guilds of London Institute (2000) *Ensuring Quality Policy and Practice for Externally Verified Assessment* (9th edn, October). London: City and Guilds.

Clow, R. and Harkin, J. (2003) *FE Teachers Perceptions of Initial Teacher Training and Implications for the Teacher Training Curriculum Journal of National Association for Staff Development in the Post-16 Sector* 47, pp. 16–24.

Coffield, F. (1999) 'Breaking the consensus: lifelong learning as social control', *British Educational Research Journal*, 23, 4, pp. 479–99.

Coffield, F., Moseley, D., Hall, E. and Ecclestone, K. (2004) *Should We Be Using Learning Styles? What Research Has to Say to Practice.* London: Learning and Skills Research Centre.

Collins, M. (1991) *Adult Education as Vocation: A Critical Role for the Adult Educator.* New York: Routledge.

Commission of the European Communities (1995) *Teaching and Learning – towards the Learning Society.* Luxembourg: EC.

Commission of the European Communities (1997) *European Directive 97/81.*

Cottrell, S. (1999) *The Study Skills Handbook.* Basingstoke: Macmillan.

Cowan, J. (1999) *On Becoming an Innovative University Teacher.* Buckingham: Open University Press.

Cowley, S. (2010) *Getting the Buggers to Behave.* London: Continuum.

Craig, M. (2000) *Thinking Visually: Business Applications of 14 Core Diagrams.* London: Continuum.

Crotty, M. (1996) *Phenomenology and Nursing Research.* Melbourne: Churchill Livingstone.

Daines, J. and Graham, B. (1988) *Adult Learning, Adult Teaching.* Nottingham Working Papers in Staff Development and Training, Nottingham: University of Nottingham.

Department for Children, Schools and Families (2010) *Young People Not in Education, Employment or Training: Eighth Report of Session 2009–2010 HC 316 I and II.* London: Stationery Office.

Department for Education and Employment (1998) *The Learning Age: A Renaissance for New Britain.* London: HMSO.

Department for Education and Employment (1999) *Learning to Succeed.* London: HMSO.

Department for Education and Employment (2000) *Colleges for Excellence and Innovation Statement by the Secretary of State for Education and Employment on the Future of Further Education in England.* London: DfEE.

Department for Education and Employment (2001) (www.lifelonglearning.co.uk/llp/remit.htm)

Department of Education and Science (1973) *Adult Education: A Plan for Development* (The Russel Report). London: HMSO.

Department for Education and Skills (2001) *Skills for Life: The National Strategy for Improving Adult Literacy and Numeracy Skills.* London: Department for Education and Skills.

Department for Education and Skills (2002) *Success for All: Reforming Further Education and Training.* London: Stationery Office.

Department for Education and Skills (2003a) *21st Century Skills: Realising Our Potential: Individuals, Employers, Nation.* London: HMSO.

Department for Education and Skills (2003b) *Qualifications and Participation in Learning at a Local Level: England 2002/2003* (www.dfes.gov.uk).

Department for Education and Skills (2004a) *Equipping Our Teachers for the Future: Reforming Initial Teacher Training for the Learning and Skills Sector.* November 2004 (www.dfes.gov.uk).

Department for Education and Skills (2004b) *National Quality Improvement Body for the Learning and Skills Sector: Progress Report 16 November 2004.* London: DfES.

Department for Education and Skills (2004c) *Standards Unit Newsletter,* Issue 4 Spring 2004.

Department for Education and Skills (2005) *Skills: Getting on in Business, Getting on at Work* (www.dfes.gov.uk).

Department for Education and Skills (2006) *Further Education: Raising Skills, Improving Life Chances* (www.dfes.gov.uk).

Department for Innovation, Universities and Skills (2008) *Skills for Life: Changing Lives.* London: Stationery Office (www.bis.gov.uk/assets/biscore/corporate/migratedD/publications/S/SkillsforLifeChangingLives) accessed 23 June 2011.

Department for Trade and Industry (2004) *Regional Competitiveness and State of the Regions* (www.dti.gov.uk).

Department of Employment (1981) *A New Training Initiative: A Programme for Action.* London: HMSO.

Dewey, J. (1916) *Democracy and Education.* New York: Free Press.

Dewey, J. (1933) *How We Think: A Restatement of the Relation of Reflective Thinking in the Educative Process.* Chicago: Henry Regnery.

Doyal, L. and Harris, R. (1986) *Empiricism, Explanation and Rationality: An Introduction to the Philosophy of Social Sciences.* London: Routledge.

Dreyfus, H. and Dreyfus, S. (1986) *Mind Over Machine: The Power of Human Intuition and Expertise in the Era of the Computer.* Oxford: Blackwell.

Ecclestone, K. (1996) 'The reflective practitioner: mantra or a model for emancipation?', *Studies in the Education of Adults,* 28, pp. 145–61.

Ecclestone, K. (1997) 'Energising or enervating: implications of National Vocational Qualifications in professional development', *Journal of Vocational Education and Training,* 49, pp. 65–79.

Education and Employment Committee of the House of Commons (1997) *Report of the Select Committee.* Evidence by the National Association of Teachers in Further and Higher Education (NATFHE), vol. 2, Appendix 53. London: HMSO.

Education and Training Monitor (December 2000) Issue 69.

Edwards, R. (1997) *Changing Places? Flexibility, Lifelong Learning and Learning Society.* London: Routledge.

Edwards, R., Harrison, R. and Tait, A. (eds) (1998) *Telling Tales: Perspectives on Guidance and Counselling in Learning.* London: Routledge/Open University.

Egan, G. (1976) *Interpersonal Living: A Skills/Contract Approach to Human Relations Training in Groups.* Monterey, CA: Brooks/Cole.

Egan, G. (1990) *The Skilled Helper: A Systematic Approach to Effective Helping* (4th edn). Pacific Grove, CA: Brooks/Cole.

Elliot, J. (1991) 'A model of professionalism and its implication for teacher education', *British Educational Research Journal,* 17, 4, pp. 310–14.

Entwhistle, N. and Ramsden, P. (1983) *Understanding Student Learning.* London: Routledge.

Eraut, M. (1994) *Developing Professional Knowledge and Competence.* London: Falmer.

Erikson, E. H. (1978) *Adulthood*. New York: Norton.

Fawbert, F. (ed.) (2003) *Teaching in Post-Compulsory Education: Learning, Skills and Standards*. London: Continuum.

Field, J. (2000) *Lifelong Learning and the New Order*. Stoke-on-Trent: Trentham Books.

Field, J. and Schuller, T. (2000) 'Networks, norms and trust: explaining patterns of lifelong learning in Scotland and Ireland', in F. Coffield (ed.) *Differing Visions of a Learning Society*, vol. 2. Bristol: Policy Press.

Fieldhouse, R. (1996) *A History of Modern British Adult Education*. Leicester: NIACE.

Flanagan, J. C. (1954) 'The Critical Incident Technique', *Psychological Bulletin*, 51, 4, pp. 327–58.

Freire, P. (1971) *Pedagogy of the Oppressed*. Harmondsworth: Penguin.

Freire, P. (1972) *Cultural Action for Freedom*. Harmondsworth: Penguin.

Freire, P. (2002) *Pedagogy of Hope: Reliving Pedagogy of the Oppressed*. London: Continuum.

Fryer, R. (1997) *Learning for the 21st Century, The First Report of the National Advisory Group for Continuing Education and Lifelong Learning*. London: NAGCELL.

Further Education Funding Council (2000) *Supporting Part-Time Teachers in Further Education Colleges, National Report from The Inspectorate* (1999). Coventry: FEFC.

Further Education Funding Council (2001) *Student Numbers at Colleges in the Further Education Sector and External Institutions in England in 1999–2000*. Coventry: FEFC.

Further Education National Training Organisation (1999) *Standards for Teaching and Supporting Learning in Further Education in England and Wales*. London: FENTO.

Gagné R. (1985) *The Conditions of Learning*. New York: Holt, Rhinehart and Winston.

Gibbs, G., Habeshaw, S. and Habeshaw, T. (1986) *53 Interesting Ways to Assess Your Students*. Bristol: Technical and Education Services.

Gramsci, A. (1971) *Selections from Prison Notebooks* (ed. and trans. Q. Hoare and G. Nowell Smith). London: Lawrence and Wishart.

Gray, D., Griffin, C. and Nasta, T. (2000) *Training to Teach in Further and Adult Education*. Cheltenham: Stanley Thornes, pp. 139–64.

Gray, E. D. and Griffin, C. (eds) (2000) *Post-Compulsory Education and the New Millennium*. Higher Education Policy Series 54. London: Jessica Kingsley.

Griffin, C. (1989) 'Cultural studies, critical theory and adult education', in B. Bright (ed.) *Theory and Practice in the Study of Adult Education: The Epistemological Debate*. London: Routledge, Chapman and Hall.

Guidance Council (2002) *Quality Standards Matrix: Quality Standard for Information, Advice and Guidance Services* (IAG) (www.guidancecouncil.com).

Hammond, M. (1998) 'Learning through on-line discussion: what are the opportunities for professional development and what are the characteristics of on-line writing?', *Journal of Information Technology for Teacher Education*, 2, 3, pp. 331–46.

Hayes, J. R. (1976) 'It's the thought that counts. New Approaches to Educational Theory', in D. K. Lahr (ed.) *Cognition and Instruction*. Hillsdale, NJ: Arlbaum.

Heron, J. (1989) *The Facilitator's Handbook*. London: Kogan Page.

Hillier, Y. (1994) 'Informal Practitioner Theory in Adult Basic Education', University of East London, unpublished Ph.D. thesis.

Hillier, Y. (1999) 'Higher Level National Vocational Qualifications: the candidates' experience', *Journal of Vocational Education and Training*, 51, 2, pp. 199–228.

Hillier, Y. (2010) 'Counting me in and Getting On', in Sue Jackson (ed) *Innovations in Lifelong Learning Critical Perspectives on Diversity, Participation and Vocational Learning*. London: Routledge.

Hillier, Y. and Jameson, J. (2003) *Empowering Researchers in Further Education*. Stoke-on-Trent: Trentham Books.

Hillier, Y. and Jameson, J. (2004) *The Ragged Trousered Philanthropists*. London: LSDA.

Hillier, Y. and Thompson, A. (eds) (2004) *Readings in Post-Compulsory Education: Research in Learning and Skills*. London: Continuum.

Hodgson, A. (2000) *Policies, Politics and the Future of Lifelong Learning*. London: Routledge.

Hogwood, B. W. and Gunn, L. A. (1984) *Policy Analysis for the Real World*. London: Oxford University Press.

Honey, P. and Mumford, A. (1992) *The Manual of Learning Styles*. Maidenhead: Peter Honey.

Horkheimer, M. (1972) *Critical Theory*. New York: Herder and Herder.

Hoppe, R. (2010) *The Governance of Problems: Puzzling, Powering and Participation*. Bristol: Policy Press.

Houston, G. (1990) *The Red Book of Groups* (3rd edn). Norfolk: Rochester Foundation.

Huddlestone, P. and Unwin, L. (1997) *Teaching and Learning in Further Education: Diversity and Change*. London: Routledge.

Hyland, T. (1994) *Competence, Education and NVQs: Dissenting Perspectives*. Cassell: London.

Hyland, T. (1998) 'De-professionalising teaching: putting ethics back into post-school education', *Adults Learning*, 9, 5, pp. 9–12.

Hyland, T. and Merrill, B. (2003) *The Changing Faces of Further Education*. London: Routledge.

Institute for Employment Studies with NIACE (2000) *Adult Learning in England: A Review*. Brighton: IES.

Ivanic, R., Clark R. and Rimmershaw R. (1999) 'What am I supposed to make of this?', in Mary R. Lea and B. Stierer (eds) *Student Writing in Higher Education*. Buckingham: SRHE/Open University Press.

Jacques, D. (2000) *Learning in Groups* (3rd edn). London: Kogan Page.

Jarvis, P. (1990) *An International Dictionary of Adult and Continuing Education*. London: Routledge.

Kelly, T. (1970) *A History of Adult Education in Great Britain: From the Middle Ages to the Twentieth Century*. Liverpool: Liverpool University Press.

Kennedy, H. (1997) *Learning Works: Widening Participation in Further Education*. Coventry: FEFC.

Kindred, M. (1987) *Once upon a Group*. Southwell: Southwell Diocesan Education Committee.

Knowles, M. (1978) *The Adult Learner: A Neglected Species*. Houston: Gulf Publishing.

Knowles, M. (ed.) (1984) *Andragogy in Action*. San Francisco: Jossey-Bass.

Kolb, D. (1984) *Experiential Learning*. Englewood Cliffs, NJ: Prentice Hall.

Lave, E. and Wenger, E. (1991) *Situated Learning*. Cambridge: Cambridge University Press.

Lea, J., Hayes, D., Dunnill, R. and Armitage, A. (2003) *Working in Post-Compulsory Education*. Buckingham: Open University Press.

Lea, M. and Stierer, B. (1999) *Student Writing in Higher Education*. Buckingham: SRHE/Open University Press.

Learndirect (January 2001) (www.ufiltd.co.uk/Update/profiles/id-factsfigures.htm).

Leitch, S. (2006) *The Leitch Review of Skills: Prosperity for All in the Global Economy – World Class Skills: Final Report December 2006*. London: Stationery Office.

Livingston, K., Soden, R. and Kirkwood, M. (2004) *Post-16 Pedagogy and Thinking Skills: An Evaluation*. London: Learning and Skills Research Centre.

Lovell, R. B. (1979) *Adult Learning*. London: Routledge.

Lovett, T. (ed.) (1988) *Radical Approaches to Adult Education*. London: Routledge.

McCarthy, T. (1984) *The Critical Theory of Jurgen Habermas*. Cambridge: Polity Press.

McGill, I. and Brockbank, A. (2004) *The Action Learning Handbook: Powerful Techniques for Education, Professional Development and Training*. London: RoutledgeFalmer.

McNair, S. (ed.) (1996) *Reflections from the Guidance and Learner Autonomy in Higher Education Programmes.* Moorfoot: DfEE.

Malseed, J. (1992) *48 Warm-Ups for Group Work.* Lancaster: Lancaster University.

Manpower Services Commission (1981) *A New Training Initiative.* Moorfoot: MSC.

Marcuse, H. (1966) *Eros and Civilisation.* London: Sphere Books.

Martinez, P. (2000) *Raising Achievement: A Guide to Successful Strategies.* London: DfEE/FEDA.

Marton, F. and Saljö, R. (1997) 'Approaches to learning', in F. Marton, D. Hounsell and N. J. Entwhistle (eds) *The Experience of Learning.* Edinburgh: Scottish Academic Press.

Maslow, A. (1968) *Towards a Psychology of Being.* New York: Van Nostrand.

Mayo, M. and Thompson J. (eds) (1995) *Adult Learning, Critical Intelligence and Social Change.* Leicester: NIACE.

Mezirow, J. (1998) 'On critical reflection', *Adult Education Quarterly,* 48, 3, pp. 185–98.

Moon, J. (1999) *Reflection in Learning and Professional Development: Theory and Practice.* London: Kogan Page.

Moser, C. (1999) *Improving Literacy and Numeracy: A Fresh Start.* London: DfEE.

Nash, I. (2011) 'Cuts strategy flawed by poor political judgement', *Basic Skills Bulletin,* 91, March 2011. Devon: Education Publishing Company.

National Committee for Continuing Education and Lifelong Learning (1999) *Creating Learning Cultures: Next Steps in Achieving the Learning Age.* London: HMSO.

National Committee for Inquiry into Higher Education (1997) *Higher Education in the Learning Society* (Dearing Report). London: NCIHE.

National Employment Panel (2004) *Welfare to Workforce Development* (www.dwp.gov.uk/docs/skillswelfaretoworkforcedevelopment.pdf).

National Institute for Adult and Continuing Education (2000) *Impact of Learning on Health.* F. Aldridge and P. Lavendar (eds). Leicester: NIACE.

Newman M. (1999) 'Constructing and critiquing reflective practice', *Educational Action Research,* 7, 1, pp. 145–61.

Nonaka I. and Takeuchi H. (1995) *The Knowledge Creating Company: How Japanese Companies Create the Dynamics of Innovation.* Oxford: Oxford University Press.

Nyatanga, L., Forman, D. and Fox, J. (1998) *Good Practice in Accreditation of Prior Learning.* London: Cassell.

Ofsted (2003) *The Initial Training of Further Education Teachers: A Survey.* London: Stationery Office.

Ofsted (2004) *Vocational A-Levels: The First Two Years* (ofsted.gov.uk/publications).

Organisation for Economic Co-operation and Development (2001) *Education Policy Analysis: Education and Skills.* Paris: OECD.

Parsons, W. (1995) *Public Policy: An Introduction to the Theory and Practice of Policy Analysis.* Aldershot: Edward Elgar.

Payne, J. (1996) 'Who really benefits from Employee Development Schemes?' in P. Raggatt, R. Edwards and N. Small (eds) *The Learning Society: Challenges and Trends.* London: Routledge.

Peters, J. M. (1994) 'Instructors-as-researcher-and-theorists: faculty development in a community college', in R. Benn and R. Fieldhouse (eds) *Training and Professional Development in Adult and Continuing Education.* Exeter: CRCE.

Piaget, J. (1978) *The Development of Thought: Equilibration of Cognitive Structures.* Oxford: Basil Blackwell.

Polanyi, M. (1962) *Personal Knowledge.* London: Routledge.

Pollard, A. (1997) *Reflective Teaching in the Primary School* (3rd edn). London: Cassell.

Popper, K. (1962) *The Open Society and Its Enemies: Volume 2 Hegel and Marx* (4th edn). London: Routledge.

Popper, K. (1968) *The Logic of Scientific Discovery*. London: Hutchinson.

Ramsden, P. (1992) *Learning to Teach in Higher Education*. London: Routledge.

Rogers, C. (1983) *Freedom to Learn for the 1980s*. Columbus: Merrill.

Ryle G. (1949) *The Concept of Mind*. London: Hutchinson.

Sawbridge, S. G. (2001) *Internet Research Resources on Raising Achievement in Post-Compulsory Education*. London: LSDA (www.raising achievement).

Schön, D. (1983) *The Reflective Practitioner*. New York: Basic Books.

Schön, D. (1987) *Educating the Reflective Practitioner: Towards a New Design for Teaching and Learning in the Professions*. San Francisco: Jossey-Bass.

Schuller, T. and Watson, D. (2009) *Learning through Life: Inquiry into the Future for Lifelong Learning*. Leicester: NIACE.

Schuller, T., Preson, J., Hammond, C., Brassett-Grundy, A. and Bynner, J. (2004) *The Benefits of Learning: The Impact of Education on Health, Family Life and Social Capital*. London: Routledge.

Skills and Education Network (SENET) (2004) *Newsletter*, April 2004, p. 2 (http://senet.lsc.gov.uk).

Skills Funding Agency (2010) (http://skillsfundingagency.bis.gov.uk/) accessed 23 June 2011.

Skinner, B. F. (1938) *The Behaviour of Organisms: An Experimental Analysis*. New York: Appleton-Century-Crofts.

Skinner, B. F. (1959) *Science and Human Behaviour*. New York: Macmillan.

Smith, J. and Spurling, A. (1999) *Lifelong Learning: Riding the Tiger*. London: Cassell.

Smyth, J. (1989) 'A critical pedagogy of classroom practice', *Journal of Curriculum Studies*, 21, 6, pp. 483–502.

Society for Research in Higher Education (2004) 'Presentation on Foundation Degrees, Further and Higher Education Network meeting', London, 6 July 2004.

Stenhouse, L. (1975) *An Introduction to Curriculum Research and Development*. London: Heinemann.

Success for All (2004), *Reform of Initial Teacher Training for the Learning and Skills Sector*, November 2004 (www.successforall.gov.uk).

Taylor, L. (1999) 'Laurie Taylor', *Times Higher Education Supplement*, 12 March.

Tennant, M. (1997) *Psychology and Adult Learning* (2nd edn). London: Routledge.

Tomlinson, J. (1996) *Inclusive Learning: Report of the Learning Difficulties and/or Physical Disabilities Committee*. London: HMSO.

Tomlinson, M. (2004) *Final Report from the Working Group on 14–19 Reform*. London: DfES.

Tuckman B. (1965) 'Development sequence in small groups', *Psychological Bulletin*, 63, pp. 384–99.

Twining, J. (2001) 'Visions and reflections', *EDUCA: The Digest for Vocational Education and Training*, 209, pp. 8–10. Guildford: Stanley Thornes.

Unit for the Development of Adult Continuing Education (1986) *The Challenge of Change: Developing Educational Guidance for Adults*. Leicester: UDACE.

Usher, R. and Bryant, I. (1989) *Adult Education as Theory, Practice and Research: The Captive Triangle*. London: Routledge.

Vygotsky, I. (1962) *Thought and Language*. Cambridge: MIT Press.

Ward, C. (1997) 'Qualifications – the next eleven years', *EDUCA*, 172.

Warnke, G. (1987) *Gadamer: Hermeneutics, Tradition and Reason*. Oxford: Polity Press.

Watson, J. B. (1913) 'Psychology as the behaviourist views it', *Psychological Review*, 20, p. 158.

Westwood, S. and Thomas, J. E. (eds) (1991) *The Politics of Adult Education*. Leicester: NIACE.

Willis, P. (1999) 'Looking for what it's really like: phenomenology in reflective practice', *Studies in Continuing Education*, 21, 1, pp. 91–112.

Wolf, A. (1995) *Competence-Based Assessment*. Buckingham: Open University Press.

Wolf, A. (2011) 'Review of Vocational Education Commissioned by the Secretary of State for Education', Michael Gove MP (www.education.gov.uk/publications).

Yalom, I. (1980) *Existential Psychotherapy*. New York: Basic Books.

Index